The
WORLD'S LARGEST
MARKET

The
WORLD'S LARGEST
MARKET

A Business Guide to Europe
1992

Robert Williams
Mark Teagan
José Beneyto

With a Foreword by
Professor George Cabot Lodge

amacom

American Management Association

This publication is designed to provide accurate and authoritative information in regard to the subject matter covered. It is sold with the understanding that the publisher is not engaged in rendering legal, accounting, or other professional service. If legal advice or other expert assistance is required, the services of a competent professional person should be sought.

Library of Congress Cataloging-in-Publication Data

Williams, Robert.
    The world's largest market : a business guide to Europe, 1992 /
    Robert Williams, Mark Teagan, José Beneyto.
        p.   cm.
    Includes bibliographical references and index.
    ISBN 0-8144-5989-7
    1. European Economic Community countries—Commercial policy.
2. Corporations, American—European Economic Community countries.
3. Europe 1992.   4. United States—Commerce—European Economic
Community countries.   5. European Economic Community countries—
Commerce—United States.   6. Europe—Economic integration.
I. Teagan, Mark.   II. Beneyto, José.   III. Title.
HF1582.5.W55   1990
658.1'8—dc20   90-55216
                                                                      CIP

Printing number

10   9   8   7   6   5   4   3   2   1

Table of Contents

Foreword

The twelve nations belonging to the European Community (EC) are aiming to remove all barriers to the free movement of goods, services, money, and people by 1992—all barriers, that is, within the EC. This is a dramatic step in a long sequence of actions beginning after World War II that were aimed at making one market out of Europe's 320 million people and thus spurring European growth. It is accompanied by numerous cooperative endeavors by European companies and governments to develop the economies of scale and generate the capital resources necessary for Europe to compete successfully in electronics, biotechnology, and the other industries of the future.

This book is a most useful description of the 1992 process.

Whether or not the ambitious deadlines are met precisely in 1992 is unimportant. An irreversible transition is under way. Europe is determined to organize its resources so as to make the most of itself in global competition.

The 1992 process is bound to produce a variety of tensions both within the Community and with other nations. Europe's great multinational corporations—Philips of the Netherlands, Siemens of Germany, and Thomson of France, for example—are joining forces with their national governments and the EC to innovate. At the same time, they are competing with one another and their Japanese and American rivals, but they are also joining with these very rivals in global alliances to promote their corporate interests. There is, therefore, tension between the interests of corporations and the governments that invest in them in the hopes of producing jobs and a higher standard of living at home. To the extent that EC funds are used to finance corporate research and development in the rich countries, there is concern among the poorer members about what they will get in return and fears on the part of the rich that the poorer nations may get too much. Volkswagen, for example, builds in Spain to take advantage of lower labor costs while unemployment in Germany rises.

So there is tension within Europe between the interests of corporations and those of the governments of the member states. These tensions are related to those with the outside world.

European business is learning from Japan that to win in global competition, government, whether national or regional, must be a partner, providing not only capital for long-run gains in market share but also protection from foreign producers. France and Italy, for example, have long protected their automobile industries. It seems likely that such protection will be essential, at least temporarily, if Europe is to achieve global competitiveness in microelectronics and other high-tech areas where it is now well behind Japan and the United States.

Europe's initiative confronts the United States with formidable challenges. In order to overcome this perfectly predictable propensity of Europe to protect itself, American companies will have either to go abroad—by investing in Europe or joining a European firm—or to seek from the U.S. government a countervailing trade strategy. Going abroad may be good for a company's shareholders, but it may not be so good for its American employees or for the country at large. Indeed the deterioration of the manufacturing sector in the United States has already steadily eroded the paychecks of American workers. It has also produced a continuing deficit of well over $100 billion in our trade account, requiring the United States to sustain itself on foreign borrowing, a practice that obviously cannot go on forever.

If U.S. companies are to stay home and compete, exporting to Europe, they will need the same kind of help from their government as their European competitors get from theirs.

For forty years U.S. trade policy has been aimed at enforcing the rules of free trade and punishing those who cheat. One of the most celebrated cases involved European steel producers. In 1981, European governments were found to be subsidizing their steel producers to help them modernize and become competitive in the world economy. This was in violation of U.S. duty laws. So, at the urging of the American steel industry, the U.S. Department of Commerce launched a series of suits against the Europeans. A good deal of bitterness and animosity ensued. The Europeans argued that the United States had no business telling them how to run their countries. Finally, through the efforts of the U.S. departments of State and Defense, which had diplomatic and military interests to protect, Commerce called off the suits after a commitment from the Europeans to limit their market share in the United States to 5.6 percent. This kind of bilateral negotiation is one way to go, but it is clumsy, slow, and expensive. Perhaps most important, for the United States it frequently results not in a more competitive domestic industry but in the protection of an uncompetitive status quo. The result is certainly not free trade.

The Trade Act of 1988 requires the President of the United States to retaliate against countries that close their markets to U.S. business, but this is a blunt instrument, difficult to use with precision or discretion and sure to engender animosity.

It would be nice perhaps if the United States could begin to organize itself, as other countries—and now the European region—have done, with government and industry acting in concert to define and promote community needs. The Office of the United States Trade Representative (USTR), with its extensive advisory committee apparatus, would seem ideally suited to such an endeavor. But this would smack of "industrial policy," which is anathema to the reigning ideologues.

The Defense Department and the Congress nevertheless indulged in just such a policy when, in 1988, they decided that the United States needed a semiconductor industry. Following an industry-led initiative, spearheaded by IBM and fourteen of the nation's leading semiconductor manufacturers, Congress appropriated $500 million to be matched by another $500 million from industry for the creation of Sematech. This became an industry consortium, sponsored by the Defense Advanced Research Project Agency (DARPA) of the Department of Defense (DOD), to produce the manufacturing know-how the United States needed to recover its lost lead in chip manufacturing. The Sematech initiative was by itself insufficient to fulfill this objective; nevertheless it represented a significant piece of industrial policy. Taken over the objections of important components of the Reagan administration, it was justified as essential for the national security, meaning military security.

The most dangerous threat to national security, however, may not be military; more likely it is economic, as measured in the loss of commercial competitiveness, especially in high-tech areas. If that is true and becomes accepted doctrine, perhaps the United States can begin to match its European and Asian competitors with an economic strategy of its own based on a new definition of national interest.

Such a strategy would require far more subtle and extensive thought than that which has gone into Sematech. In the first place, non-Americans are not allowed into the consortium. Europeans resent this, especially companies such as Philips, which has a major U.S. subsidiary (Signetics) engaged in semiconductor research and manufacture. "Why," they ask, "should we let Americans into European microelectronics markets when we are barred from theirs?" Europeans have much to offer that the United States needs; an effective strategy should be aimed at making the most of foreign achievements, not denying them outright. Second, a healthy U.S. semiconductor industry requires healthy suppliers of equipment and materials as well as a healthy chip-using industry—consumer electronics and computers, for example. Chips are part of a food chain. A weak or missing link can destroy the whole.

Astute observers such as Raymond Vernon doubt the capacity of the

United States, politically or ideologically, to use trade policy effectively to promote an economic strategy. The vagaries of Congress, the pulls and pushes of interest groups, the fragmentation of the executive branch, and the adversarial and suspicious relationships between business and government all conspire to subvert any such effort. Europeans and Asians can do such things, but not Americans.*

Vernon suggests that the best course for Europe and the United States to follow in dealing with the friction the 1992 process can be expected to create is to set up something similar to the U.S.-Canada free trade agreement, which broke new ground by establishing elaborate machinery for the settlement of disputes between the two governments. "One especially interesting provision allows each party to protest an action by the other through an appeals procedure governed by an international tribunal; a tribunal composed of two judges from Canada and the United States each, with a fifth judge chosen by them."**

Whatever the unfolding of Europe 1992 brings, it will pose new challenges to American business, challenges that require managers as never before to align their policies and objectives with those of the United States government. No company can win alone for long. In today's world, companies are not competing with each other the way they used to. It is country versus country, region versus region, system versus system. Successful companies must understand the components of winning systems and how to design, build, and manage them.

This book is an essential beginning. It provides managers with what they need to know about the European Community and the drive for unity. It charts the rocks and shoals that lie ahead and is a helpful pilot for both companies and countries to the safe waters of expanded trade with growth and prosperity for all.

George Cabot Lodge
Harvard University

*Raymond Vernon, "Can the U.S. Negotiate for Trade Equality?" *Harvard Business Review,* May-June 1989.
**Ibid.

Preface

The integrated market is defined in the Single European Act as "an area without internal frontiers in which the free movement of goods, persons, services and capital is ensured. . . ."

The concept is simple, the execution anything but. This book strives to inform American readers how the execution is going and what it means to them. We refer to the whole process simply as 1992, for it is by December 31 of that year that the European Community (EC) hopes to have the program fully in place. Although there are still many skeptics, their numbers lessened around 1988 when it became evident that progress was exceeding even the optimists' expectations. But there is still a long way to go and many obstacles to overcome.

We hope that reading this book will enable you to reach your own conclusions about how 1992 might affect your business (and it most likely will, even if you have no intention of addressing the European market) and to interpret the consequences of new developments that are bound to occur. It also provides practical advice on how to track 1992's progress and to do business in Europe, and offers numerous references to additional sources of information. These include not only articles and other books but also, for instance, the names of individuals at the Department of Commerce and the Department of State who can provide much assistance.

Chapters 1 and 2 provide background material about the EC. Chapter 1 gives a very brief history of the institution, to place 1992 in context, and introduces the major treaties and developments that lie behind the program. Chapter 2 introduces the institutions, the legal process, and the directives, the EC's major tool for making 1992 happen.

Chapter 3 discusses some controversial issues, such as reciprocity, that have the potential for creating a "Fortress Europe," a possibility that concerns many Americans, Japanese, and other EC trading partners.

Chapters 4 and 5 go together, the former introducing a matrix that will enable you to formalize your thoughts about 1992, the latter reviewing the legislation and other developments that will most likely affect different industrial sectors. If you are already knowledgeable about 1992's background, you might want to go directly to these chapters to focus on your industry. Even if you are not directly involved in one of these sectors, one or more might be end users of your products or services. Further, by getting an idea of how 1992 is playing out in these sectors, especially in the ongoing conflict between the thrust towards a unified market versus the retention of national preferences, you will be better equipped to make decisions regarding Europe.

Chapter 6 is for those who have no experience in exporting to or running operations in Europe and who, because of 1992, believe that now is a good time to start. It is a primer, outlining the basic issues and processes you'll need to consider before making a move.

Chapters 7 and 8 discuss the European Monetary System and the role of 1992 vis-à-vis Japan, the Council for Mutual Economic Assistance (COMECON), and the European Free Trade Association (EFTA), parties with considerable interests in and concerns about the single market. And, to say the least, political events in Eastern Europe in 1989 certainly increase the EC's interests in and concerns about these countries. It is noteworthy that commentators on what these events mean often point to the EC, rather than to its individual member states, as the political body most likely to influence the changes that are certainly coming.

Chapter 9 reviews trade law and the General Agreement on Tariffs and Trade (GATT) from a practical point of view. You will find it useful if you are thinking of doing business with EC companies or individuals or if you are concerned about European companies, strengthened by the internal market, competing in your markets here at home. It refers to trade laws you can use and suggests whom you can contact if you think a competitor is behaving unfairly.

Chapter 10 summarizes our conclusions about 1992 in the light of the research, both primary and secondary, we conducted in writing this book.

We have tried to make each chapter able to stand on its own; this occasionally required repeating descriptions of important legislation and developments to spare you the necessity of having to flip back and forth among chapters.

Five directories follow these chapters. The first three represent a nuts-and-bolts review of EC and American programs and organizations that can help you to obtain financing, get involved in joint R&D programs, and find EC importers for your products. Some of these are particularly oriented toward small business. You'll probably find that there is more assistance available than you thought. These directories contain numerous names, addresses, and phone numbers to enable you to contact people who can help you get started. Directory D lists some of the more important directives, categorized by possible Euro-hazard (corresponding to the discussions in Chapter 3) and industrial sector (corresponding to Chapter 5). Directory E lists the members of the EC Commission and their responsibilities, as of 1990.

While not intended to be fully comprehensive, this book is self-contained and provides more facts about 1992 than we have been able to find in any other single source. But beware; even though we have updated the book through the last minute before press run, the issues surrounding 1992 change rapidly; so, to keep current, you will have to read newspapers, magazines, and other sources of information that address them. Naturally, we refer you to these too.

Acknowledgments

One of the many challenges in writing this book was to convey numerous facts in a context that would help make them useful to the reader. For many of the facts and (we trust) an understanding of their relevance, we relied on a large number of people. We found that the community of those who were generous with their knowledge and time was hearteningly large and widespread.

First we would like to extend special thanks to Mike Brown, independent consultant and entrepreneur, for providing the section "Managing a Pan-European Operation" in Chapter 6.

Our thanks also go to Pamela Entwistle, of the Kangaroo Group, for her own input and for contacting several people in the London financial district on our behalf. We also received generous assistance from Lindsay Armstrong, of the Commission of European Communities office in Paris, Chris Boyd, of Directorate-General II in Brussels, Guy Doucet, of ESPRIT, and Ms. Clayman, at the EC office in Washington, D.C.

Lois Smith, of Harvard Business School, supplied essential support and assistance throughout, and Dick Snijders, Director of Corporate Finance at Philips International B.V. in the Netherlands, gave us excellent guidance on developments in the European Monetary System. Several people at the Department of Commerce proved that many of our tax dollars are well spent, and Stephen Cooney of the National Association of Manufacturers provided excellent insights into how American companies might approach 1992. Alan Tousignant, at the U.S. EC Mission in Brussels, Tim Richards, at the USTR, George Willingmyre, at HIMA, and numerous others at European companies and EC institutions supported us throughout this project. These included Neil A. Hartley, of National Westminster Bank, John Young, of Lloyds Bank, Juan A. Riviere Marti, of Directorate-General XVII, and P. S. Sanson, of the European Committee for Standardization.

Other acknowledgments go to Beatrice Verschueren, of UNICE, Gaston Michaud, at CEN, and Pam Snook, at ANSI.

Any errors are those of the authors and no one else.

A special thanks to Euromonitor for allowing us to use the maps of EC countries shown in Directory B.

And last but not least, we would like to recognize the patience and support of our friends and families, who had to put up with our late-night writing sessions and ongoing enthusiasm for this project.

The
WORLD'S LARGEST
MARKET

Chapter 1 | The Changing Landscape of Europe: One Way or the Other, It'll Affect You

The EC is embarked on a revitalized program finally to complete what it started in 1958: a single internal market with freedom of movement for goods, services, people, and capital. The result will be a $4 trillion market of 320 million people.

C. William Verity
Former U.S. Secretary of Commerce

The stakes of the 1992 venture are nothing less than the full realization of the original vision of a unified European Community. Further, its success would gain for the EC international economic power at least equal to that of Japan and the United States, a goal Europeans candidly admit to.

Why You Need to Know About the New Europe

These rather heady geoeconomic consequences aside, what does all this mean to you, the individual business decision maker? Most likely a whole lot. Certainly enough so that you can't afford to ignore the new Europe even if you have no intention of doing business there. Ignorance of the internal market could become a prelude to disaster. If you are in any form of manufacturing, you can almost count on new European competitors coming to the United States. Further, those already here will most likely compete more effectively. Some of these will simply expand as they reap the benefits of economies of scale a single European market affords them. Others will look to U.S. markets because of increased competition at home. Many of them will enter joint ventures, helping to make your current competitors more formidable—unless, of course, you become one of the partners. At the very least, to remain competitive, you must have the information necessary to make sound decisions in the face of the new possibilities.

If you are in distribution or retailing, you will either be confronting new competition for the reasons just listed, or you will be able to choose from an expanding assortment of competitive European products to add to your product lines. Failure to be aware of these developments may put you at a competitive disadvantage.

1

On the other hand, becoming fully knowledgeable about the new Europe could present you with numerous new opportunities. As the 1992 program is implemented, you will find it increasingly easy to market to the entire EC under a single set of rules rather than to twelve individual markets, none of which comes even close in size to the market you enjoy. Distribution, whose complexities alone have made Europe seem beyond practical reach to many American companies, will become subject to rules no more difficult to comply with than those in effect in the United States. Even manufacturing in Europe will be simplified as the social, environmental, and legal policies that must be adhered to become unified. Not to seriously address these opportunities could leave you behind your competitors who do.

Finally, as Eastern Europe opens up, and the EC assumes a significant role in establishing new East-West relations, playing by the EC's rules in any of the EC's twelve member states* could, in turn, provide entry to these new untapped markets and sources of educated, comparatively inexpensive labor.

This book will make you fully conversant with 1992 developments and issues. Further, if you decide you must take action, it provides you with the information you need to get started, which, as we all know, is often the hardest part of any new undertaking.

The Opportunities

The EC is in fact already a trade giant. Its exports amount to 23 percent of world trade, compared with 18 percent for the United States and 10 percent for Japan. U.S. trade with the EC's twelve member states climbed to $165 billion in 1988; the EC is the United States' biggest export market and its fastest-growing one. Between 1986 and 1988, the fall in the dollar and improved EC economic growth rates helped significantly increase U.S. exports to the EC, which grew by 9 percent in 1986, 14 percent in 1987, and an incredible 25 percent in 1988. The *increase* in U.S. exports to the EC, from $49 billion in 1985 to $76 billion in 1988, was nearly equal to *all* U.S. exports to Japan in 1987. It is as though the United States has suddenly found a new export market the size of Japan.

The European market could become even more important as the successful completion of the 1992 program creates the largest single market in the world (325 million in the EC compared with 250 million Americans and 123 million Japanese). Although there are large differences among member states, average living standards are high, the average gross do-

---

*Belgium, Denmark, France, Greece, Ireland, Italy, Luxembourg, the Netherlands, Portugal, Spain, the United Kingdom, and West Germany.

mestic product (GDP) per capita being over $13,500, ranging from just under $3,000 in Portugal to nearly $20,000 in Denmark.

The creation of a single market creates opportunities for economies of scale, particularly in high-technology sectors where the spiraling costs of research and development often cannot be justified by sales to a restricted national market. The economies of scale created by an EC-wide market will make EC-based companies much more competitive in relation to their rivals in the United States and Japan.

How likely is it that 1992 will actually result in a unified market, create economies of scale, and make EC companies formidable world competitors? Opinions vary all across the board, so you'll have to come up with your own evaluations, a task this book is designed to help you with. But, first, you must learn how it all came about.

1992: A Brief History

During the 1970s, the term *Eurosclerosis* gained wide currency. It referred to the stagflationary crisis (double-digit inflation and unemployment) then occurring in Europe and to the high-technology gap that characterized European industry on into the 1980s.

Europe's poor performance was considered a consequence of its failure to adapt management systems, labor relations, capital market institutions, and government policies to meet the needs of a postindustrial economy. Bound by specialization in medium-technology products, European firms performed poorly. Although Europe was outspending Japan in research and development, the lack of collaboration between scientific institutions and industry together with the presence of different national standards throughout Europe made success hard to achieve. In 1987, for instance, EC countries ran a high-technology deficit estimated at $10 billion compared with corresponding surpluses of $1.3 billion in the United States and $8.6 billion in Japan.

Finally, the lack of an EC-wide market imposed real constraints. The fixed costs of R&D in developing telecommunications products, for example, required a large market with common standards. But the "uncommon market," in which each nation sought to advance its own "national champions," precluded the emergence of companies with genuinely European strategies.

The American Way and the European Way

With EC industry languishing, the rewards of addressing a large market became obvious. Big U.S. companies such as IBM and Ford had, for decades, approached Europe as a single market, coordinating manufacturing and distribution from many factories through a single headquarters. IBM, for example, makes one product at each of its thirteen European plants—e.g., personal computers in Greenock, Scotland, and mainframes in Montpellier, France—and ships them around the continent. Many European companies started to emulate IBM and other multinationals, an acknowledgement of the success of the American way.

In a parallel development, most of the EC member states embraced market economies; the stark ideological divisions of the past waned into insignificance. In particular, Mitterand's France and Spain's socialist government exemplified how the moderate left rapidly abandoned its traditional predilection for increased state intervention in favor of more market-determined economies and increased economic freedom. Although much of this change was caused by the demands created by a structural shift towards high technologies and capital servicing, the role of political decisions should not be underestimated. France's abandonment of the socialist policies associated with the first phase of the Mitterand presidency was an event of far-reaching significance.

Meanwhile, Europe's deteriorating economic performance was only too obvious to European industrialists like Wisse Dekker, vice-chairman of Philips, and Jacques Solvay of the French company of the same name, who, since the early 1980s, had campaigned energetically for completion of the Common Market, claiming that it was essential to meeting the challenges posed by the United States, Japan, and the rising newly industrialized countries (NICs) of East Asia. In 1983, these men and others launched the Roundtable of European Industrialists, an influential group composed of Europe's industrial aristocracy. By 1985, it could rely on active partners within the Commission itself, the Commission being the major initiator of EC legislation (see Chapter 2). The new commissioner in charge of the internal market, Lord Cockfield of the United Kingdom, undertook the task of assembling 300 measures required to eliminate the internal barriers to free domestic trade. Like many other EC initiatives, this "White Paper for the Completion of the Internal Market" would probably have enjoyed a modest reception but for the general political and economic environment, not to mention the Commission's brilliant use of public relations.

Building the Road to 1992

Fortunately, the EC had institutions in place that could capitalize on these developments. These, and the European Economic Community itself, had been established by the 1957 Treaty of Rome whose objective was to create a union of European nations with common economic goals.

Further, by 1985, the EC had made progress even beyond the significant elimination of internal tariffs and quotas that had taken place in 1969. It had relatively few nontariff barriers compared to other industrialized countries, and the European Monetary System (EMS) had successfully stabilized fluctuations in the currencies of seven participating member states.

This unique combination of problems and opportunities led to a sequence of developments that, in turn, have created a widely shared belief that the time for a true European Common Market has come, a belief whose prevalence would have been unimaginable even in the mid-1980s, and whose full magnitude became evident only in 1988–1989. The most important of these developments were:

- The Cassis de Dijon Case (1979)
- The White Paper (1985)
- The Single European Act (1987)
- The Cecchini Report (1987)

Cassis de Dijon (1979)

For more than twenty-five years, the EC's attempts to rationalize the business environment under the Treaty of Rome centered around "harmonization," the creation of rules on a Communitywide basis for every product so there would be integration through uniformity. The instrument for achieving this goal (and for initiating Community legislation to this day) was the *directive*. Starting in 1969, approximately 200 directives were adopted to establish harmonized technical regulations for all member states. However, the process proved far more difficult than expected. For example, one of the most substantial achievements during this period, the "low-voltage" directive, was under discussion for seven years before its final adoption in 1973; no fewer than 150 meetings had been devoted to it.

This slow progress reflected the practice of legislating extremely detailed specifications. The Commission was often ridiculed for striving to harmonize for its own sake and for trying to achieve excessive and artificial uniformity. Lack of interest in the whole program became rampant.

The Spirits of a Liqueur.   This gloomy situation was reversed by the seminal 1979 *Cassis de Dijon* decision of the European Court of Justice. The case concerned a German firm, Rewe, which attempted to import Crème de Cassis, a traditional French liqueur. Because German law required such liqueurs to contain a specified minimum amount of alcohol, an amount higher than that contained in Cassis, the West German government prohibited the import of Cassis de Dijon. The French firm appealed to the European Court of Justice, which ruled that German authorities could not block the import of a product that was sold in France except for reasons relating to health, fiscal supervision, fair trade, or consumer protection.

More important, the Court also established that the burden of proof in such cases lies with the importing member state, which must show that products lawfully produced and marketed elsewhere in the EC do not comply with health or safety demands or with those of consumer or environmental protection.

This legal prejudice in favor of imports that meet other member states' requirements led to a new approach to harmonization of technical standards. Two principles were established:

1. A product or group of products that meet *essential* safety criteria must be allowed free circulation. The EC no longer attempts to legislate detailed technical standards.
2. For product differences based on nonessential requirements, there is *mutual recognition* of national regulations and industrial standards.

The White Paper (1985): Deregulation Within a New Regulatory Environment

This brings us back to Lord Cockfield's "White Paper for the Completion of the Internal Market," which builds on the principle of mutual recognition established by *Cassis de Dijon*. The White Paper proposes to remove the physical, technical, and fiscal barriers that conflict with the goal of a single unified market. It would do this through a broad range of liberalizing and deregulating measures contained in its three hundred directives (since reduced to 279). Equally important, it has set December 31, 1992, as the deadline for the program to be fully implemented. Following is a broad outline of its content:

- *Physical* barriers at borders that impede the free flow of goods and persons:
  —Eliminate border customs facilities.
  —Eliminate veterinary and phytosanitary controls and harmonize food inspection.
  —Relax control of individuals.
- *Technical* barriers that prevent goods produced or traded in one member state from being sold in others:
  —Define "essential requirements" only where health and safety are at stake.
  —Mutually recognize standards, diplomas, and licenses.
  —Develop European standards in new areas.

—Adopt EC-wide patents and trademarks.
—Develop industrial cooperation and European company law.
- *Fiscal* barriers, such as different national tax systems, that impede cross-border trade:
  —Harmonize value-added taxes (VAT).
  —Harmonize excise taxes.
  —Tax transnational corporations uniformly.
  —Liberalize capital movements.

Obviously, the White Paper does not "concentrate on minimal proposals that would be easily acceptable to the Member States."[1] Rather, it is comprehensive, striving for maximum mutual recognition and minimal legislative harmonization. In the financial area, for instance, authorizing and supervising a financial institution would be the responsibility of that institution's home country. Provided it meets essential requirements, it would be free to operate throughout the EC without needing to be licensed and supervised by the other member states, which would recognize the home country's authority and competence.

The White Paper does not shy away from the issues surrounding the integration of the member states' economies. In its introduction, it openly states that resolving such issues is an intrinsic part of its goal:

- Any import quotas or restrictions maintained by a member state will have to be applied on a communitywide basis.

- Increased coordination of economic policies and the European Monetary System will inevitably challenge the jurisdiction of member states, gradually shifting the present structure of public policy regulation, market intervention, income redistribution measures, and macroeconomic policies from the national to the Community level. Transportation, social, and environmental and consumer protection policies will necessarily undergo a significant degree of unification.

The White Paper effectively set the agenda for 1992. Its principles of harmonization and mutual recognition are at the heart of the program, and much legislation applying these concepts has been passed. But many of its goals are yet to be achieved. The harmonization of VAT rates and total removal of border controls are among the most elusive.

The Single European Act (1987)

The Single European Act (SEA) contains the first major amendments to the Treaty of Rome. Its most significant modification replaced the requirement for a unanimous vote in the Council of Ministers by one requiring only a qualified majority for measures pertaining to the internal market (except those concerning taxes, financial and monetary policy, and labor movement). This means that progress can no longer be "slowed to the pace of the most reluctant Member State."[2]

Via the new "cooperation procedure," the Act also conferred new powers on the European Parliament, providing it with new veto and amendment powers over legislation. Both the Commission and the Council must work more closely with Parliament during the legislative process (see Chapter 2).

The Act also encompassed new policy areas such as the environment, research and technology, regional development, and economic and monetary coordination.

A central goal established by the SEA is a stronger "social and economic cohesion" within the Community. It increased financial backing for this objective through measures such as doubling the European Regional Development Fund, which provides "structural funds" to the less developed countries, specifically, Spain, Portugal, Greece, and Ireland. These funds are designed to encourage modernization and to counteract the increase in regional imbalances within the Community that few doubt will be a major cost of 1992.

These policies in the social area were, in fact, the price that had to be paid for the introduction of qualified majority voting within the Council. Without the social policies, the poorer member states would not have agreed to relinquish their veto power.

Other concessions to the poorer member states are provisions that enable them to delay implementation of much of the EC's legislation, an option already extensively used, though it carries economic costs and creates legal difficulties. The possibility of delay is likely to tempt governments into resisting common disciplines in ways that could distort the market, and make final adjustments more difficult for the weaker member states most likely to delay implementing them.

The Cecchini Report (1987)

In 1987, the Commission published "The Costs of Non-Europe," widely known as the Cecchini Report after its lead author, Paolo Cecchini. Based on analyses conducted by Ernst & Whinney, Price Waterhouse, Group MPC, and many others, the report declared the end of "the era of the national soft option," and drew an optimistic picture of an integrated EC market. "Post-1992" was expected to bring:

- Removal of barriers such as customs formalities, protective public procurement, divergent national standards, and restrictions on services and manufacturing that hinder trade, limit competition, and sustain excess costs and overpricing

- A significant reduction in costs through increased economies of scale in production and business organization. This would be accompanied by a more cost-effective supply of labor, capital, plant, and components for industrial production, and improved allocation among firms, sectors, and countries
- A boost in profit margins for individual companies based on cost savings, the ability to take on foreign competition in global markets, and a structural increase in European demand. Despite the downward impact on prices, increased operating efficiencies would reduce many companies' overhead by 10 percent or more
- Increased innovation, resulting in the creation of new businesses and products. Larger markets and the restructuring of Europe's productive potential would enable many firms to finance and undertake R&D projects previously considered too costly and risky

The report claims that these and other developments would result in a 5 percent growth in the EC's GNP, a 6 percent reduction in prices, and 2 million new jobs. The Cecchini Report is by far one of the most optimistic evaluations of 1992, and has even been called EC propaganda (though an even more optimistic report from an independent source[3] appeared in late 1989). Although many think it is unrealistic, its central analytical tool, "the costs of non-Europe," dramatically portrays the advantages of achieving the internal market versus continuing to pursue economic success solely through national policies.

In 1988, a 125-page summary of the thirty-five-volume Cecchini Report entitled "The European Challenge—1992: The Benefits of a Single Market" was published by Gower Publishing.

A New Business Environment?

Even skeptical observers concede that the developments that lie behind 1992 have already changed the way some business is done in Europe and are likely to bring further changes. In early 1990, the United States upgraded the EC's representative in Washington to ambassadorial status. And, at a special summit in April 1990, EC heads of state called for an intergovernmental conference by the end of 1990 on the subject of political union. This would necessitate revision of the treaties now in place. Many major corporations are behaving as if the whole program will indeed be realized. The results started appearing in 1988. Although the number of mergers and takeovers undertaken by the 1,000 largest EC firms had already been growing rapidly, from 117 in 1982-1983 to 303 in 1986-1987, they more than doubled in 1988-1989.

Companies may encounter other developments as well. For example:

- Customers in previously local markets may prefer to buy directly from the main sales organization to get better prices. This may open up service opportunities.
- Local customers may disappear. This may well become the case for components manufacturers. As 1992 forces industrial buyers to rationalize production facilities, a company that has served a specific factory may be forced to close down.
- The decline in border-crossing costs will enable suppliers to address new EC markets, though most likely at the cost of facing stiffer competition as others do the same.

Over the long haul, 1992 should help increase the efficiency of the product development process, thereby speeding up product innovation and substantially modifying traditional patterns of competition. Winners are likely to be Locusts (low-cost producers like IBM), Lions (strong national companies), and Monkeys (niche players). Losers will likely be Dinosaurs (large, protected companies), Dodos (companies that look interesting but have high overhead costs and few opportunities for economies of scale), and Nouveau Dodos (those who buy a dodo).

For the consumer, the promise of the internal market is wider choice and lower prices for both goods and services, wider choice through the removal of barriers that currently keep companies out of particular markets, and lower prices through economies of scale being passed on to the retail level. In addition, companies will no longer be able to keep prices artificially higher in one member state than in another. Buyers or arbitragers will compare prices in different markets and purchase products where prices are lowest.

Although something like an EC-wide recession could derail the 1992 process, it is still likely that 1992 will have a major effect on American business. In fact, if there is a recession, the fears of Fortress Europe could become confirmed (see Chapter 3). On the other hand, if there isn't, you might want to get ready for a new business environment in Europe (see Chapters 4 and 5). But for those not familiar with them, let's first review the EC's decision-making bodies and legislative process.

Notes

1. *Europe Without Frontiers—Completing the Internal Market* (Luxembourg: Office for Official Publications of the European Communities, 1988), p. 20.
2. Ibid., p. 23.
3. Richard Baldwin, *The Growth of Effect of 1992*, Economic Policy no. 9 (Cambridge University Press, November 1989).

Chapter 2 | Your Host: The European Economic Community

The four Community institutions responsible for achieving the 1992 program are:

The Commission:	Initiates legislation and administers Community policy.
The Council:	Approves legislation.
The European Parliament:	Can modify and impede legislation.
The European Court of Justice:	Interprets laws and frequently establishes precedents of far-reaching impact.

The following provides an overview of these institutions. Their addresses and phone numbers can be found in Directory E.

The Commission

On a day-to-day basis, the Commission is the most visible of the four institutions, largely because of its executive role in the EC and its guardianship of the treaties, for whose implementation it has responsibility. Other duties include initiating EC policy and pursuing EC interests in the Council. It is the Commission, for example, that put forward the initial proposals for the 1992 program, including the White Paper.

The Commission has seventeen members (two each from France, Germany, Italy, the United Kingdom, and Spain and one each from Belgium, Denmark, Greece, Ireland, Luxembourg, the Netherlands, and Portugal). Member state governments appoint members for four-year renewable terms, with the president and six vice-presidents holding office for two-year renewable terms. Although appointed by member states, the commissioners' charter is to act independently and consider the interests of the Community as a whole.

Each commissioner is responsible for one or more areas of Community policy and for formulating proposals in these areas that will help achieve the goals of the treaties (see Directory E). In this effort, commissioners are assisted by a small staff called a cabinet. Proposals are reviewed by the Commission as a whole, which decides on precisely what will be presented to the Council and Parliament.

Beneath the commissioners are directorates-general (DGs), which administer the Commission's work. Within the directorates-general, officials draft proposals and then report to their director-general. Each DG has a commissioner who is responsible for its work and who coordinates efforts with the director-general in charge. As of 1990, there were twenty-three directorates-general.

In drafting proposals, the Commission maintains contact with political and business interests throughout the EC. It often incorporates opinions expressed by these interests, particularly those put forward by major European trade associations, business leaders, and labor. *It is possible to influence Community legislation by contacting the individual officials in charge of the first draft of a piece of legislation.*

The Commission also maintains contact with the other Community institutions. It is invited to most of the meetings of the Council in an advisory capacity, and commissioners regularly attend sessions of the Parliament. Commissioners and/or Commission officials may also attend parliamentary committee meetings.

The Council of Ministers

The Council is the Community's primary decision-making body. Legislation cannot pass without its approval; only rarely, however, can it make decisions without a proposal from the Commission. Consisting of one minister from each member state, it is the only institution that directly represents the governments of the member states within the EC. There are two distinct types of Council meeting:

1. *General Affairs Council.* These coordinate the overall activities of the Council and are usually attended by the foreign ministers of each member state, who are considered the main representatives of their governments.
2. *Specialized councils.* These deal with specific subjects, including finance, the internal market, research, commercial policy towards third countries, education, and justice. These Council meetings are attended by ministers from the relevant ministries in each of the member states.

In addition, *European Councils* or *Summits* are attended by the heads of state or government to discuss broad areas of policy. These normally occur twice a year, in June and December, and usually receive considerable media coverage. Summits play a large role in the integration process, deciding on controversial issues, developing new policy areas, and initiating intergovernmental conferences that are required to revise or make treaties (such as the one in 1986 that led to the adoption of the Single European Act).

Council meetings are chaired by a president, an office that rotates among the member states every six months. Through 1992, this rotation will be as follows:

	First Half	*Second Half*
1990	Ireland	Italy
1991	Netherlands	Luxembourg
1992	Portugal	United Kingdom

This rotation can be significant because a member state's own priorities can heavily influence the Council's agenda during its presidency. Further, the president can exercise considerable power through appointing chairmen of working groups.

Once drafted, Commission proposals are forwarded to the Council, which decides via one of three methods:

1. *Unanimity:* Required for votes concerning tax harmonization, the free movement of persons, and the rights and interests of employed persons.
2. *Simple majority voting:* Requires the vote of seven member states.
3. *Qualified majority voting:* Requires 54 of 76 votes. Although most legislation needs only a qualified majority for approval, the Council has developed the practice of adopting virtually all proposals by unanimity. When an issue forces a qualified majority vote, member states have the following number of votes:

   - Germany, France, Italy, the UK (10 each)
   - Spain (8)
   - Belgium, Greece, Netherlands, Portugal (5 each)
   - Denmark, Ireland (3 each)
   - Luxembourg (2)

The change from requiring unanimity to qualified majority voting may prove relevant to U.S. companies. They will no longer be able to rely on one country to block changes they oppose; conversely, they can afford to be less concerned about individual countries that oppose favorable internal market reforms.

The actual work of the Council is prepared by the Committee of Permanent Representatives of the Member States (COREPER), which officially comprises the member states' ambassadors to the EC. Meetings are normally attended by the permanent representatives of each member state in Brussels, or by their deputies. A permanent representative plays a particularly important role when his or her government holds the Council presidency. Commission proposals may be substantially altered while under discussion by the Council, COREPER, or other working groups.

The European Parliament

The Parliament consists of 518 members of the European Parliament (MEPs) who are elected by a direct vote in the member states. Representation varies according to member state size, from eighty-one for each of the four largest member states to six for the smallest. Parliament normally meets in Strasbourg for one week a month; these plenary sessions are open to the public. Committee meetings are held in Brussels.

Parliament has three main functions:

1. *Legislative.* Parliament is consulted about most legislation proposed by the Commission and can make amendments to it. Parliament can delay legislation by withholding its opinion until the Commission responds to its proposed amendments. Its decisions are presented to the Council but are not binding on it. Parliament can also make reports on its own initiative.
2. *Financial.* Parliament can request changes in some expenditure items and unilaterally make changes in others as well as reject the Community budget.
3. *Control.* Parliament can put oral and written questions to the Council and the Commission, and can bring both to the European Court of Justice for failing to act in accordance with the Treaty of Rome. It can also dismiss the Commission from office through a two-thirds majority vote.

Parliament considers its major task to be speeding up the process for completing the 1992 program. It expects also to increase its influence in the social area (Parliament has long advocated the establishment of a European charter of social rights) and on environmental issues.

MEPs sit in ten political party groupings, such as the European People's Party (Christian Democrats) or the Socialist Group (Social Democrats), rather than in national groups. Elections for the European Parliament occur every five years, the most recent one having taken place in June 1989. The Socialists again won the most seats; there are also a number of Communist MEPs (mostly Italian and French). The Greens increased their representation, as did also the extreme right.

Within the Parliament, three kinds of groups play a significant role:

1. *Political groups.* Because a majority of 260 votes is required for a measure to pass the second reading of legislation in Parliament (after a Council decision), both transnational and cross-party alliances are essential. At present, an alliance between the two largest groups, Socialists and Christian Democrats, guarantees ample support for speeding up the 1992 legislative process.

2. *Committees.* There are eighteen parliamentary committees dealing with various aspects of Community policy. For every piece of legislation, a *rapporteur* is nominated by the committee responsible for the particular area being addressed. The rapporteur assumes responsibility for writing a report about its specific content, and after discussions within the responsible committee, presents the committee's report to the Parliament as a whole. In preparing the report, the rapporteur works closely with the Commission and Council but also consults other interested bodies and lobbying groups. This process confers considerable power on the rapporteur.

3. *Inter-groups.* These are unofficial pressure groups formed by MEPs of different parties and member states that focus on specific areas such as the internal market, research and development, human rights in a particular country, and minority concerns. The "Kangaroo Group, the Movement for Free Movement," comprising approximately 200 MEPs, has played an influential role in articulating a free market position across national boundaries. Inter-groups and other unofficial groupings of MEPs can play an important role in influencing the Parliament's position on a specific issue, but the trade-offs among political groups (and in particular the possible alliances between Christian Democrats and Socialists, and Socialists, Communists, and Greens) are normally the decisive factors within Parliament.

Finally, Parliament now has the power to ratify all EC treaties with nonmember countries, and may veto any negotiation of commercial agreements (as was the case with the EC-Israel commercial treaty of 1988). This could prove important to U.S. interests.

The European Court of Justice

The European Court of Justice (ECJ) comprises thirteen judges, one from each member state plus one appointed by the large member states in rotation. They are assisted by six advocates-general, each appointed by agreement among the national governments. Both judges and advocates-general serve six-year renewable terms. A Court of First Instance has been attached to the ECJ to help relieve its heavy work load.

Based in Luxembourg, the ECJ can settle disputes and award penalties. It enjoys extensive powers of judicial review of Community and member state legislation, and all its judgments are binding. Judgments may be given on issues referred by the national courts or on those brought directly before the Court itself by member states and by EC citizens, institutions, and organizations. National courts are bound to ask the Court's opinion whenever they are in doubt about whether legislation adopted by their member states is in conformity with Community law.

The Court has played a significant role in framing competition policy and through its famous *Cassis de Dijon* judgment it laid the foundations for the new approach towards harmonization of national regulations, a major component of the 1992 process. ECJ judgments have also affected Commission proposals on value-added taxes, the application of competition rules to air transport, and the initiation of a Community insurance policy. The Commission's proposal on liberalizing transport is a result of Parliament's Court case against the Council relating to the Council's passivity in establishing the common transport policy advocated by the Treaty of Rome.

Although a hearing before the ECJ is difficult to obtain, an American party may attempt to do so. If appropriate, however, it is probably better to approach the national courts that are sworn to uphold Community law.

The EC Legislative Process

The first stage in the Community's lawmaking process is the drafting of a proposal by the Commission. This proposal is forwarded to the Council, which is empowered to reject, amend, or approve it. In those areas where the Treaty calls for consultation with the Parliament, the Council must first obtain Parliament's opinion, expressed during the first reading, before making its final decision. If you wish to try to influence Community legislation, it is best to do so before Parliament expresses its opinion during this first reading. For proposals relating to economic and social matters, the Council must also formally consult with the Economic and Social Committee of the Community, a body that represents the interests of European industrialists, merchants, and workers.

Whenever the *cooperation procedure* with the Parliament applies, as it usually does for 1992 legislation, the Council adopts what is known as its *common position*, or legislative proposal. The common position is referred back to Parliament for a second reading. The Parliament has three months during which it can approve, reject, or amend the Council's common position. Rejection requires an absolute majority of its members, approval a qualified majority. Normally, however, Parliament decides to amend the Council's position. Whatever its decision, Parliament then refers its second opinion to the Council and the Commission.

If Parliament has amended the proposal, the Commission must also put forward its views on the common position within one month. The Commission may adopt or reject some or all of Parliament's amendments, and forwards the proposal to the Council, which then has three months to reach a decision. After receiving the Parliament's amendments and the Commission's opinion on them, the Council may take a final decision on the proposal.

If Parliament rejects the common position, the Council can adopt it only through a unanimous vote. If the Commission does not approve Parliament's amendments to the common position, the Council can adopt the position, with Parliament's amendments, also only through a unanimous vote. Thus, the whole procedure has the goal of favoring a qualified majority vote within the Council on a final proposal that includes the views of both the Parliament and the Commission. Figure 2-1 presents an overview of the legislative process.

Under the Single European Act, the cooperation procedure applies to nearly all internal market proposals, except those falling under the rule of the unanimity (harmonization of taxes, free movement of persons, rights and interests of employed persons), and three other important areas: free movement of capital, liberalization of services, and sea and air transport.

The Nature of Community Law

While the primary source of Community law—its "constitution"—is the Treaty of Rome, secondary legislation also strives to realize the basic provisions contained in the Treaty. Secondary legislation consists of regulations, directives, decisions, and recommendations and opinions.

A *regulation* is a legal act that has general application, is binding in its entirety and immediately, and is directly applicable in all member states. They do not need to be confirmed by member states, and supersede even existing national laws. Both the Commission and the Council are empowered to issue regulations. Although their main goal is to secure the uniformity of laws, they have been limited mostly to establishing and developing market organizations for agricultural products.

Directives are binding, but only as to the results member states must achieve. The method of implementation is up to the national govern-

Figure 2-1. Community legislative process: new cooperation procedure.

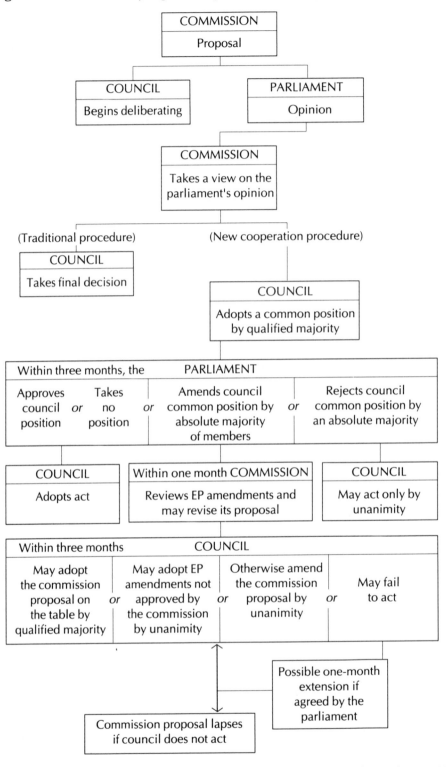

Source: United Kingdom Department of Trade and Industry, "The Single Market," February 1989, p. 14.

ments. In practical terms, the legislative changes required of each member state depend on the degree to which its laws differ from the Community directives. Both the Council and the Commission may issue directives, though they are usually issued by the Council. Member states are generally given a limited time to implement the directives. Most 1992 legislation is in the form of directives, and the Commission has made known its concern about the failure of member states to implement enabling legislation. This problem has been substantially increased as the Council has issued more directives. At the end of 1989, the United Kingdom, France, and the Netherlands had the best implementation record, Greece, Spain, and Portugal, the worst. The Commission is so concerned that it has threatened to replace directives with regulations, which, as noted above, take effect immediately.

Decisions are acts directed specifically to particular parties, which may be member states, companies, or individuals. Decisions are binding and are the usual instrument the Community uses to deal with individual cases. They have had their greatest impact in the competition field.

Recommendations and opinions are not binding and do not give rise to legal obligations. Only in some limited cases can they affect individuals or companies. By suggesting a specific course of action, their goal is to prepare the ground politically and psychologically for subsequent legal acts.

The 300 Directives: Why Only a Few Are Important to You

The directive, then, is the EC's main vehicle for implementing 1992. Because of the merging of some and the dropping of others, the original 300 directives of the White Paper have been reduced to 279. The Commission may also propose other directives to further the goals of achieving a single market.

Of the numerous directives, it is likely that only a few will be of interest to you, depending primarily on the industry you're in. Agriculture and environmental policy, for example, account for more than 200 of them. And even if you are in one of the most affected sectors, e.g., financial services or information technology, you need concentrate primarily on only a few areas, because these sectors, though subject to the most change, are going to be affected mostly by only a few, albeit major, developments, e.g., industry deregulation in financial services and harmonized standards in information technology.

The exception is company law, which will affect all sectors. The following is a brief analysis of developments in this area.

Company Law

A most difficult area has been company taxation. The former goal of a standard corporate rate throughout the EC has been replaced with that of mutual recognition. In this area, the Commission, in April 1990, issued revisions of three proposals:

1. The parent-subsidiary directive that would eliminate withholding taxes on dividends paid to a parent company in one member state by a subsidiary in another
2. The merger directive that would defer the capital gains tax on acquisitions so long as the acquired company continues paying taxes in its home state
3. The arbitration directive that would establish a panel to address tax disputes

The Commission is also likely to issue a controversial proposal that would enable companies to write off losses of a subsidiary in one member state against profits in another.

The regulation of a European Economic Interest Grouping (EEIG), which came into effect on July 1, 1989, enables EC companies, individuals, and some institutions to enter joint ventures that can operate under one Community law rather than several national ones. "Capitalization is not required. Once formed and registered, an EEIG will be able to acquire rights, incur obligations, make contracts, sue and be sued."[1] Although profits are allowed, the primary goal of EEIGs is to enable companies, especially small and medium-size ones, to share costs and risks in the fields of research and making tenders and to provide less costly joint services. One common use may be a collaboration between manufacturers and exporters to save setup and management costs.

The EEIG itself may have no more than 500 employees, and must be ancillary to the sponsoring companies, not a form of integration. There is no limit on the size of sponsoring organizations, but they must be EC legal entities and must have been operating in the EC before the grouping was created. Further, at least two members must have been operating in different member states. Although an EEIG may not issue shares to the public, participants are free to define financing arrangements and contractual relations among themselves and the EEIG's internal organization. An EEIG may even operate outside the EC.

The Fifth Company Law Directive, proposed in 1973, would harmonize the structure of public limited companies in the areas of composition and responsibilities of boards, employee participation in management, and auditing standards.

For certain types of companies, the Eleventh Company Law Directive would eliminate the current need for branches to publish accounts separate from those of the parent company.

The Fourth and Seventh Company Law Directives concern annual and consolidated accounts. The Commission has issued a proposal that would amend the scope of these directives by requiring harmonized practices in preparing financial statements. A yet-to-be-written Ninth Company Law Directive, concerning administration and audits as well as relationships between parent companies and their subsidiaries, is being opposed by the European business community, which fears that it could impose excessive administrative costs. It could also affect relationships between U.S. companies and their European subsidiaries. Small and medium-size enterprises may be exempt.

Small Business Can Play the Game Too

Keeping track of developments in EC legislation, tariff barriers, standardization, and administrative procedures can be particularly burdensome to small and medium-size enterprises (SMEs). Recognizing this problem, the EC has taken several steps, including:

- Establishing a Euro-Info Centres network throughout the EC. These offices provide access to Community data banks that have information on "legislation, aids, loans, research programs, internal market, third country markets, etc."[2]
- Initiating the Cooperative Research Action for Technology (CRAFT) program to help SMEs jointly commission research from third organizations such as universities and large companies.
- Reviewing all legislation for its impact on SMEs. A "proposal which would result in a noticeable increase in costs for SMEs can be blocked or modified before its adoption by the Commission."[3]
- Publishing *Euro-Info,* a monthly bulletin on EC initiatives that might affect SMEs.
- Implementing the Euronet-Diane system, "which makes more than 300 computerized data bases accessible to firms."[4]
- Providing seed capital through several funds.[5]

In addition, SMEs have access to BC-Net, a computerized network that helps them find advisers and business partners throughout the EC. You simply submit your company profile, and the system will compare your needs with those of other companies, often finding a match. If no match is found, the request is distributed to advisers in the areas you are interested in. So, even if you're in a small business, 1992 might be of great interest to you. By establishing operations in the EC or forming a partnership with an EC-based company, you can gain access to resources tailored to your needs. For further information on BC-Net, contact the EC Information Office in Washington, D.C. (see Directory E) or one of the EC Information Offices that are located throughout the EC.

Notes

1. United States Department of State, *The European Community's Program to Complete a Single Market by 1992* (July 5, 1988), p. 11.
2. *The Community and business: the action programme for small and medium-sized enterprises* (Luxembourg: Office for Official Publications of the European Communities, February 1988), p. 8.
3. Ibid., p. 5.
4. Ibid., p. 9.
5. See European Seed Capital Scheme, Enterprise Directorate, Rue de la Loi 200, B-1049, Brussels, Belgium.

Further Readings

"European Unification. The Origins and Growth of the European Community," European Documentation 3/1986. Luxembourg: Office for Official Publications of the European Communities, 1986.

Cooney, Stephen. "EC-92 and U.S. Industry. A National Association of Manufacturers Report on the Major Issues for U.S. Manufacturers in the European Community's Internal Market Program." Washington, D.C.: NAM, February 1989.

Chapter 3 | Euro-Hazards: Is the Trade Wall Going Up or Down?

Abroad it is feared that the liberalization within the Internal Market will be compensated by turning the Community into a fortress. . . . The internal market will create opportunities both for Community enterprises and for foreign firms; much will depend on their respective capacity to seize these opportunities.

Willy De Clercq
Former EC Commissioner for
External Relations and Trade Policy
From an interview, June 1989

The 1992 process will not create a closed European market. At nearly 25 percent of the EC's gross domestic product (GDP), exports are too important to be placed in jeopardy. However, while something resembling free trade is certainly in the EC's interest, particular sectors could impose barriers to non-EC countries for a variety of political and social reasons. Further, changes in the rules concerning mergers and acquisitions, intellectual property rights, and social legislation will affect everyone to some degree, regardless of whether they're European, American, or Asian. Some areas like social policy will affect all companies equally, but in other areas, like standards, European companies may be favored. Euro-hazards will affect different companies differently; sometimes this will depend on how a business operates in Europe, or, in the case of some protectionist measures, on the particular industry involved.

This chapter will help you to identify the Euro-hazards that could affect your business so that you can prepare for the upcoming developments. It is divided into two sections: The first covers new laws that could affect all companies in the Community, and the second discusses protectionist measures that will affect specific sectors.

The important thing to remember here is that some of the 1992 program will probably have negative effects on the way foreigners conduct business, a development that could become more pronounced if there is a sharp recession in the Community. It is important for you to keep track of these developments and to be aware of how you might have to alter your company policies to adapt to the new rules.

Why Euro-Hazards?

Because 1992 is intended to improve European competitiveness and because, in certain industries, EC companies still lack the scope and scale to compete, it isn't surprising that these companies seek protection as a way of buying time to develop the skills needed to play in the global game. If implemented, this protection will place non-EC companies at a disadvantage vis-à-vis their European competitors.

How do you know if you're in an industry that the EC may protect? Although any industry may try to persuade government officials that it needs a subsidy or tariff to shield it from import competition, there are two simple ways to identify those industries most likely to receive some form of protection. One is to discover which sectors the EC has targeted for development. These sectors include:

- Advanced materials
- Manufacturing processes
- Energy
- Ocean sciences
- Electronics
- Biotechnology
- Telecommunications

Another way is to identify those sectors that have historically been shielded from foreign competition either by individual member states or by the EC as a whole. Such areas include:

- Aircraft
- Agriculture
- Autos
- Textiles
- Steel
- Water
- Utilities

If you operate in one of these areas, you probably will confront some form of protectionist barrier, be it a tariff or something more complex like direct government subsidies or protected government purchasing contracts. You can follow these developments by reading Community statements and by observing Community actions, both in its protectionist activity and in the amount of money the Community has allocated to develop these industries in its cooperative R&D programs.

Will such government action encourage European companies to become more efficient, or will it just make them feel more secure behind a wall of protection? Although free traders may not like it much, the proper combination of government policies and management incentives can produce winners. Japanese and Korean efforts in steel, electronics, and shipbuilding prove that protection is a viable strategy if properly executed. But less happy examples abound: Sweden's attempts to support its shipbuilding industry resulted in the government's total cost being higher than if it had provided direct welfare payments to each displaced worker.

Still, the Europeans have had their share of successes. One noteworthy example, which they point to as a model for future endeavors, is Airbus. This case demonstrates that even the largest U.S. companies are not immune to European competitive efforts. Boeing, which once commanded 90 percent of the world's plane market, learned this lesson the hard way. Airbus Industrie, a European consortium, backed by the Community and several member states, is now the world's second largest aircraft manufacturer, with 30 percent of the world market.* Back in 1970, when Airbus opened for business, Boeing never dreamed that it would have the staying power to wrench away so much of its market share.

At first glance, it's clear why Boeing thought this. The industry certainly didn't have attractive entry features. Airbus faced:

- Huge investment requirements (R&D and manufacturing)
- Long payback periods (10 years or more on a model)
- High customer switching costs (parts, repairs, and training)
- A world-dominant competitor (Boeing)
- Industry overcapacity (Boeing could supply the world's annual needs)

This is about as formidable a set of conditions as a company can face, and it is unlikely that a nongovernment-supported enterprise could ever take them on. But the Community felt it was important to have the capability to produce aircraft. Why? For several reasons: Aircraft sales are a big-ticket item; they not only provide jobs at the aircraft company, they provide them for its suppliers as well, while simultaneously increasing local labor skills. Exports of aircraft naturally make a major contribution to a country's balance of trade, and aircraft manufacturing capability is considered important for national security. Finally, its technical development provides spin-offs for other industries and fosters growth in scientific institutes and universities.

Europe is not alone in its willingness to subsidize an industry to get it going; Japan and Korea have both done so, and the United States has

---

*Airbus was formed in 1970 as a French and West German joint venture. Great Britain joined in 1979, and Belgium became an associate member that year. When Spain joined the EC in 1986, it took a minority investment in Airbus.

recently pledged $500 million to Sematech, a consortium comprising fourteen U.S. semiconductor companies.

Economic justification for such government support always becomes entangled with political concerns (such as jobs in politicians' constituencies), thus reducing the ability of government to decrease support once the project (or company/industry) is self-sustaining. Airbus faces this complication now. It is strong enough to stand on its own, but its investors are concerned that an independent Airbus would move manufacturing overseas, thereby reducing jobs.

Airbus could have achieved its success only with government support and protection. Although this industry has characteristics that have made government participation essential, the EC may also take an active role in developing such industries as electronics and biotechnology. This might not involve such elaborate action as creating a consortium, but a combination of subsidies, tariffs, local content rules, and the encouragement of European companies to cooperate could make your European sales more difficult while forcing you to face stiffer European competition at home.

The justification for making business in the Community more difficult for foreigners goes beyond simply enhancing European corporate competitiveness. Many Europeans believe that the benefits from 1992 should be reaped by the Community first, and that "outsiders" should have to earn the right to share in the benefits. There are several factors, however, that support instead those who predict increased world trade as a result of the 1992 process. At the top of the list is Europe's position as the world's largest trader. Second, 1992 has been driven largely by the multinational companies of Europe, and it's in their best interests to ensure that a global trade war doesn't erupt. Finally, the underlying philosophy of the 1992 process is to open up Europe, to spark competition so that increased efficiency and innovation develop. Protectionist actions would defeat these lofty ambitions.

The challenge for executives in the United States is to keep abreast of the issues and to understand the ramifications for their businesses, no matter what scenario develops.

The sections that follow will help you to sort out the trade issues. Each topic presents a summation of the issue, a projection, essential background information, and sources for additional help. A list of the major relevant directives and legislation appears in Directory D, where they are listed under topic and (for Chapter 5) by industry.

Section One: General Legislative Issues

The section pertains to the hazards that potentially affect all companies. In most cases, EC and non-EC firms are in the same boat, for instance, in the area of intellectual property. But in others, like standards, EC firms may be favored. Besides intellectual property and standards, merger control and the social dimension are discussed here.

Intellectual Property

Patents, copyrights, and trademark protection should be strengthened by the 1992 process. The Commission hopes to be empowered to uphold international intellectual property (IP) agreements that are being worked on in the Uruguay round of the General Agreement on Tariffs and Trade (GATT) (see Chapter 9 for complete information). Expect national trademark systems to exist in parallel with the EC system during the harmonization process. The resolution of intellectual property conflicts and disagreements about where to locate the Community Trademark Office made IP one of the four areas identified by the Commission as being farthest behind schedule.[1]

Background: During the 1970s, patents and trademarks could be obtained only by filing separately in each of the member states, whose procedures and tests differed considerably. The European Patent Convention (1978) made it possible to obtain a European patent by applying to the European Patent Office in Munich, West Germany. This office, however, is not a Community institution; Denmark, Ireland, and Portugal don't belong, but Austria, Switzerland, and Sweden do.[2]

Although a European patent can be obtained through a single application (recognized only by the member countries of the Patent Office), its enforcement and validity are determined by national law and national courts; thus different rulings within the different member states are possible.

The Community is striving to establish a Community patent conven-

---

Three European Patent Options

1. Apply separately to each member state.
   - Time-consuming, but most reliable at the moment.
2. Apply through the European Patent Convention.
   - Not all member states belong.
   - Patents subject to individual country law.
3. After 1992: Apply through the Community Patent Convention.
   - Valid throughout the Community.
   - EC patent courts in each member state would have jurisdiction.

tion under which one patent would be valid throughout the EC and subject to EC-wide jurisdiction. Virtually all provisions have been agreed to, but the specifics as to how and when the convention is to be implemented have not.

Trademarks are in much the same position as patents. There are ten separate systems for registering trademarks—a common system for the three Benelux countries (Belgium, the Netherlands, and Luxembourg) and one each in the remaining member states. New directives to create a Community trademark would enable business to secure Communitywide protection through a single application to a Community Trademarks Office.

The EC-wide trademark system will run in parallel to the national systems. Because two firms in different parts of the EC could be using the same trademark, an EC-wide grant will not always be possible. Therefore, to avoid conflicts, member states have been required to harmonize their national laws on a number of significant points, such as the rights conferred by a registered trademark.[3]

Procedures for resolving conflicts, and the location of the Community Trademarks Office, have not been settled, so it is questionable whether the system will be in place by the target date of January 1, 1993.

In terms of copyright, software and prerecorded music/video stand to benefit most from harmonization and strengthening of member states' copyright laws. Some losses are substantial; for example, up to 50 percent of all videocassette sales in Greece are reported to be pirated sales, but all member states appear to have violations.[4] The 1988 Green Paper on copyright spells out several ways of stiffening penalties and improving enforcement throughout the Community.

U.S. Position: The U.S. government estimates that American industry lost about $50 billion from inadequate foreign protection of intellectual property in 1987. Other industrialized countries report similar losses. The current GATT round is attempting to develop a framework to reduce these infringements.

Although most EC countries have good trademark, patent, and copyright protection, Greece, Italy, Spain, and Portugal are perceived by many in American industry as offering less than adequate protection. Most U.S. companies and government officials believe that harmonization and strengthening of Community laws and enforcement will reduce most of these violations.

Thirteen major American corporations dedicated to the negotiation of a comprehensive agreement on IP in the current GATT round formed the Intellectual Property Committee (IPC) to formulate a U.S. position and to work with their European and Japanese counterparts on IP issues. Although the IPC represents such firms as IBM, Dupont, and Pfizer, it has actively sought other corporate input.

In 1988, the American, European, and Japanese groups issued a joint report outlining a basic framework for IP within GATT. Using this report as a foundation, United States Trade Representative (USTR) negotiators are pressing forth in the Uruguay round. The report calls for an IP code to be established in GATT, similar to the existing standards code, which commits signatories to abide by guidelines such as not using standards as a barrier to trade. The code would aim at reducing IP infringements by implementing adequate rules to protect intellectual property and by creating effective deterrents. All parties hope to reach multilateral settlements as opposed to bilateral agreements.

Merger Control

In December 1989, the EC finally agreed to a merger control regulation that gives the Commission, effective September 21, 1990, the right to review mergers of companies whose combined worldwide sales are in European Currency Units 5 billion or more, provided that EC sales of at least two of the companies involved exceed ECU 250 million.

Background: Member states have been reluctant to let the Commission veto mergers they considered important to their national interest, or to have their authority diluted or superseded by Community-level regulation. On the other hand, the Commission had hoped to achieve a one-stop merger review process under which companies involved in mergers and takeovers would have had to deal with only one government authority—and that in Brussels. The regulation on merger control is a compromise, the following being its other major provisions:

- The ECU's 5 billion threshold will be reviewed after four years.
- The threshold for banks is based on one-tenth of assets, for insurance companies on one-tenth of net premiums.
- Affected companies have one week to notify the Commission. The Commission then has three weeks to notify the companies if it plans to investigate.
- If it does investigate, the Commission has three months to make a decision.
- If the Commission chooses to block a merger, that is the end of the matter. If it does not, a member state can block an approved merger on grounds of national security, or when the deal violates its standards concerning media ownership or prudent practices by financial institutions.
- Further, smaller member states, lacking experience in such matters, may ask the Commission to investigate deals involving over ECU 2 billion.

Although the regulation will be enforced by the Commission's Competition Directorate-General (DG IV), some observers believe that the regulation's also addressing "economic and technical progress" might result in its being used as an element in industrial as well as competition policy.

The Commission's DG IV (Competition) has other powers to control European competition. Whereas the Council of Ministers normally has the greatest decision-making authority, the Commission and the Court of Justice play a larger role in regard to competition policy. Article 90 of the Treaty of Rome grants the Commission wide powers to attack market restrictions and to issue direct orders to member states regarding monopolistic industry structure without the involvement of the Council or Parliament. In 1988, the Commission used this tool to require the opening of markets by 1990 for telecommunications terminal equipment (telephone companies have long benefited from national protection).[5] It used it again in 1989 to open markets in value-added services like videotex and on-line data services. France has taken the Commission to the European Court of Justice over the matter.

Hostile takeovers are the subject of controversy, with Great Britain arguing that it and France account for more than 80 percent of takeover activity in the EC because only their companies tend to be predominantly publicly owned. German companies, for instance, are often cross-owned by banks and issue limited voting rights when the public is involved. In other countries, family control is the norm.

Although many argue that such ownership patterns would prove hard to control, the EC is considering some measures to help make the takeover environment more equitable. These include improving company disclosure practices, limiting cross-ownership, enabling a majority of shareholders to dismiss directors, and making it more difficult for target companies to buy their own shares.

U.S. Position: U.S. companies attempting to engage in merger activity in the EC will have to follow the regulation on merger control. Further, the regulation contains reciprocity language like that in the Second Banking Directive (see Chapter 5), meaning that the Commission could prohibit merger activity in the EC by a third-country firm if its home country were deemed to discriminate against EC firms attempting merger activity there. It is unlikely that this would affect American firms, and the Commission would first negotiate.

As long as decisions are based on sound competition policy, the United States has encouraged the development of this regulation. However, if it is used as an industrial policy tool, American companies will be at risk. USTR officials report no evidence to indicate that the EC would exercise this regulation beyond its stated intent.

In the United States, increasing concern about foreign direct investment (FDI) gave rise to the Exon-Florio Amendment to the 1988 trade bill, which enabled the President to review foreign takeovers of American business. If the President considers that an acquisition will threaten national security or adversely affect the national interest, he can block the sale. Foreign companies are concerned because the definition of national security was purposely left vague, allowing the President ample flexibility. If the President were to block a sale to an EC company, the merger control regulation's reciprocity provision could come into play.

The results of a 1989 poll reported in the *Economist* indicated that 85 percent of Americans think purchases by foreigners of U.S. companies should be limited.[6] This could prompt more legislation from an anxious Congress that wants to be in the forefront on a popular issue. As both EC and U.S. corporations increase acquisition of one another's firms, there is clearly potential for conflict.

Standards

EC-wide technological standards, be it a single voltage standard for common wall outlets or a standard operating system that enables computers to "talk" with each other, would ease the movement of goods throughout the community and cut production costs.[7] This contrasts with the costs of meeting many different standards; "for example, NV Philips, the Dutch-based electronics giant, carries 23 percent of its annual revenues in inventory while its U.S. counterparts need carry only 14 percent."[8] Eventually, manufacturers will be able to produce to one set of basic specifications instead of having to meet the different ones of each country. Product approval in one EC country will carry with it the right to sell throughout the Community.

However, new EC-wide standards could act as a barrier to non-EC products. For example, the U.S. forest products industry (with $900 million in exports to Western Europe) claims that the EC could set standards that are tied to specific properties found in European woods but not in American wood.[9] Foreign participation in standards formulation could alleviate some of this concern. Another reason standards might not become a trade barrier is that European companies striving for scale to compete globally will not benefit from solely European standards; it is in their best interests to have harmonized global standards.

Background: The elimination of technical barriers is an essential part of the 1992 program. Barriers are being removed in three ways:

1. *Avoiding New Barriers.* A 1983 directive required member states to notify the Commission in advance of all draft regulations and standards concerning technical specifications. This enables the Community to develop a harmonized EC standard before national standards become entrenched. In January 1989, the directive was extended to cover previously

excluded areas—agricultural products, foodstuffs, pharmaceuticals, and cosmetics.

2. *Harmonized European Standards.* In the past, agreement on EC-wide standards was a lengthy process because of the need to agree on a mass of technical detail and because, prior to the Single European Act, decisions had to be unanimous. For example, the Commission had to legislate such specifications as the width and length of the screws used to secure the driver's seat of a tractor. Once a standard was approved by the Council of Ministers, manufacturers wanting to change it had to petition the Commission to change the underlying law.

Under the new approach (begun in 1985), directives concerning standards are limited to setting only those requirements essential for health, safety, and consumer and environmental protection, with the technical details being worked out later by such bodies as the European Committee for Standardization (CEN) and the European Committee for Electrotechnical Standardization (CENELEC) (see description under "Standards Organizations" later in this section). All products that comply with these requirements are then entitled to carry an "EC" mark, which allows them to circulate freely in the rest of the EC.[10]

Of course it isn't possible for the Community to set standards for every product or all features of products; thus product attributes not covered by Community-defined *essential* standards are classified as *nonessential* and must be accepted by all member states, assuming the essential standards have been met.

Directives have already been agreed to for construction products, simple pressure vessels, toy safety, electromagnetic compatibility, and machinery safety. Agreement in principle has also been reached on personal protective equipment. Further proposals under discussion cover measuring instruments, gas appliances, powered implantable (and not implantable) medical equipment, nonactive medical devices, mobile machinery, and lifting equipment.

3. *Testing and Certification.* Testing to make sure that a product meets essential standards takes place in the more than 2,000 labs within the Community. In 1989 the Commission was attempting to establish criteria by which lab approaches could be harmonized to ensure that testing meets minimum requirements, thus enabling results to be recognized throughout the Community.

Lab harmonization will take several years beyond 1992 to effect. Lab quality varies greatly, especially in the southern European countries. Work your product through established labs in countries like Britain, France, and West Germany.

Attempts to harmonize the certification process (confirming that a product meets the established EC standard) are also taking place. The

Number of White Paper Standards Directives*

Agriculture	65	Machinery	7
Motor vehicles	22	Chemicals	5
Pharmaceuticals	9	Generic	3
Telecommunications	8	Miscellaneous	14

*More than half of the original 300 directives deal with standards.
Source: United States Industrial Trade Commission (USITC).

Union of Industrial Employers' Confederations of Europe (UNICE), the organization that represents industry (all sectors, all member states) in discussions with the Commission, has called for a "manufacturer's declaration of conformity" as the general rule for certification as opposed to a mandatory third-party certifier. In certain high-risk product categories (e.g., nuclear power plants), however, UNICE supports a third-party inspector. Member states are divided on the issue. Britain supports UNICE's position, whereas West Germany prefers to have third-party certification for all products.

Both lab testing and certification harmonization appear to be moving more slowly through the legislative process than standards harmonization, perhaps being five to ten years from completion.

To redress this situation, the Council, in December 1989, proposed the creation of a flexible, nonbureaucratic organization to encourage mutual recognition of test results and certificates. The details were being formulated in the Spring of 1990.

Mutual Recognition: The principle of *mutual recognition,* formally established in the EC in 1979, states that any product legally manufactured and marketed in one member state must also be admitted to the markets of all member states. The 1979 Cassis de Dijon decision by the Court of Justice set the precedent by forcing Germany to allow a French alcoholic beverage to be sold in Germany even though it fell below long-standing German alcoholic content standards.

Although the mutual recognition precedent has been set, its application is not consistent, especially where standards affecting human health and safety and the environment are concerned. Under Article 36 of the Treaty of Rome, member states have the right to prevent the free circulation of a good if they deem it unsafe for their citizens. Alleged concern for consumer protection has been the rationale behind several restrictive practices that have affected such products as Cassis de Dijon, German beer, and Italian pasta.[11] In 1988, for example, the European

Rank of Existing Technical Trade Barriers
(in descending order of importance)

- Motor vehicles
- Electrical engineering
- Mechanical engineering
- Pharmaceuticals (and some chemicals)
- Nonmetallic mineral products
- Other transport equipment
- Food and tobacco
- Leather
- Precision and medical equipment
- Metal articles

Source: Paolo Cecchini, *The Benefits of a Single Market* (Hampshire, England: Wildwood House), 1988.

Court of Justice upheld a Danish ruling that banned imports of soft drinks and beer in plastic bottles from other EC countries.

The Single European Act requires the Commission to base proposals for environmental standards on a high level. As these standards are established, fewer abuses of Article 36 will occur, and the principle of mutual recognition will finally be realized for all products. However, even in those areas where EC-wide standards have been set, member states are slow to adopt national legislation to reflect the Euro standard. The White Paper's fourth progress report in June 1989 stated that no member state had as yet incorporated the toy safety directive even though by law national legislation should have been enacted to meet the end-of-1989 deadline. For this reason, it's best to check with one of the boards listed under "Standards Organizations" in this chapter to identify the proper procedures for your products.

The following are industry groups that stand to gain the most from harmonized standards:

Standards and Trade: The Tokyo round of GATT established a code for standards that prevents them from being used as trade barriers. There is concern, however, that the EC will not permit American input into the standards process. Robert Mossbacher, the U.S. Secretary of Commerce, initiated discussions with the Commission in the summer of 1989 to provide American companies with the opportunity to comment on the early drafts of directives concerning EC-wide standards. Mossbacher was also concerned about mutual recognition of data for the purpose of certifying that U.S. products meet European standards and vice versa. Although criteria are being set for accrediting foreign laboratories, and a code of good conduct established for certification bodies, it is unclear what those procedures will be.[12]

As a result of the meetings with Mossbacher, CEN/CENELEC have informally allowed nonmember input into the technical committees. These committees will consider this input and, where appropriate, respond to requests. Although direct foreign participation on technical committees is not allowed, in certain instances an ad hoc forum may be created to further the dialogue. CEN/CENELEC have also agreed to make public all drafts and new work via the *Official Journal*. A House of Representatives Report on 1992 stated, however, that the EC compromise was not a significant improvement, and that there were no guarantees that the information provided would be complete or timely.[13]

Standards Organizations: There are several groups that govern standards policy around the world that you should be familiar with (see Figure 3-1). Addresses and phone numbers appear at the end of this chapter.

Community Organizations: The EC has restructured its standards formulation process to bring coherence to the Common Market. The task of formulating and harmonizing the technical specifications for standards has been assigned to nongovernmental, European regional standardization bodies. Although influencing the standards process takes place only at the member state organization level, the community groups may be able to provide you with general information and contacts on the national level.

1. *CEN:* The European Committee for Standardization promotes European standards in the nonelectrotechnical field. CEN is the world's largest regional standards group. Both EC and EFTA countries participate.
2. *CENELEC:* The European Committee for Electrotechnical Standardization promotes European standards for electrotechnical products.
3. *CEPT AND ETSI:* The European Conference of Postal and Telecommunications Administration (CEPT) publishes recommendations on harmonizing and improving administration and operational services. CEPT established the European Telecommunications Standards Institute (ETSI) to prepare standards for a unified telecommunications system. ETSI hosts a series of technical committees in which all European companies can participate. If you operate in the Community, you should be eligible. Ask for the ETSI monthly newsletter that highlights its activities.

These three organizations coordinate the work of the national standards groups in each member state. Each publishes material on its activ-

Figure 3-1. Interrelationships of entities influencing the development of European standards.

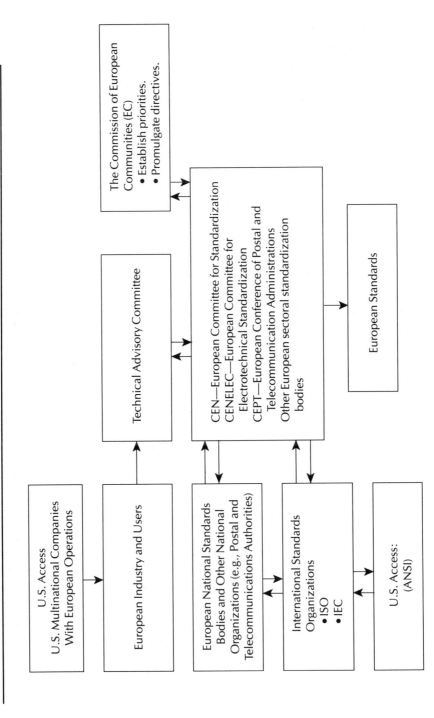

Source: U.S. International Trade Commission.

ity, most of which can be obtained through the American National Standards Institute (ANSI). There is talk of merging CEN/CENELEC/CEPT into one body to reduce fragmentation and increase coordination. The national organizations are brought together through a number of technical working committees that the Community organizations supervise (there are 200 technical committees and 400 working groups in CEN alone). The three best recognized national standards groups are the Association Française de Normalisation (AFNOR), the British Standards Institution (BSI), and the Deutsche Institut für Normung (DIN). Each national organization can assist you in tracking standards development. Some have data bases, newsletters, and seminars to help companies keep abreast of developments.

American National Standards Institute (ANSI): ANSI is a private sector organization that coordinates the establishment of voluntary standards for the United States. Over 1,000 companies and twenty government agencies belong to ANSI, and standards for all sectors of industry are under ANSI jurisdiction. ANSI also coordinates the activities of several more specialized standards groups like ASTM (the American Society of Testing and Materials). This fragmentation has at times caused friction that has resulted in multiple U.S. positions. One reason for this incoherence is that the United States is one of the few countries in which the government does not supervise the standards formulation process.

ANSI represents the United States at International Organization for Standardization (ISO) meetings and acts as the only official U.S. representative at CEN/CENELEC/CEPT conferences.

ANSI provides an important forum in which U.S. companies and government agencies can discuss standards issues. Through working groups, representatives of the different sectors meet to hammer out U.S. positions. ANSI provides technical details on EC developments, maintains a data base, conducts seminars, and publishes a biweekly newsletter.

International Organization for Standardization (ISO): ISO serves as an international forum for establishing and coordinating global standards. ANSI is the U.S. representative at these meetings. It joins a variety of other standards bodies from around the world, including CEN/CENELEC and most of the member state standards boards, in coordinating international standards. Although companies do not participate directly as members of ISO, there is opportunity for corporate participation through ISO working groups. The International Electrotechnical Commission (IEC) is the electrical version of ISO and is set up in a similar fashion. In recent years the two organizations have increased coordination. Between them they have established more than 85 percent of the world's international standards. There are over 3,000 ISO/IEC working groups, and on any given day there are about ten ISO or IEC meetings under way somewhere in the world.[14]

EC officials have stated that whenever possible they will adopt ISO standards. A new agreement was reached between CEN/CENELEC and ISO in 1988. The resulting CEN communiqué stated that, "It is the intention of CEN . . . to ensure that the CEN work in progress is transparent to the relevant ISO members, and that when CEN standards are to be different than ISO standards, ISO will be duly notified."[15] As it happens, this cordial relationship stems from the fact that Western Europe administers more than 70 percent of the ISO technical committee secretariats and pays nearly 40 percent of the membership dues.

In many instances, however, American standards diverge from international ones. This is partly because the United States believes that it need not comply with the world but rather that the world should accommodate itself to the United States, and partly because the U.S. process is fragmented and voluntary, making consensus with ISO very difficult to achieve. The U.S. Outdoor Power Equipment industry's recent successful participation in formulating standards for lawnmowers, hedge trimmers, and lawn trimmers through ISO may indicate that things are changing. These ISO standards are now being reviewed by CEN. If they are approved, U.S. companies will easily be able to comply with the European standard because they will have been part of the process through the ISO working groups. According to John F. Liskey of the Outdoor Power Equipment Institute, who headed the U.S. delegation, "This is one of the first standards of its kind to go to CEN. . . . U.S. manufacturers will be able to build one product for the EC, thus saving money."[16] On the other hand, when the 1988 CEN voluntary standard for forklift truck battery cables was enacted, only European producers manufactured cables that conformed to the standard; it took U.S. producers until mid-1989 to adapt their products to meet the standard.[17]

What to Do: Companies that operate in Europe can participate in the standards formulation process directly. To make your influence felt, the best way is to contact a member state standards board like BSI and join the appropriate technical working groups. Although U.S.-based exporters will have a more difficult time influencing EC standards than U.S. firms that either operate directly on the continent or in association with European firms, there are still options available:

1. Contact the U.S. standards organization ANSI.
2. Participate in its working groups.
3. Utilize its monitoring services (e.g., data bases and newsletters).
4. Use ANSI as a lobbying force.
5. When possible and if necessary, participate in ISO working groups. Contact ANSI to do this. Otherwise, make sure ANSI is representing your view at ISO meetings.

Trade associations and U.S. government agencies are other vehicles to contact; however, only ANSI is an official member of ISO and the only U.S. body recognized by CEN/CENELEC.

Besides ANSI, there are several U.S. government agencies that can assist in tracking the standards process. The National Center for Standards and Certification Information (NCSCI) maintains material on standards, regulations, and rules of certification for many countries. A reference collection is available for on-site review only. NCSCI can also assist in tracking specific directives and individual standards. The USTR and Commerce Department likewise can be of assistance (see Directory A).

Social Dimension

The social dimension concerns issues such as the rights of workers, health and safety requirements, length of the work week, transfer of private pension rights, equal rights for men and women, and rights for the elderly and disabled. While labor wants to protect and expand its rights in these areas, many in management fear that too rigid policies could encumber the flexibility and competitiveness of European industry. Further, there is disagreement over how much these policies should be the responsibility of the EC as a whole versus that of the individual member states.

Although the White Paper of 1985 did not address worker-related issues, the "social dimension" of 1992 has received increasing attention as the question of who will really benefit from an integrated EC came to the forefront of the whole debate. Labor mobilized this interest in 1987 and capitalized on it by getting part of the Single European Act to address social issues. Conservative losses in the 1989 European Parliament election further strengthened labor's position.

No other issue generates such acrimonious debate. Clearly, the issue cannot be ignored, as the White Paper had originally assumed. Discussions will probably continue well into the 1990s over what areas Brussels should dictate and what areas should be left to the discretion of member states.

The Community Charter of the Fundamental Social Rights of Workers details the labor issues under discussion. Although it was ratified at the Strasbourg Summit in December 1989, Great Britain refused to endorse it, claiming that the Charter was short on specifics.

Background: It was the famed *Vredling Proposal* of 1980 that touched off the heated social debate. This pro-labor document called for strong worker participation and involvement in corporate activity. Although the proposal was shot down, it has been credited with mobilizing European industry, providing the catalyst for the European Roundtable (an organization composed of the top European CEOs), and as a factor in creating the 1985 White Paper.

Because management wants the flexibility to respond to dynamic changes in the global market, whereas labor wants to maintain the hard-won privileges it has earned over the past years, the challenge will be to find the proper balance.

This isn't just a blue-collar issue. For example, engineers in Germany and Great Britain went on strike in 1989 to gain shorter working hours, claiming that productivity and profits had risen. Workers at Ford in the United Kingdom are also pressing for a shorter work week in the light of the company's record 1989 earnings. Managers fear that institutionalizing social rights will raise the costs of doing business throughout Europe and force many to manufacture elsewhere.

Nevertheless, most member states agree to a general framework of rights that would provide for health and safety measures, the transfer of private pension rights across frontiers, and the mutual recognition of individuals' technical qualifications. The problem lies with such specifics as the maximum allowable number of hours in the work week, or how many hours at night people under a certain age should be permitted to work.

The Community Social Charter, drafted by the Commission in September 1989, is the product of compromise and careful maneuvering. Its thirty articles were submitted to the European Council for approval at the Strasbourg Summit in December 1989. The wording was deliberately made vague in the hopes of soothing even such vocal opponents as Margaret Thatcher. Phrases like "fair and equitable" and "to satisfactory levels" appear throughout, precise definitions being purposely left for another time. Though this effort proved insufficient to comfort Mrs. Thatcher, the 11-to-1 vote by the Council in favor of the Charter was enough to carry forward its momentum. Notwithstanding that it is a symbolic statement without legal force, the Charter does point to the Commission's seriousness about ensuring that workers are not left behind in the mad rush to complete the internal market. It declares the Commission's intention of keeping a sharp lookout for loopholes that could lead to abuses in such areas as transferring pension rights for those who work in two or more member states.

Areas (and rights) covered by the Charter include:

- *Freedom of Movement.* Every worker will have the right to move anywhere within the EC and to be treated equally regarding access to employment, working conditions, and social protection.
- *Employment and remuneration.* All workers are entitled to a fair and equitable wage.

- *Improvement of Living and Working Conditions.* The 1992 process must lead to an improvement in the conditions of EC workers, and conditions of employment must be stipulated by law.
- *Social Protection.* Every worker has the right to adequate social protection.
- *Freedom of Association and Collective Bargaining.* Every employee has the right to join or not to join a union. (Some national unions have problems with this because their organizations promote closed shops.) Mediation and arbitration should be encouraged, but all workers have the right to strike subject to the obligations arising under national practice.
- *Vocational Training.* Every worker must have access to vocational training.
- *Equal Treatment for Men and Women.* This must be assured, and equal opportunities for men and women must be developed.
- *Information, Consultation, and Participation for Workers.* These must be provided, particularly in cases involving technological change, restructuring, and collective redundancy procedures.
- *Health Protection and Safety at the Workplace.* Every worker must enjoy satisfactory health and safety conditions.
- *Protection of Children and Adolescents.* Specific rules must be devised to prevent abuses in youth employment.
- *Elderly Persons.* Every EC worker, at the time of retirement, must be able to enjoy resources affording a decent standard of living.
- *Disabled Persons.* All disabled people are entitled to additional concrete measures aimed at improving their social and professional integration.[18]

The Charter declares that it is the "responsibility of the member states to guarantee the fundamental social rights . . . and to implement the social measures indispensable to the smooth operation of the internal market."[19]

The main fight will be over the Commission's action program, published in November 1989, which spells out the implementation plan for the Charter. Keen to avoid unnecessary conflict, the Commission states that "It will limit its proposals for directives or regulations to those areas where Community legislation seems necessary to achieve the social dimension of the internal market and, more generally, to contribute to the economic and social cohesion of the Community."[20] The action program contains more than forty-five proposals for directives. The document further claims that "the role to be played by Community standards, national legislation and contractual relations must be clearly defined." No one disagrees, but *how* the Community's role is to be defined is another matter.

One thing seems certain: The Commission has no intention of committing itself to any such administrative nightmare as attempting to ensure equal working conditions for every work force in every sector of every country within the European Community.[21]

Although the social debate takes place principally in the political arena, there are formal channels through which labor and industry can put forth their views. The European Trade Union Confederation (ETUC) represents all labor unions in Europe, and provides labor's input to the Commission. UNICE, the federation of European employers, is the formal corporate voice to the Commission. Naturally, trade groups and individual companies also have access to the Commission.

Just how many new jobs will actually be created as a result of the 1992 process is another issue that crops up during the social debate. The Cecchini Report projects that the 1992 process will create as many as 5 million jobs.[22] Economists of a more pessimistic turn predict that initially jobs will be lost while European business goes through a wrenching restructuring process. Only then, as business becomes competitive globally, will the job picture improve. The European Council, for its part, has called for making job creation a top priority in the completion of the internal market; its initial goal was the creation of 5 million jobs between 1988 and 1990.[23] Mrs. Thatcher claims that institutionalizing social benefits will result in a reduction in jobs. A 1990 report stated that 1.3 million new jobs were created in 1989 versus a loss of 600,000 in 1988. The report also credited the 1992 process for a 7 percent increase in investment in 1989 and 3.5 percent economic growth versus 1.5 percent in 1988.[24]

European Company Statute: A company incorporated under the proposed statute would be subject to just one single code of law. This would ease the creation of mergers and joint ventures and would enable companies to write off losses in one member state against profits in another.

At present, companies must incorporate in each country in which they are located and are subject to differing tax, accounting, and labor laws. Although accounting rules aren't scheduled for harmonization, companies would benefit from having to follow only one set of tax and labor laws.

In exchange for these benefits, companies would have to choose one of three worker participation systems:

1. *The West German Model* (Mitbestimmung). Worker representatives would have a seat on the supervisory board (similar to the board of directors in a U.S. company).
2. *The French Model.* There would be a separate system of independent internal employee councils, but workers would not have a seat on the board of directors.

3. *The Scandinavian Model.* Collective bargaining would determine the form of worker representation, but a member state would be free to disallow a representation option it did not like.

These systems are designed to provide information to workers and to provide a mechanism whereby employees can voice their concerns to management. But in all cases, management retains the right to make decisions.

Although adherence to the corporate statute is voluntary, some companies are afraid that unions will force them to incorporate under the law so as to increase worker input. There is certainly a danger in institutionalizing worker participation because the potential for abuse is great. On the other hand, many companies are realizing that workers can be an important partner, not just a variable cost. Providing information to employees and seeking their input on major decisions in most cases is just good business.

Section Two: Protectionist Measures

This section describes Euro-hazards that pertain to specific industries, including government procurement, harmonization of veterinary and phytosanitary measures, import quotas, reciprocity, and rules of origin and local content. You'll find industry alert labels at the beginning of each category that identify those areas most susceptible to the hazard being discussed. But it's a good idea also to scan those protectionist measures that don't apply to your industry because the protectionist winds could blow in your direction at any time.

Government Procurement

Industry Alert: Services, public works contracts, telecommunications, water, energy, and transport.

Access to highly coveted government procurement contracts, estimated at bringing in $490 billion a year to companies in the EC, holds great opportunity for many companies. The new rules are intended to encourage member states to buy on the basis of the cost and quality of the product rather than according to the nationality of the supplier. The EC estimates that savings of more than $21 billion will result from an open public procurement system.[25] But since so much money is at stake, and many national firms require more time to become competitive, you can expect delays in approvals and implementation.

Estimated Savings via Open Government Procurement

Pharmaceuticals: 52% in Germany, 40% in the UK
Office Machinery: 12% in France, 27% in Italy
Telephones: 20% in Belgium, 43% in France, 39% in Germany

Source: Paolo Cecchini, *1992, The Benefits of a Single Market* (Hampshire, England: Wildwood House, 1988), p. 19.

Background: Member states have used government procurement as a form of industrial policy for many years. Although roughly 20 percent of public contracts are subject to open tendering, only 2 percent in the mid-1980s were awarded to nonnational firms.[26] This figure is a bit deceiving because it doesn't capture the cross-border value of subcontracts; however, no data have been collected on this.

EC decisions in the 1970s to open up the process together with the 1984 recommendation for opening telecommunications contracts have proved ineffective. The most serious infringements include:

- Failure to publish invitations to tender
- Misuse of exceptional bid award procedures
- Incompatibility of bid conditions with legislation
- Unlawful exclusion of tenderers
- Discrimination in the evaluation of tenderers
- Discrimination in tender awards[27]

In early 1990, the Commission made significant progress by approving a directive opening up procurement in previously excluded sectors—water, energy, telecommunications, and transport.

To truly open government procurement, *transparency* must be required. That is, procedures must be conducted in a public manner that allows equal participation by both EC and non-EC firms. In most cases, government procurement requests for bids and lists of contracts awarded will be found in the EC's *Official Journal* (similar to the U.S. *Federal Register*). The long-range goal is to open 80 percent of public purchasing to EC-wide competition.[28]

There is concern that a national champion, that is, a company that has been nurtured by way of a monopoly on government contracts, will seek *infant industry status* on the basis that it needs such protection in order to gain the scale necessary to compete against imports. This would naturally result in preference being given EC firms over non-EC companies.

Restricted or negotiated procedures are permitted for certain government contracts (for instance, those dealing with telecommunications and postal services, water companies, airports, maritime ports, railway companies, gas and electric utilities, and gas and oil explorers). However, all interested suppliers are entitled to objective and nondiscriminatory reasons for their exclusion.

EC officials want to ensure that Community companies gain access to the home markets of any non-EC firms that are awarded Community government procurement contracts. Therefore, the possibility exists that the EC will seek *reciprocity* from countries before offering equal access to their lucrative government contracts.

Another option is for EC officials to adopt a *linkage* approach to other countries. This refers to quid pro quos negotiated between governments. For example, the United States might agree to provide Europe with access to its military procurement process if the EC provided U.S. companies with access to government telecommunications projects.

Most legislation is aimed at opening the government procurement process for all firms; however, because national firms dominate this area, Community efforts will be considered a success if they can simply increase intra-EC contract awards. Expect Euro firms to get the initial contracts, followed by foreign firms operating in the Community, and only then by exporters. In most cases, exporters will be awarded contracts only when their products are unavailable locally or through package deals that involve technology transfer.

The GATT Government Procurement Code negotiations being conducted in the Uruguay round deal with trying to make government procurement fair for all bidders, regardless of origin. The EC represents all member states, so it is hoped that consistent, predictable, and competitive procedures can be established.

Technically speaking, government procurement barriers should not affect non-EC companies already operating in Europe. *Article 58 of the Treaty of Rome* states that companies conducting business in the Community, regardless of where their corporation's home base is, will be considered European. This provides equal status for U.S. companies based in Europe and should give adequate protection against discrimination based solely on corporate parentage.

U.S. Position: The United States claims that its companies will be treated far less favorably in Europe than Euro companies are treated in the United States when it comes to government procurement. While U.S. companies will get non-discriminatory access only up to 25 percent of the EC government market, EC companies will get 80 percent non-discriminatory access to U.S. government purchases.[29]

This inequity arises from a series of memoranda of understanding (MOU) with European nations governing the purchase of defense ar-

TED (Tenders Electronic Daily) is an on-line data base that lists public calls for tender offered by more than eighty countries. Documents are available on the morning of their publication (see Chapter 4, Step 2 under "How You Should Deal With 1992," for details on all EC data bases).

ticles. These agreements ensure that U.S. and EC defense contractors are not discriminated against in each other's home country. Because the U.S. defense procurement budget is much greater than the combined member states' budgets, European firms enjoy more nondiscriminatory access.

A good example of the potentially negative impact of the 1992 procurement directives on U.S. exports occurs in the heavy electrical equipment industry. For the past twenty years, the EC government procurement market for heavy electrical equipment, worth between $5 billion and $10 billion per year, has been virtually closed to American producers. From 1975 to 1988, U.S. companies did not win a single order from an EC purchaser for a large steam generator, an essential ingredient in energy generation. By contrast, the U.S. market for large power generators is completely open, with EC member countries supplying 50 percent of U.S. imports of this equipment.[30] Because many of these American companies are small, they don't manufacture in Europe. Meeting the local content requirement is therefore all but impossible for them.

Harmonization of Veterinary and Phytosanitary Measures

Industry Alert: Agricultural products, biotechnology.

The 1992 process includes a number of measures to improve animal, plant, and fish health, and to facilitate trade between member states. However, progress on this front has been slow. The White Paper's fourth progress report in June 1989 identified this area as one that was seriously behind schedule. The Community has had difficulty agreeing to EC-wide standards for these areas.

A major bone of contention between the United States and the EC concerns the EC's 1989 prohibition on the import of U.S. hormone-fed beef. Expect lengthy trade debates and delays.

Background: The question of food product purity inspires bold political activity because it's a guaranteed vote generator. The beef hormone debate not only rallied consumer and farmer support for politicians who called for the ban; it also attracted those who enjoy seeing Europe stand up to U.S. demands. Technically, the hormone issue falls under GATT's standards code. This states that standards generally cannot be used to block international trade. The USTR claimed that the hormone directive violated this code because it was not based on scientific evidence, but, rather, was a protectionist measure. The EC disagrees, claiming that the rules apply to all producers, including EC farmers. The EC also points out that it granted American exporters a longer grace period than it granted its own farmers to comply with the directive.

A US/EC task force was formed in early 1989 to resolve the issue. Although discussions are not slowing other trade negotiations, a prompt resolution of the hormone issue is unlikely. Other areas likely to create similar tensions include pesticide usage and pesticide residues on produce; however, agreement was reached in December 1989 on compulsory tolerances for residues of veterinary medicines and foodstuffs.

U.S. Position: In general, the United States is fighting stringent enforcement of these EC directives, and supporting instead recognition and acceptance of equivalent U.S. production and marketing processes.

After the EC ban of U.S. beef in 1989, John Hightower, agricultural commissioner for Texas, encouraged small farmers to raise hormone-free beef to sell in Europe. Unfortunately, he has not received the support of the U.S. Department of Agriculture (USDA) or of the cattlemen who make use of hormones because of their fears of drawing the public's attention to the whole question of chemicals in cattle. Hightower favored USDA certification of hormone-free beef, which would then have eased the European registration process; but the USDA doesn't want to label products in any manner that would suggest to the public that the hormone used is dangerous.

Import Quotas

Industry Alert: Textiles, autos, footwear, urea, consumer electronics, bananas, sewing machines, motorcycles, dishware and certain ceramic articles.

Quantitative restrictions (QRs) are member state quotas placed on specific imports. Although QRs are illegal under GATT, member states protect more than 1,000 products through national QRs. Italy, France, and Spain top the list in this practice. Because the 1992 process entails the free flow of goods within the Community, it will be impossible for member states to control these QRs, and most will be eliminated. Because of strong local political pressure, however, there has been talk of elevating some QRs to Communitywide levels.

Background: Examples of quantitative restrictions include the following facts:

- Greece allows no imports of bananas.
- A few highly visible QRs are attached to automobiles:

—*Italy:* Only 3,500 Japanese cars allowed per year.*
—*France:* Only 3 percent of French market allowed for Japanese cars per year (Britain, Spain, and Portugal also have restrictions on Japanese cars).
- Spain has QRs on many agricultural and industrial products.
- Most QRs are on textiles and have been set under the terms of the multifiber agreement for Community and/or member states. None apply to exports from the United States.

Because it is economically and politically difficult simply to remove existing QRs, a transitional phase will be needed to ease manufacturers and growers into the competitive process that has been restrained by these quotas. One possibility is a series of *voluntary restraint agreements (VRAs)*, sometimes referred to as voluntary export restraints (VERs). A VRA is an import quota negotiated between two countries that is voluntarily adhered to. The United States established a VRA with the Japanese on autos throughout much of the 1980s. Don't be surprised to see the EC enter into a Community-wide auto VRA with the Japanese. There has been talk of including Japanese cars produced in the United States within the VRA, a development that would rankle American officials because a U.S.-produced Nissan shipped abroad helps the United States' trade balance. The Community could also use local content requirements and rules of origin as other ways of cushioning the elimination of QRs. The EC assures GATT participants that any communitywide QRs will be negotiated through proper GATT channels.

U.S. Position: The United States claims that QRs are not justified according to Article XIX of GATT, which provides for relief through tariffs for sectors facing potential injury from import competition. However, politically and economically, it will be difficult for the EC to avoid establishing some VRAs.

The EC has responded to American complaints by expressing concerns of its own. The Commission claims that the United States has also violated Article XIX. It points to President Bush's 1989 decision to extend an existing VRA agreement on steel until March 1992 as a prime example. The EC feels that the U.S. steel industry is healthy enough to stand on its own. It also points out that EC steel exports to the United States have been substantially reduced from their 1982 levels.[31]

Reciprocity

Industry Alert: Banking, securities, insurance, other services, and public procurement.

---

*Statistics vary on how many Japanese cars are actually sold in Italy. Some Italian officials claim that the number is much higher than the QR.

Foreign access to EC markets could be in jeopardy, depending on how reciprocity is applied to specific sectors. Because the term can be defined in many ways and because the Community has been unclear as to its precise use of the word, the potential for trade friction is great.

Background: The EC is preparing more than sixty directives affecting the service sector, and is also developing a general policy framework for services. Pending directives will address the following sectors:

- Transportation
- Banking
- Securities
- Insurance
- Mortgage credit
- Payment cards
- Engineering
- Mobile telephones
- Information services
- Medical services
- Broadcasting

In 1988 the Commission stated that it would seek "reciprocity" from non-EC countries as a condition for granting access to newly integrated markets in services, investment, and other areas not covered by GATT. USTR officials are concerned that the EC is seeking to gain concessions from third countries in payment for access to the unified EC market. In 1989 there were indications that the EC would consider backing down from its initial position of mandatory reciprocity to a more liberal stance of national treatment (see below).

Reciprocity can be defined as requiring that the status of, and opportunities for, EC firms conducting business abroad be equivalent to those they enjoy at home in the EC. U.S. companies could face restrictions in the EC if U.S. rules in specific sectors are not equivalent to, or are more restrictive than, the EC's. For example, in the area of banking, the United States would be accorded the same benefits as EC banks in the Community only if the banks of each member state enjoyed an access to the American market similar to what U.S. banks enjoyed in the EC.[32] The fact that some states limit foreign banking could in itself be viewed as denying EC banks access.

National treatment, or equality of competitive opportunity, on the other hand, means that the competitive rules are the same for domestic and foreign companies operating in a country regardless of what conditions exist outside the market. EC banks, therefore, could operate in the United States under the same laws as U.S. banks do even though U.S. rules are more restrictive than the Community's. In turn, the EC would permit U.S. banks to operate in Europe under the same laws as their banks operate under without requiring any conditions or linkage to EC banking activity in the American market.

The issue of reciprocity versus national treatment has caused heated debate between the United States and the EC, especially with respect to the Second Banking Directive. The problem stems from the differences in banking laws in the two regions. The U.S. Glass-Steagal Act prohibits institutions from engaging in both commercial and investment banking, whereas in Europe no such law exists.

A revised draft of the Second Banking Directive (April 13, 1989) defined reciprocity in terms of national treatment, thus reducing U.S. fears that the EC would require the United States to allow EC banks to conduct commercial and investment banking services in America as a condition for permitting U.S. banks to operate in Europe under the same conditions as EC banks. In April 1989 the Commission stated: "Any country providing genuine national treatment to Community banks would be under no threat."[33]

The scope of the EC's new definition and clarification of reciprocity is restricted to the banking sector. Whether national treatment will be applied to government procurement and other financial services is still unclear. U.S. officials hope that the new Second Banking Directive will be the model for other directives.

There are other forms of reciprocity that you should be aware of. *Mirror-image reciprocity* means that the EC would insist that opportunities for EC firms abroad be equivalent to those provided foreign firms in the EC before it granted access to post-1992 Europe. The conditions would be applied to specific sectors. Mirror-image tests normally result in discrimination because countries are unlikely to modify their systems to suit the demands of foreign governments. *Overall balance of concessions*, on the other hand, is a reciprocity test based on the degree of market access provided EC firms in *all* sectors, not just a specific industry.

U.S. Position: With some exceptions, national treatment is the general policy of the United States. The United States claims that reciprocity as defined above violates GATT Article I [stipulating Most Favored Nation (MFN) treatment, which requires all signatories to treat all others equally as regards custom duties, rules, and regulations governing trade (see Chapter 9).] A key objective for the United States in the Uruguay round of GATT is to liberalize trade and investment in services, which in turn would result in national treatment as the standard the EC would have to apply to all sectors.

Rules of Origin and Local Content

Industry Alert: Autos, electronics, services.

Would Honda cars made in Ohio and then shipped to Europe be considered American or Japanese? A tough call, you say. That decision, however, will determine rates of import duties, antidumping measures, and eligibility to participate in certain commercial opportunities.[34] The problem is that no agreed-upon standard of determination of origin exists between the United States and the EC. The GATT Uruguay round negotiators hope to create an international rule of origin standard, encompassing criteria such as predictability, transparency, consistency, neutrality, and nondiscrimination. Although the EC has said it will adhere to GATT standards, don't be surprised if rules of origin are used as protectionist measures in EC-targeted sectors.

Background: A common method used to determine the origin of a product is its local content percentage, that is, the percentage of added value (labor and material) contributed by the local economy. This standard was established largely to prevent products produced in "screwdriver" plants (where components manufactured elsewhere are merely assembled) from being deemed Community products, when, in actuality, very little of the product is made locally. Local content rulings force U.S. companies to increase overseas activity (parts and labor) or to face having their products reclassified as imports and thereby subject to tariffs.

There is no uniform percentage that establishes products as being European. It varies by sector. For example:

- For products of "screwdriver" plants, a local content value of at least 40 percent is required. In March 1990, a GATT panel ruled that duties on products of such plants violate GATT rules.
- For VCRs, 45 percent is required.
- For radios, TVs, and ball bearings, 35 to 45 percent is required.
- Most imports from EFTA must have at least 60 percent EFTA content to be included under the EC-EFTA Free Trade Agreements.

The *safeguard rule* requires that components of a finished product be 45 percent European for it to be considered European. Otherwise, the components are subject to possible tariffs, thus increasing the cost of the finished product.[35]

Another way to determine origin is through *substantial transformation* (defined as the essential added-value component of the product) rather than through its overall local content percentage. A recent EC ruling on semiconductors was based on this concept.

In early 1989, the U.S. semiconductor industry was caught off guard when the EC ruled that the diffusion process involved in chip making had to be conducted in the Community for a chip to be considered European. Although the semiconductor ruling was intended to curtail Japanese dumping of chips, the law was enacted without prior notice to the United States.[36] Because the plants required to conduct the diffusion process cost around $100 million each, U.S. manufacturers must reexamine their investment plans and decide whether it is preferable to pay the 14 percent tariff or to commit the funds necessary to avoid the import status. Intel, for instance, announced in late 1989 that it would set up a chip plant in Ireland to better service its European customers.

Other EC local content rulings have caused manufacturers problems. In 1988, for example, when Nissan agreed to use 60 percent local content in its British plant in exchange for generous United Kingdom government incentives, other member states were reluctant to accept the car as European (France wanted 80 percent). After heated debate, a compromise was reached; 60 percent would be considered sufficient for 1988, but Nissan would have to increase the European content of its automobiles to 80 percent within three years (the percentage difference representing engine development).

The French were considered the losers in this debate for a couple of reasons. Not only did the British get the 60 percent concession (for the short term), but they also received major investment commitments from Toyota and Honda in addition to Nissan's investment. French hostility naturally cooled Japanese enthusiasm for investment in France. French government authorities now must scramble to convince the Japanese that their investment is welcomed.

Television programming provides another striking example. What's at stake is the $1 billion worth of U.S. films and television shows that are broadcast on European airwaves each year.[37] In an attempt to improve the quality and quantity of European television efforts, the Commission considered a ruling to reserve a large percentage of the European airwaves for indigenous productions. After much pressure from the United States, however, the "TV Without Frontiers" directive specified no percentage, but did stipulate that, where practicable, the majority of programs should be European-produced.[38] This is another example of how rules of origin can be used as a trade barrier because of their potential to hinder the sale of foreign programming. USTR officials claim that if Euro producers want more access to the airwaves they should simply create programs Europeans want to watch. While trade officials bicker across the ocean, companies like MCA are considering setting up European production facilities.

On the positive side, the EC Commissioner for Internal Market and Industrial Affairs (DG III), Martin Bangemann, has called for an end to all local content rules not specifically related to the enforcement of antidumping regulations. Further, in March 1990, the European Court of Justice ruled that some importers and middlemen can appeal against dumping duties; previously, only manufacturers could.

The U.S. Position: The United States opposes local content requirements, claiming that they restrict investment choices, artificially reduce trade, and distort international investment flows. European rules of origin rulings could spark a flurry of similar requirements around the globe. The United States is pushing for a transparent and predictable process for determining these rules.

Although local content legislation has been discussed on Capitol Hill, it has never passed. The only local content rules in the United States pertain to certain military equipment, for reasons of national security.

There is concern that increased European local content percentages will force U.S. companies to relocate to Europe, in the process causing loss of jobs domestically and a decrease in exports. The National Association of Manufacturers (NAM), a U.S. trade association representing 80 percent of U.S. manufacturing production and manufactured exports, doesn't agree. During an interview in the summer of 1989, Stephen Cooney of NAM said, "Market access is the principal reason U.S. companies produce abroad. If a company wants to be a major player in a market, it just can't do it without local production. Although it is common to hear that this hurts U.S. exports and jobs, this isn't the case. Normally a company's move overseas results in increased U.S. exports because the subsidiary relies on U.S. capital equipment to get the operation going.*

Richard E. Heckert, NAM chairman of the board and former CEO of E. I. DuPont de Nemours and Company, testifying at a Senate hearing in May 1989, said:

> Since EC companies are trying to be more competitive, they are going to need access to advanced and competitively priced technologies and products from U.S. companies as well as European companies. Our strongest trade surpluses are in capital goods and in technologically advanced industrial materials such as chemicals. For this reason, the EC is unlikely to want to keep out competitive and innovative U.S. goods.[39]

One coy move suggested by some is to enter the EC through the backdoor, via an EFTA country. For example, EFTA's automotive local content percentage is only 50 percent; therefore, one could set up an operation in Austria, maintain 50 percent EFTA content, and then enter the EC under the EC-EFTA Free Trade Agreement.

---

*NAM based this conclusion on the fact that close to 35 percent of all U.S. exports to Europe go to U.S. affiliates operating in the EC.

Notes

1. Commission of the European Communities, *Fourth Progress Report of the Commission to the Council and the European Parliament*, COM (89) 311, June 20, 1989, p. 12.
2. Excerpt from a United Kingdom Department of Trade and Industry brochure, "Europe Open for Business: Single Market Factsheet #14," 1988.
3. United Kingdom Department of Trade and Industry, "The Facts About the Single Market," 4th ed., 1989.
4. USITC, "The effects of greater economic integration within the European Community on the United States," USITC publication 2204, July 1989, pp. 12–19.
5. United States Department of State, *The European Community's Program to Complete A Single Market by 1992*, July 5, 1988, p. 4.
6. "Storming the Fortress," *The Economist*, July 15, 1989, p. 66.
7. Congressional Research Service, "The Europe 1992 Plan: Science and Technology Issues," by Glenn J. McLoughlin, *CRS Report for Congress*, March 16, 1989, p. 7.
8. *Institutional Investor*, July 1988, p. 48.
9. U.S. House of Representatives, Report by the Subcommittee on International Economic Policy and Trade of the Committee on Foreign Affairs, May 31, 1989, p. 21.
10. Excerpt from the Scottish Development Agency brochure "1992 Issues: Product Regulatory Standardization," May 1989.
11. USITC, "The Effects of Greater Economic Integration Within the European Community on the United States," pp. 6–11.
12. Michael Calingaert, *The 1992 Challenge From Europe* (Washington, D.C.: National Planning Association, 1988), p. 61.
13. U.S. House of Representatives, Report by the Subcommittee on International Economic Policy and Trade of the Committee on Foreign Affairs, May 31, 1989, p. 22.
14. Excerpt from a speech by Dr. Lawrence D. Eicher, Secretary-General of ISO, at the Annual Public Conference of ANSI, March 1989.
15. Ibid.
16. ANSI press release, August 23, 1989.
17. United States Department of Commerce, *EC 1992*, Vol. I, May 1989, p. 64.
18. European Community, "Community Charter of the Fundamental Social Rights of Workers," December 1989.
19. Ibid.
20. European Commission, "Communication from the Commission concerning its action programme relating to the implementation of the Community charter of basic social rights for workers," COM (89) 568, November 29, 1989, p. 8.
21. "The Looming Labour Crunch," *International Management*, February 1989, p. 26.
22. Paolo Cecchini, *1992, The Benefits of a Single Market* (Hampshire, England: Wildwood House, 1988), p. 102.
23. EC Office of Press and Public Affairs, "EC Summit Brings Agreement on

Monetary Union," *European Community News*, Release no. 21/89, June 28, 1989, p. 4.

24. "Single Market Programme already has positive effects," *Journal de Geneve*, February 15, 1990, p. 9.

25. Michael Calingaert, *The 1992 Challenge From Europe* (Washington, D.C.: National Planning Association, 1988), p. 27.

26. United States Department of State, "The European Community's Program to Complete a Single Market by 1992," July 5, 1988, p. 7.

27. Calingaert, *The 1992 Challenge*, p. 27.

28. Congressional Research Service, "1992 Plan for Economic Integration," by Glennon Harrison, *CRS Issue Brief*, June 20, 1989, p. 7.

29. U.S. House of Representatives, Report by the Subcommittee on International Economic Policy and Trade of the Committee on Foreign Affairs, May 31, 1989, p. 3.

30. Ibid., p. 47.

31. "EC Commission reacts to US steel decision," *European Community News*, Release no. 25/89, July 26, 1989.

32. Congressional Research Service, "1992 and Reciprocity," by Glennon J. Harrison, *CRS Report for Congress*, April 11, 1989, p. 3.

33. "EC Commission Clarifies Reciprocity Provisions in Proposed Second Banking Directive," *European Community News*, Release no. 10/89, April 13, 1989.

34. Excerpt from the testimony of James M. Murphy, Jr., Assistant U.S. Trade Representative for Europe and the Mediterranean, before the Ways and Means Trade Subcommittee, hearing on "Europe 1992," March 20, 1989.

35. U.S. House of Representatives, Report by the Subcommittee on International Economic Policy and Trade of the Committee on Foreign Affairs, May 31, 1989, p. 31.

36. Ibid., p. 32.

37. "Buddy, can you spare a reel?" *The Economist*, August 19, 1989, p. 56.

38. "European Commission Adopts Television Without Frontiers Directive," *European Community News* Release No. 33/89, October 4, 1989.

39. Excerpt from testimony given by Richard E. Heckert, former DuPont CEO, before the Committee on Finance, United States Senate, May 10, 1989.

Further Readings

Government Procurement

The European Community Official Journal. Similar to the *U.S. Federal Register.* Contact EC offices in Washington, San Francisco, or New York for a copy.

A Guide to the Community Rules on Open Procurement or *Vademecum*, 12/31/87, an EC publication. Describes government procurement liberalization proposals.

Intellectual Property

EC Green Paper: Copyright and the challenge of technology, (88)172.

EC Green Paper: Harmonization of copyright in the EC, 6/16/88.

Standards

Common Standards for Enterprises, by Florence Nicolas, European Communities Publication, ISBN 92-825-8554-9, 1988. Provides a good overview of the standards process and its implications for European competitiveness, but skirts the protectionist issues.

The European Community Official Journal. See listing under Government Procurement.

Global approach to technical specifications and certification. A policy statement and draft resolution from the Department of Trade and Industry of the United Kingdom, November 1988.

Standards Action. A biweekly publication by the American National Standards Institute, 1430 Broadway, New York, N.Y. 10018. Provides updates and listings, and calls for comments on standards being formulated in the United States and abroad. Although you have to filter through the morass of standards undergoing formulation, from fittings, flanges, and valves to video recording devices, it's a good source for keeping abreast of U.S. efforts.

Social Dimension

Community Charter of the Fundamental Social Rights of Workers. Luxembourg: Office for Official Publications of the European Communities, December 1989.

The Social Dimension of the Internal Market. Luxembourg: Office for Official Publications of the European Communities, 1989.

Communication from the Commission Concerning Its Action Programme Relating to the Implementation of the Community Charter of Basic Social Rights for Workers, EC Commission, COM(89)568, November 29, 1989.

General Hazards

The Effects of Greater Economic Integration Within the European Community on the United States, USITC Publication 2204, July 1989. A detailed account and analysis of the major potential trade barriers in the EC, based on solicited, direct corporate and trade industry input. Dry at times, with numerous footnotes, it is nevertheless comprehensive and well researched.

Phone Directory

ANSI
American National Standards Institute (ANSI)
1430 Broadway
New York, N.Y. 10018
Phone: 212/354-3300
Fax: 212/398-0023
Contact: Ms. Pam Snook

AFNOR
Association Française de Normalisation Pour Europe (AFNOR)
Cedex 7
92080 Paris la Defense
France
Phone: 33/1 42 91 55 00

BSI
British Standards Institution (BSI)
2, Park Street
London W1A2 BS
England
Phone: 44/908 22 09 08

BNA
The Bureau of National Affairs
1231 25th Street, N.W.
Washington, D.C. 20037
Phone: 1-800/372-1033

CEN or CENELEC
2 Rue Brederode
Bte. 5
B-1000 Brussels,
Belgium
Phone: 32/2 519 6811
Fax: 32 2 519 6819

CEPT
Office Liason CEPT
BP 1283
3001 Berne
Switzerland
Phone: 41/31 62 20 81

DIN
Deutsche Institut für Normung (DIN)
Burggrafenstrasse 6
Postfach 11 07
D-1000 Berlin 30
West Germany
Phone: 49/30 26 01 1

ETSI
BP 152-06561

Valbonne, Cedex
France
Phone: 33/92 94 42 00

ISO
Central Secretariat
1, rue de Varembé
Case postale 56
CH-1211 Genève 20
Switzerland
Phone: 41/22 34 12 40

NCSCI
The National Center for Standards and Certification Information
National Bureau of Standards
Administration Building, Room A629
Gaithersburg, Md. 20899
Phone: 301/975-4040
GATT Hotline: 301/975-4041 (a recorded message listing pending
standards formulation around the world)

USTR
Office of the U.S. Trade Representative Director
Technical Barriers to Trade
Room 513, Winder Building
600 17 Street, N.W.
Washington, D.C. 20006
Phone: 202/395-3063

Chapter 4 | What Your Company Should Do About 1992: A Four-Step Approach

As you have seen, 1992 is a complex, multifaceted phenomenon. There is no single strategy applicable to every company that wants to take advantage of its opportunities or guard against its potential hazards. There is, however, an *approach* that all companies can profitably adopt. This chapter presents a four-step process for dealing with 1992 that you can adapt to your own company's situation. It features a "1992 analysis matrix" that will help you pinpoint those aspects of 1992 that will have the greatest impact on your business and allow you to devise strategies to address them.

To place this approach in a useful context, we will first show briefly how a few representative U.S. companies are coping with 1992.

How Some U.S. Companies Are Dealing With 1992

IBM

Although most companies have neither the resources of IBM nor its ability to command the attention of Brussels bureaucrats, there's still much that even a small exporting firm can learn from the giant's know-how.

Symon Visser, IBM's governmental affairs director in Brussels, said the company began to take 1992 seriously at the end of 1987. IBM governmental affairs people analyzed the White Paper and presented their findings to the management committee at the European Community's headquarters in Paris. Part of the analysis, Visser said, "was to establish the potential dollar value of the changes 1992 would bring in terms of IBM business."[1]

The company established working groups and identified twenty-five strategic questions. Through this approach, IBM generated a set of recommendations, and by July 1988 it had an action plan for finance, marketing, distribution, and personnel. Although IBM already had a pan-European manufacturing strategy, whereby thirteen plant locations in six countries produce one product for all of Europe, it searched for further efficiencies that could emerge from 1992, especially in inventory control and distribution.

Visser felt that 1992 would profoundly influence several areas of IBM's business. Pricing was one: "At the moment, each country's management team sets its own pricing. Over time this has resulted in differences, which have led to some cross-border shopping. As VAT rates harmonize and goods flow more easily, price differentials will have to come in line."

Customer needs are another area that IBM is concentrating on. "Some of our large international customers," Visser stated, "only want to deal with one IBM in Europe, and yet, we still need to service them decentrally. We must respond to customer needs, but creating the organizational links to mobilize our work force is challenging. If, for example, we make the Netherlands responsible for selling to Royal Dutch Shell, how will we credit the French operation that services Shell operations in France?"

Although Visser agreed that local content, reciprocity, and quotas were big issues with most U.S. companies, "We've worked very hard at being good Europeans. Most of our manufacturing has at least 90 percent local content."

IBM has already seen a savings from the 1992 process. "The single administrative document," Visser claimed, "has saved us a lot of time and money."

Monsanto

Because Monsanto is in several different types of businesses (chemicals, agrochemicals, pharmaceuticals, synthetic sweeteners, and valves and control instrumentation), the direct impact of 1992 on the company will vary. The company expects the greatest changes to occur in its pharmaceutical business. Anil C. Parikh, director of planning and business development for Europe-Africa, says: "Since member states have regulated almost all aspects of this business from registration and pricing to patents, many changes are ahead. At the opposite end of the spectrum, we don't expect dramatic differences in our chemical business. That has been operating on a pan-European basis for many years."[2]

Although the White Paper contained 300 directives, Monsanto extended the list to some 400 to include additional areas such as environmental legislation. Parikh says: "We took a close look at all of them, but only about forty are really relevant to Monsanto. Some, like transportation, affect all our businesses, and others, like drug regulation, affect one unit. Those that touch all units are dealt with by staff functions. The others are dealt with solely by each unit."

The company is assessing the 1992 impact by asking what the direct and indirect impacts of the directives are. As Parikh says, "It's much tougher to assess the indirect forces. How, for instance, will a directive affect the industry structure, our customers' pricing, competition? And then of course, the question is, what should we do about it?"

Smaller Companies

As U.S. exporters begin to face increased pressure to conform to European business practices, from harmonized standards to local content requirements, many are keeping a close eye on developments. Many use U.S. government agencies, trade associations, and international partners to keep abreast of 1992 activities. Some have formed 1992 task forces to identify opportunities and dangers.

Several exporters have decided to set up shop in Europe. By doing so, they hope to establish closer ties with their customers, avoid tariffs, and skirt new rules of origin and local content laws. William Gibson, president of Digital Microwave Corporation of Silicon Valley, 60 percent of whose revenues already come from Europe, recently made a $2 million investment in the United Kingdom in the hope of securing existing customer relationships with two British communications companies. Digital also set up a plant in Scotland as a springboard for increasing sales in Europe.[3]

On the other hand, H. Joseph Gerber, president of Gerber Scientific, has opted to stay at home to service Europe, believing that his company has better control of the process in Connecticut, where it produces high-tech equipment for the apparel, electronics, and other industries. Gerber claims that as long as the dollar stays put and labor costs are higher in Europe, his company can remain competitive even if it has to pay a tariff.[4]

Trade Associations

Trade organizations can play a crucial role in shaping industry strategy and in providing a voice for smaller companies. Many are taking an active role in educating their members about 1992. The Health Industry Manufacturers Association (HIMA) is a fine example of how an association can play an integral part in your 1992 plans.

Representing manufacturers of medical devices that range from syringes to artificial heart valves, HIMA has an eye towards 1992 for several reasons. Standards formulation, testing, and certification could all develop into major stumbling blocks for U.S. products. HIMA members are concerned that standards could be formed in such a way as to prevent U.S. products from entering the EC market; and testing and certification could also impose delays. Rather than take a wait-and-see attitude,

HIMA took the offensive. In late 1988 a number of its officials gave speeches at a CEN/CENELEC* conference, presenting HIMA member concerns and encouraging a dialogue between the countries.

After Secretary of Commerce Robert Mosbacher returned from Brussels in early 1989, HIMA quickly seized on the momentum he had created by inviting senior CEN/CENELEC officials to Washington, D.C., to meet association members and members of Congress.

According to George Willingmyre of HIMA:

> We've identified four directives that are critical to our members' efforts in Europe. They all revolve around standards. Our goal is to influence the process as much as possible. We've gone directly to the Commission to present our position, in addition to working with the European trade associations that are similar to us. We also work through the technical committees of ANSI, and with the Commerce Department and USTR.[5]

It appears that HIMA efforts are paying off. The standards process for medical devices is slowly opening up to U.S. companies. According to Willingmyre: "The door to U.S. participation is open, but companies have to walk through it to make things happen."

As you can see, there are many ways to deal with 1992, both internally and externally. There are, however, some common threads to these stories. Each organization is identifying those parts of the 1992 process that will most affect its business; it then devises specific steps it must take to adjust to the new environment. With these examples in mind, let's proceed to our four-step approach to analyzing 1992.

How You Should Deal With 1992

Step 1: Performing a Strategic Diagnostic and Industry Analysis

A 1992 analysis cannot be done in a vacuum. You must first understand your company's competitive position and the dynamics of the industry you operate in. This involves performing a strategic diagnostic on your company and its industry, assessing your relative strengths and competitive position to take advantage of market opportunities.

Strategy is a planned approach to business development as opposed to simply reacting to market developments. By outlining an overall international plan for your company, you give coherence to the day-to-day

---

*CEN, the European Committee for Standardization; CENELEC, the European Committee for Electrotechnical Standardization; ANSI, the American National Standards Institute; USTR, the U.S. Trade Representative.

The Four-Step Approach to 1992 Decision Making

Step 1:   Perform a strategic diagnostic and industry analysis.
Step 2:   Factor 1992 into your strategy.
Step 3:   Focus on the EC directives driving change in your industry.
Step 4:   Generate specific action steps.

tactical decisions you must make. Most companies have a mission statement, and perhaps now is as good a time as any to reevaluate yours and to refine it. What business are you really in? This simple question has forced many companies to make major overhauls in their operations. Many large corporations have found it best to return to core businesses. During the late 1970s and early 1980s, the Monsanto Chemical Company, for instance, shed most of its commodity chemicals business in favor of new specialty chemicals and biotechnology because it felt its strength lay in technology development rather than commodity manufacturing. It went so far as to drop the word *Chemical* from its corporate name.

Once the mission is set, the company must assess how it performs compared to other businesses operating in similar sectors. What are your company's competitive advantages? Procter and Gamble prides itself on product development and marketing, Sony on R&D, BMW on engineering.

How sustainable are your strengths? Wang found itself in the unenviable position of being a leader in an obsolete technology, dedicated word processing. For almost ten years, it has tried to diversify, with only limited success, while holding onto its existing customer base. You must periodically evaluate your strengths and resources to sustain leadership. Are you in a position to innovate continually to protect yourself from being leapfrogged the way Wang was?

How have your relationships with suppliers and customers evolved? Has new technology given you an opportunity to establish better ties? Just-in-time manufacturing entails forging partnerships with suppliers, creating trust instead of arms-length impersonal relationships, so that both can share information that will help to reduce costs and improve service. Have you explored innovative ways of improving these relationships so as to create a greater competitive advantage?

Understanding the dynamics of your industry and new developments in it is critical to the long-term health of your company. Peoples Express misread the changing dynamics of a deregulated U.S. air market despite the fact that its initial success was based on airline deregulation itself. Blinded by its initial market acceptance, it continued to expand, amassing overhead to the point where it eroded its competitive advantage as a low-cost provider of air passenger transport.

How has the competitive environment changed for your industry? And, more specifically, how will the completion of Europe's internal market affect your sector? Returning to the airline business, British Airways, KLM, Lufthansa, and Air France are all vying for competitive advantage in a deregulated European airline market. Each is forming new alliances, trimming costs, and improving marketing in preparation for the changes ahead. The next step in this exercise will help you pinpoint those aspects of 1992 that will have the greatest impact on your business.

Step 2: Factoring 1992 Into Your Strategy

By identifying the main areas of the 1992 process and then gauging how they affect the sources of competitive advantage, you can determine how your industry will be affected.

Take a look at the 1992 Analysis Matrix. The left-hand column lists the areas in which businesses can create a competitive advantage. The categories are a combination of business functions, technology, and external relations, a holistic approach to operations reflecting the fact that companies operate in a complex environment. For example, supplier relationships can be as essential to a company's success as employee relations are. The top row of the matrix portrays the essential thrusts of the 1992 process. Immediately underneath are listed the chapters or sections

The 1992 Analysis Matrix
Major Areas of the 1992 Process

Areas of Competitive Advantage	Harmonized Standards (Chapter 3)	Opened Government Procurement (Chapter 3)	Industry Deregulation (Chapter 5)	Fiscal Harmony (Chapter 7)	Community R&D Policy (Directory C)	Reduction of Physical Barriers (Chapters 2, 5)	Content-Quota/ Tariff Reform (Chapter 3)	Social Dimension (Chapter 3)
Supplier relations								
Manufacturing								
Scale Location								
Product								
R&D Products								
Marketing								
Sales Distribution Price								
Customer service								
Organization								
Info tech HRM Linkages								
Finance								

of this book in which these thrusts are discussed. Understanding how these 1992 forces may affect areas in which companies compete will reveal how they might influence the dynamics of an industry. The 1992 Analysis Matrix will appear again in this book eight different times to allow coverage of the automotive industry, chemicals, consumer products, financial services, information technology, pharmaceuticals and medical devices, service industries and the professions, and shipping and transportation.

Begin with Harmonized Standards at the top left of the matrix. How will this important 1992 development affect the areas of competitive advantage listed on the left-hand side of the chart? Mark each box with *H* for high, *M* for medium, *L* for low, or simply leave low-impact areas blank. If, for instance, you feel an area might fall between low and medium, mark it as *L-M* (see Figure 4-1).

Telecommunications and Standards: The Matrix in Action.   Take the telecommunications sector (shown in Figure 4-1) as an example. EC-wide standards for such things as fax machines, videotex, and teletex will dra-

Figure 4-1.   Application of the matrix to telecommunications.

Areas of Competitive Advantage	Harmonized Standards (Chapter 3)
Supplier relations	M-H
Manufacturing	
Scale	H
Location	L-M
Product	
R&D	M-H
Products	H
Marketing	
Sales	M
Distribution	M
Price	M
Customer service	M-H
Organization	
Info tech	M
HRM	M
Linkages	M
Finance	M

matically affect the cost structure of this industry because manufacturers will be able to trim product lines and increase manufacturing efficiency through scale. Large-scale operations will result in bigger purchase orders, and this in turn will significantly affect supplier relations. And, to invest in larger-scale operations, a stronger role for finance will be required. Therefore production, procurement, and cost-cutting skills will be important if companies want to stay competitive in the new environment.

Further, as compatible European telecommunications systems are installed, new product opportunities will develop as users take advantage of an integrated network. Close ties to the market to identify new customer needs and rapid product development capability are additional skills companies will need.

Not having to subject the product to twelve different testing and certification boards will also add to the cost savings. In addition, marketing the same product throughout the EC will be far different from marketing several products that have to meet different national standards. And, of course, servicing will be easier because the technical specifications will be similar, if not the same.

Managing a pan-European operation will place new demands on the organization. New links must be formed for improved communications and decision making. Information technology and new approaches to personnel management will be required to meet these challenges.

Manufacturers of telecommunications equipment subject to high transportation costs and/or requiring an educated labor force might prefer a central location in a member state with a large economy. Manufacturers of, say, lightweight components whose manufacture does not require an educated work force might prefer a less central location where labor rates are lower.

Harmonized standards will have a degree of impact on all areas of competitive advantage. If you operate in the telecommunications industry, it will be important to understand how standards formulation, testing, and certification will change in Europe. Completion of steps 2 and 3 will help you get the information needed to prepare your company for the new Europe.

Once you've completed the standards column in Figure 4-1, move to the next 1992 area, government procurement; repeat this process until you've performed it for each of the major 1992 areas. You may be able to save time by referring to one of the completed sector matrices in the next chapter. If so, all you'll have to do is to fine tune the matrix.

If you are unsure as to the impact a particular area or directive may have on your business, you should explore the specific legislation in some detail. To obtain the latest information on a directive or to delve deeper into a specific issue, refer to Directory A on U.S. government assistance. There you'll find a number of sources of free 1992 advice, from the Commerce Department, which has a number of experts in a variety of sectors, to state export assistance agencies, many of which operate offices in Europe. Other options include:

- Contacting the European Community offices in Washington, San Francisco, or New York. Besides offering an array of EC information, including the *Official Journal* and other publications, they offer several on-line data bases covering such specific areas as agriculture, textiles, chemicals and pharmaceuticals, food and drink, trade, technology, energy, the environment, science, and law. Many of the data bases are specialized: Phone the EC office at 202/862-9500 for more information.

    —CELEX: An easy-to-use directive data base that provides the *Official Journal* listings of all directives and proposals. Current listings take three to six weeks to come on line. ABLE, a new directive data base, provides real-time posting of the *Official Journal*.

    —SCAD: Contains over 100,000 references to 1992 issues from periodicals around the world.

- Contacting the directorate-general in the Commission that oversees the areas that will affect your European operations. Most will provide you with information on request; their names and a central phone number are given in Directory E.

- Consulting with your trade association or a national organization like the National Association of Manufacturers. Most of them are analyzing 1992.

- Contacting the American Chamber of Commerce in Brussels (see Directory A) or a local Chamber near you.

Step 3: *Focusing on the Directives Driving Change in Your Industry*

Take a look at the grid boxes on your 1992 Analysis Matrix and focus on the 1992 areas (columns) having more than one H. These, of course, are the parts of the program that will have the greatest impact on your business. You should follow the directives driving these 1992 areas, and perhaps strive to influence their development.

For example, having identified standards as having a potentially high impact on several aspects of the telecommunications business, you can refer to Chapter 3 for a discussion of standards and to Directory D for a listing of the important directives relating to them. Additional information on telecommunications can be found in the Information Technology section in Chapter 5.

Once you have a listing of the relevant directives (in the worst case this would be forty or so), create a file on each directive using the Directive Status Report form shown in Figure 4-2, or something similar.

Completing the Directive Status Report.   The Directive Status Report is designed to help you keep track of pending directives and your efforts to influence the legislation. The directive progress section lets you track the directive through the different European institutions. The member state implementation area should be used to identify any possible problems with one or more countries' implementation of the directive once it is approved by the Council.

The form also provides areas for business impact analysis and for tracking your action steps. Contact the Commerce Department or the EC library to obtain a copy of the actual directive, which is described in the EC's *Official Journal;* keep this with your directive file.

If the directives have not been approved, there may be time to influence the decision-making process in Brussels, perhaps through your trade association, ANSI, the AMcham in Brussels, or U.S. trade officials. The commercial counselor at the American Embassy in Brussels can also provide you with a list of reputable lobbyists.

If you are ambitious enough to want to present your position to the Commission directly, it is possible, but be aware of the differences in lobbying styles in Europe. Most Europeans who work for U.S. subsidiaries in the Community cringe at the thought of having to take Americans to see European civil servants. The most common complaints cited include brashness, impatience, and excessive directness. Also, it is doubtful that you will make any headway in attempting to go around the Commission by influencing member states directly; you're better off making your pitch in Brussels. The European Parliament committee responsible for reviewing a particular directive is another group worth presenting your position to, preferably before Parliament's first reading of the directive.

Step 4: Generating Specific Action Steps

Incorporate your analysis of 1992 into your strategy and business plan. You might start by answering these two questions:

1. *How does your company perform in those areas listed on the left side of the matrix that will be most affected by 1992?* Look for multiple H's across the rows.
2. *Are these areas where competitive advantage can be established?* Are you in a position to seize it? If so, what steps need to be taken? If not, what can you do to ensure that the company performs to minimum acceptable industry standards? Can you possibly discover ways to break out of the pack?

Figure 4-2.   Sample Directive Status Report form.

Directive Status Report

Directive Name: _____   Directive Number: _____

Directive Progress:
____ Commission   ____ Parliament   ____ Council of Ministers

Member State Implementation: _____

_____

_____

DG Contact

                              Name: _____

                              Address: _____

                              Phone: _____

                              Fax: _____

Parliament Committee Contact

                              Name: _____

                              Address: _____

                              Phone: _____

                              Fax: _____

Directive Description: _____

_____

_____

Impact on Business: _____

_____

_____

Action Plan: _____

_____

_____

Date		Action		Results

Here's a set of 1992 business questions to help get the discussion going for each of the areas listed on the left side of the matrix.

- *Supplier Relations.* As Europe's internal market is completed, how will this affect your relationships with your suppliers?
  —How will your supplier needs change? (e.g., to meet new technical standards, to take advantage of new market opportunities, to become more cost-competitive, to increase quality, to serve new manufacturing scales and locations).
  —Will new sources of supply be required?
  —Can existing suppliers be streamlined to reduce the number of items purchased and to increase volume with reliable suppliers?
  —Will the cost/value ratio of your suppliers make your product more competitive or less so in a tougher European market?
  —How aware are the suppliers of your changing needs in the new Europe? Are they equipped to handle them?
  —How can you involve suppliers in your 1992 plans?
  —Can new ways of communicating with suppliers improve the information both of you need to increase efficiency and decrease costs?
  —Can your suppliers meet the demands of just-in-time manufacturing?
  —Do your purchasing skills include the ability to deal in different languages?
- *Manufacturing.* What opportunities will the new Europe present to improve manufacturing ability? (If you don't produce in Europe, refer to the section "Moving Overseas" in Chapter 6.)
- *Plant Scale.* Will new harmonization of standards create opportunities for rationalizing, building scale, improving inventory carrying costs?
  —How efficient are current operations?
  —Does it make sense to relocate existing operations or to set up shop in a new country?
  —Must you produce close to your customers?
  —Are there attractive government relocation incentives in areas that fit your strategy? (Refer to Directory B.)
  —How productive is the current work force? Can labor relations be improved? How competitive are wages? What skills are available in the local work force? Are training grants obtainable from government?
  —What new manufacturing technologies are needed to deal with the new competitive environment?
  —Are manufacturing skills in-house? Does it make sense to subcontract assemblies? Would a joint venture make sense?
  —Is the local infrastructure adequate to meet your new needs?

- *Product.* What changes are required in the current product line to deal with 1992?
    —Do you have the capability to adjust the product mix to meet new customer demands? If not, options include collaborating with other firms in a joint venture, participating in a Community or member state cooperative R&D program (or, if only in the United States, doing the same there), subcontracting, or licensing the technology you lack.
    —Is your product suitable for all of Europe, or must you tailor it to local tastes?
- *Marketing.* How will 1992 affect the components of your marketing strategy?
    —What new customers can you reach?
    —How will new competition affect marketing decisions?
    —Do you have the market research on which to make sound decisions?
    —Are your products positioned properly in each market?
    —Should product managers be responsible for one country or for all of Europe?
    —How will the advertising mix change? Will the message have to be tailored to each market even if you are selling a standardized product to all of them?
- *Packaging:* Are multilanguage labels appropriate? Interestingly enough, a 1989 American Management Association survey indicated that two out of three companies would stick to a single language on their products.[6]
- *Sales Management:* Is your sales force equipped to deal with the new Europe?
    —Should you translate the sales literature? Does it address local needs?
    —Should you assign European account reps for large multinational customers?
- *Distribution:* How will easier border crossings and the deregulation of the transportation sector affect your distribution?
    —How will the frequency, speed, and size of shipments change? Will you require new destinations?
    —Should new transportation relationships be established?
    —How will the information needs of the system change?
- *Pricing.* How will ease of cross-border shopping and harmonization of VAT rates affect your current pricing strategy?
    —How will new competition alter industry pricing?
    —Is your product cost accounting system accurate enough to permit you to make solid judgments on product profitability?

- *Customer Service*. How will 1992 affect your customers? How can you make it easier for them to do business with you?
  —Can you meet the service needs of local customers and large multinationals?
  —Should you subcontract some service?
  —Should you centralize/regionalize or localize the service operation?
  —Does a Euro-warranty make sense?

- *Finance*. Identify how 1992 will affect operating costs in: transport, distribution, product rationalization, and standardization.
  —How will managing the cash flow change in the new Europe? What opportunities will there be for equity raising, debt financing, and currency hedging?
  —How will tax changes affect the way your books are kept?

- *Organization*. How must your organization change with the completion of the internal market? The organization can be analyzed in three ways: by information technology, by human resources management, and by organizational linkages.
  1. *Information Technology (IT), Strategic and Back-Room:** What new demands will be placed on the current system? Both from an operational standpoint (billing, payroll) and an informational perspective (providing market data, cost analyses)?
     —What new parts of the business will require IT support?
     —Do you have the in-house capability?
     —Can you subcontract any of your activity?
     —Are suppliers equipped to handle your new needs?
     —How will improving telecommunications infrastructure throughout the Community affect your system?
     —How will harmonization of telecommunications systems affect you?
     —How will your competitors adapt to the new environment?
  2. *Human Resources Management (HRM)*. How will the free flow of workers, the different forms of labor participation mandated by the European Company Statute, and the need for multilanguage and cultural understanding affect current HRM practices?
     —Do you have sufficient training?
     —How will you handle the salary/benefits of an employee relocated from Spain to the Netherlands?
     —Do you prefer to hire only local people in each country or a mix of nationalities? Is there equal opportunity all the way to the top of the company for all nationalities?

*An example of strategic IT use would be providing automatic teller machines (ATMs) to retail bank customers.

3. *Organizational Linkages:* Should new organizational links be created? If so, how do you get different areas of the company to communicate and share information for the first time?

A final word on the 1992 Analysis Matrix: While there's always a danger in trying to put the real world into neat little boxes, we've tried to create a framework that is flexible enough to take you wherever you want it to go. The important thing is to think systematically about 1992, focusing your attention on those areas that really count, and then to decide on specific action steps to address those areas that pose the greatest challenge to your European business.

You should also consider the repercussions of ignoring 1992. Chances are, if you've come this far in the exercise, you've generated at least a couple of responses, but if this isn't the case, review your analysis. Not making a decision is a decision in itself.

Finally, remember that 1992 is a golden opportunity for reenergizing your company. Use the 1992 process as a rallying cry to stimulate and challenge your organization into a renewed focus and commitment to doing what you do best.

Notes

1. This and the following statements by Symon Visser are from an interview conducted July 1989.
2. This and the following statements by Anil C. Parikh are from an interview conducted July 1989.
3. "Should small US exporters take the big plunge?" *Business Week*, December 12, 1988, p. 65.
4. Ibid.
5. From an interview conducted September 1989.
6. American Management Association, 1989.

Chapter 5 | The Outlook for Business by Industrial Sector

The effect of 1992 on your business will depend to a great extent on what industry you are in.

This chapter explains how specific industry groups are most likely to be affected by EC legislation, both passed and pending. Forecasts in these areas have proved unreliable so we avoid them. Rather, we describe the legislation, and strive to consolidate different views of its possible consequences (see Directory D for key directives that affect industry groups). The uncertainty is increased because of secondary effects; for instance, legislation specific to the transportation sector will most likely affect the cost structures of other industries as well. With these caveats in mind, we'll look at the following industry groups:

- Automotive
- Chemicals
- Consumer products
- Financial services (banking, investment services, UCITS, and insurance)
- Information technology (electronics, computers, and telecommunications)
- Pharmaceuticals and medical equipment
- Services
- Shipping and transportation

The EC's annual *Panorama of EC Industry,* available from EC information offices for twenty one ECU, provides a good overview of many sectors.

The Automotive Industry

General Areas to Watch: Taxation, VAT, subsidies, local content, and quotas.

The 1992 process will transform the EC's fragmented automobile market into the world's largest. Clearly, the future for this sector will be dynamic as member state national champions jockey for competitive position with an already well-prepared U.S. effort. Throw in a group of eager Japanese companies that have not yet had an equal shot at European consumers, and this sector is sure to be a donnybrook. A rash of mergers and joint ventures has already taken place. Ford has swallowed Jaguar, GM has made a fifty-fifty deal with Saab, Fiat has grabbed Maserati, Honda has taken fifty percent of Rover, Renault and Chrysler have entered a cooperation deal—and the list goes on.

Prices will decline and cars will improve unless further protectionist measures encourage more sloppy management by shielded EC manufacturers; grants, loans, equity injections, and debt writeoffs to national auto makers like Renault have distorted competition and encouraged lackadaisical management. The Commission has recently ordered member states to curtail such payments and in some instances has forced repayment of sums already allocated. In addition, increased industry overcapacity could develop as non-EC carmakers build up their European manufacturing capacity from fear of being locked out of the Community.

The Cecchini Report estimated that the 1992 process could result in savings to this sector of more than $3 billion.[1] These savings would be generated by a combination of reductions in fiscal, physical, and technical barriers.

VAT, sales taxes, and registration taxes in some countries add substantially to the cost of a vehicle, close to 200 percent, for example, on large cars in Denmark and Greece. An overall decrease in these charges through harmonization would increase demand. In September 1987 the French reduced the VAT rate on autos from thirty-three percent to twenty-eight percent and witnessed an increased demand of 40,000 vehicles, or 2.2 percent, which far surpassed prior estimates as to elasticity of demand.

Quantitative restrictions (QRs) on imports are another barrier that the 1992 process should gradually eliminate. To date, Japanese cars have had limited access to many European markets, specifically Italy, France, Portugal, Spain, and Britain. But with the elimination of border barriers within the Community, it will be impossible for member states to maintain these arrangements because goods will be able to move more easily from EC countries without QRs. The EC, however, is negotiating with the Japanese to bring about a temporary voluntary restraint agreement (VRA) on the number of cars Japan exports to the EC. The number of cars to be allowed and how long the transition period would last are yet to be specified. That the Commission is also considering including Japanese output from plants in the United States and even from within the EC as part of the VRA is certain to create controversy.

Further, local content requirements will force automakers to manufacture in Europe or be subjected to import quotas and tariffs. This has already fueled increased investment in the EC and has made overcapacity in the world industry more likely. An EC-wide local content percentage is a possibility; however, no proposals have come forth.

Border formalities, inspection requirements, and customs all contribute to increased costs for all manufacturers, regardless of sector. Basic incompatibility of such things as electrical circuitry and telecommunications equipment have also burdened EC carmakers. The Single Administrative Document and improved coordination of communications among member states are integral parts of the 1992 process aimed at reducing the costs of conducting business in the Community.

EC-wide automotive standards could reduce inventory levels and produce manufacturing efficiencies. However, they are unlikely to eliminate differing member state requirements for such features as reclining driver's seats (West Germany), yellow headlights (France), side repeater-flasher lights (Italy), and dim-dip lights (Britain), all of which can be viewed as economy-of-scale bashers designed to frustrate Japanese efforts to capitalize on their ability to maximize scale advantages.

Greater coordination of the standards formulation process and of testing and certification will greatly improve conditions for EC car manufacturers. Replacing the need for obtaining approval from each member state, a Euro-process would save EC manufacturers substantial time and money.

The opportunity exists for harmonizing emission standards, but this entails a coordinated environmental policy that until now has been difficult to accomplish. Denmark, West Germany, and the Netherlands have been in the forefront of stringent emission controls requirements; the Germans and the Dutch both offer fiscal incentives to encourage sales of cars that meet higher emissions and noise standards. These policies are encouraged by the EC, which in 1987 took action to harmonize large passenger car emission standards. Although greater coordination will occur through the 1990s, some member state differences will most likely remain. Community R&D policy will facilitate modernization in auto design and manufacturing. The pooling of resources via cooperative R&D projects will not only improve research efficiencies but also foster the creation of common standards and protocols. Some of the savings derived from 1992 will be pumped back into EC R&D efforts, resulting in improved vehicle technology.

Will European car preferences converge to enable manufacturers to eliminate the potpourri of models currently offered? Generally speaking, consumer tastes are firmly grounded in tradition and local road conditions. Italians enjoy scooting around in small vehicles; Germans prefer zooming down the autobahn in larger, more powerful cars. Because it's doubtful that 1992 will influence these preferences, reductions in model offerings will probably not be as great as some companies wish.

The impact on manufacturing, however, will produce significant savings in both variable and fixed costs. Improved manufacturing and design techniques, coupled with a reduction in the number of assembly line platforms that form the foundation for models, will produce substantial savings. Changes in Eastern Europe are providing new manufacturing options. Volkswagen, for instance, is sourcing engines in East Germany, and others are exploring joint ventures to exploit low wage rates and to gain market access. Added to the savings gained from the other areas of the 1992 process, prices to consumers will undoubtedly fall, spurring additional demand, thus further increasing the opportunity for scale savings. The following table shows the potential savings estimated by the Cecchini Report:

Savings in Fixed Costs in the Automobile Sector

	ECU Millions
Tooling	571.7
Engineering	700.7
Warranty	175.3
Administration/finance	213.3
Advertising	42.3[2]

Although improved labor productivity and restructuring might reduce employment levels, the Community expects that this will be offset by the increased demand for European products both inside the EC and abroad.

Parts distribution should become centralized as car components are harmonized to leverage scale opportunities. The ease of product movement across borders and transportation deregulation should more than offset the additional costs of being farther away from end users. Dealer networks will become closer to manufacturers because pan-European companies will reduce their member state overhead, forcing better communications and a new relationship with dealers. This is important because dealers, who are now tied to only one manufacturer, will be allowed to diversify after 1995.

Service, naturally, will be conducted locally. A Euro-warranty, fully valid at dealer networks throughout the Community, will encourage increased Euro branding (even if brand name and marketing are different in each member state, the basic model could remain the same), thus making it easier for drivers to obtain service wherever they live in the EC.

U.S. automakers are well positioned for 1992 because they have treated Europe as one market for several years. However, protectionist measures may develop to provide time for some of the weaker European companies to expand their single-country strategy into a true European effort. Over time, European companies will become more competitive, so

The 1992 Analysis Matrix
Automotive Sector
Major Areas of the 1992 Process

Areas of Competitive Advantage	Harmonized Standards (Chapter 3)	Opened Government Procurement (Chapter 3)	Industry Deregulation (Chapter 5)	Fiscal Harmony (Chapter 7)	Community R&D Policy (Directory C)	Reduction of Physical Barriers (Chapters 2, 5)	Content-Quota/ Tariff Reform (Chapter 3)	Social Dimension (Chapter 3)
Supplier relations	H					M–H	M	
Manufacturing								
Scale	H				M	M–H	H	M
Location	H						H	M–H	M
Product								
R&D	H	M			M–H			
Products	H	M			M–H		H	
Marketing								
Sales	H	M						
Distribution	H					M	H	
Price	H			M		M–H	M–H	
Customer service	M–H					M–H		
Organization	H							
Info tech								M
HRM	M							
Linkages	M							
Finance	H	M		M–H				

U.S. firms must aggressively keep pace with new developments. The Big Three have all made moves in this direction within the EC. These include Ford's agreement with Volkswagen to study the joint development of a multipurpose vehicle, GM's agreement with Isuzu to develop a four-wheel drive vehicle, and Chrysler's letter of intent with Renault to develop a utility vehicle. U.S. suppliers to this industry must also keep abreast of technological changes in components and manufacturing techniques in order to secure their existing customer bases and to take advantage of new opportunities.

You are now in a position to apply the 1992 Analysis Matrix to the automotive sector, using the directions given in Chapter 4 under Step 2.

The Chemicals Industry

General Areas to Watch: R&D policy, standards, environmental protection.

The EC has the largest chemical industry in the world, supplying about 27 percent of world output. Chemicals are the third-largest manufacturing industry in the EC, with about 10 percent of manufacturing value added and 7 percent of the manufacturing work force.[3] Its products encompass artificial fibers, dyes, paints, fertilizers, detergents, and plas-

The 1992 Analysis Matrix
Chemicals Sector
Major Areas of the 1992 Process

Areas of Competitive Advantage	Harmonized Standards (Chapter 3)	Opened Government Procurement (Chapter 3)	Industry Deregulation (Chapter 5)	Fiscal Harmony (Chapter 7)	Community R&D Policy (Directory C)	Reduction of Physical Barriers (Chapters 2, 5)	Content-Quota/ Tariff Reform (Chapter 3)	Social Dimension (Chapter 3)
Supplier relations								
Manufacturing								
Scale						M		M
Location						M		
Product								
R&D					M			
Products								
Marketing								
Sales						H		
Distribution								
Price				M				
Customer service								
Organization								
Info tech				M				
HRM								M
Linkages								
Finance				M				

tics, and these in turn can be subdivided into hundreds of product categories.

The industry is often accused of operating like a cartel, the EC having brought five such cases against it since 1983. This is bothersome not only from a public relations point of view but because the industry occasionally needs the Commission's approval for sizable joint ventures and for the accusations it has leveled against non-EC firms, e.g., its request that antidumping charges be imposed on American soda ash.

Initiatives concerning the environment will have the greatest effect on the chemicals sector. Underlying EC policy in this area are the principles of preventive action, rectification of environmental damage at the source, and payment by polluters for damage done.

In October 1987, the Council adopted a resolution that includes provisions for "the reduction at source of pollution and nuisance in various areas; the control of chemical substances and preparations; the prevention of industrial accidents; [and] measures on the evaluation and best use of biotechnology with regard to the environment. . . ."[4] In 1989, the Council decided to establish an Environmental Protection agency.

According to Britain's Department of Trade and Industry, "Over 100 environmental directives are already in force."[5] These have to do with controlling the discharge of dangerous substances into water, reducing emissions from large combustion plants, minimum standards for the disposal of PCBs, the use and storage of fertilizers, and acceptance of the Montreal Protocol on chlorofluorocarbons, compounds suspected of helping to deplete the ozone layer. Another directive addresses shipment of toxic and dangerous wastes from one member state to another; the exporting country must inform the other of the shipment and receive its approval.

The 1992 Analysis Matrix for the chemicals sector can now be applied.

Consumer Products

General Areas to Watch: Consumer protection, standards.

The EC recognizes that consumer protection is essential to the goal of free movement of goods and services. If consumers in one country are suspicious of goods and services originating in another because of their perceived lack of safety, or quality, the goal is obstructed. Also, if one or more countries impose less stringent standards, producers might tend to locate their facilities there; although this might be a reason for a country to impose less stringent standards, it clearly violates the goal of "constant improvement of the living and working conditions" of EC residents, one of the main objectives articulated in the original Treaty of Rome.

Harmonization in this area has proved difficult, the greatest success having come in the area of minimum levels of protection agreed to. In other areas, individual member states retain most of the responsibility. Through the early 1980s, the problem revolved around the EC's attempt to create technical specifications that would apply on a communitywide basis. Although this was essentially an attempt at technical harmonization, it encompassed safety as well. The procedures were labyrinthine (they even tried to harmonize lipstick standards in detail) and, often, by the time agreement was reached, the products involved had undergone enough technical and/or market-driven changes to make the agreement meaningless. The seminal Cassis de Dijon case changed all this (see Chapter 1).

The EC must now harmonize only the essential standards relating to the "effectiveness of fiscal supervision, the protection of public health, the fairness of commercial transactions and the defense of the consumer." All products complying with these (and with the standards of its home member state) can be sold freely across borders. CEN (European Committee for Standardization) and CENELEC (European Committee for Electrotechnical Standardization) are entrusted with establishing standards that meet mandatory requirements.

The main EC legislation in this area includes the following:

- *Misleading Advertising Directive.* Adopted in 1984, this enables consumers, individually or in organizations, "to bring a complaint in law or before a competent administrative authority."[6] Its most remarkable feature is that it allows the courts to put the burden of proof on the advertiser: Consumers may not have to prove that advertising claims are false, but an advertiser may have to prove that they are true. Courts may also stop publication of misleading advertising.

- *Product Liability Directive.* Adopted in 1985, this makes manufacturers and importers strictly liable for personal injuries and deaths resulting from defective products, regardless of whether the manufacturer is guilty of negligence. "No limit is set on this liability, although governments may impose a limit of not less than 70 million ECU on a producer's total liability for deaths and personal injuries caused by identical items with the same defect."[7]

Damage to personal property worth over 500 ECU is also covered. Nonmaterial damage is not. There are no provisions in EC law or in that of its member states enabling class action suits.

- *Doorstep Selling Directive.* Adopted in 1985, this imposes a seven-day cooling-off period for certain sales contracts entered into at the consumer's home or place of work. It does not apply to insurance, securities, mail order sales, "or to contracts with a value of less than 60 ECU."[8]

- *Consumer Credit Directive.* Adopted in 1986, this protects consumers entering into credit agreements, which must be in writing, with the cost or annual percentage rate specified. "Nearly every form of credit is covered: personal loans, credit card accounts, bank accounts, permanent credit allowed by suppliers and installment sales."[9]

- *Toy Safety Directive.* Adopted in June 1988, it harmonizes toy safety standards and prevents dangerous toys from being sold within the EC.

- *Price Indication Directives.* Adopted in June 1988, these require selling prices and, in some cases, unit prices to be displayed.

- *Recommendation on Payment Systems.* Proposes common rules applicable to the rights and liabilities of payment card issuers and holders.

- *Nutrition Labeling Directive.* Adopted in 1990, this requires nutritional labeling only on foods for which nutritional claims are made.

- *Household Appliances: Airborne Noise Directive.* Implemented in December 1989, this prescribes that the noise level of household appliances be specified on labels and that it be determined through harmonized standards on testing. Manufacturers will no longer have to comply with the different standards of each member state.

• *Lawnmower Noise Directive.* To be implemented July 1, 1991, this prescribes limits on noise from lawnmowers, and also sets forth testing procedures.

Other legislation pertains to broadcast advertising, in connection with which the Commission has proposed five broad principles: "Advertising must not offend against prevailing standards of decency and good taste; it must contain no racial or sexual discrimination; it must not be offensive to religious or political beliefs; it must not exploit fears without good reason; it must not encourage behavior prejudicial to health or safety."[10] This last would include a prohibition against tobacco advertising on TV and restrictions on advertising alcohol. Further, advertising aimed specifically at children would not be allowed.

Member states could impose stricter requirements on their own broadcasters, but they would have to allow broadcasts from other EC states that meet the EC requirements.

Equally important as this legislation are some coordination measures the EC has taken to address issues of safety and consumer protection. In 1984, the EC established an early warning system, under which "any government which has decided to take urgent action to control the marketing or use of a product must inform the European Commission, which in turn informs the other Member States."[11] The individual governments can then take whatever action they choose. The European home and leisure accident surveillance system (Ehlass), established in 1987, monitors causes of domestic accidents in representative hospitals throughout the EC. Monthly reports sent to Luxembourg enable the EC to determine if any products need to be looked at more closely. Because accidents in the home have replaced those in the workplace as the leading cause of injury, the EC hopes that this system will have a success similar to that already enjoyed by the various programs that monitor work-related injuries instituted in EC member states and elsewhere.

Although there is no EC requirement that pricing be the same across the Community, the Commission has promoted cross-border shopping "by publishing guides on the consumer's right to buy goods in other Community countries," and by supplying "regular information on prices, together with up-to-date practical advice as to where the good buys are to be found."[12] The goal is for prices to converge to a lowest profitable level as consumers become more informed and knowledgeable.

In April 1975 the EC established a consumers' "bill of rights," specifying the right to health protection and safety, to protection of economic interests, to redress, to information and education, and to representation. In 1981, these rights were reaffirmed and value for money was added as a legitimate goal.

The main EC organization in this area is the Directorate-General for

The 1992 Analysis Matrix
Consumer Products
Major Areas of the 1992 Process

Areas of Competitive Advantage	Harmonized Standards (Chapter 3)	Opened Government Procurement (Chapter 3)	Industry Deregulation (Chapter 5)	Fiscal Harmony (Chapter 7)	Community R&D Policy (Directory C)	Reduction of Physical Barriers (Chapters 2, 5)	Content-Quota/Tariff Reform (Chapter 3)	Social Dimension (Chapter 3)
Supplier relations	H					H	M	
Manufacturing								
Scale	H					M–H	H	
Location	M–H			M–L		M–H	H	M
Product								
R&D	H				H		M	
Products	H				M–H	M	M	
Marketing								
Sales	H			M		M	M	
Distribution	H			M–H		M	M	
Price	H			M–H		M–H	M	
Customer service								
Organization								
Info tech	M			L–M		H	M	
HRM	M				M	M–H	M	M
Linkages	M				M	M–H	M	
Finance	M			M		M–H	M	

the Environment, Consumer Protection and Nuclear Safety. Others are the Consumers' Consultative Committee, which represents the European Bureau of Consumers' Unions (BEUC), the Committee of Family Organizations in the European Communities (Coface), the European Community of Consumer Cooperatives (Eurocoop), and the European Trade Union Confederation (ETUC).

The 1992 Analysis Matrix will show how consumer products are affected by developments within the European Community.

Financial Services

General Areas to Watch: Banking, investment services, UCITS, and insurance:

In the opinion of an *Institutional Investor* writer, "There is no sector riper for competition than financial services—and no set of consumers more desperately in need of it."[13]

The promise of 1992 for financial services firms is that they will be able to offer products and services in all member states without having to obtain additional licenses and approvals beyond those required in their home country. The promise for consumers is that prices, which are often inflated because of protective arrangements and which vary far more

than do prices in other areas, will become both lower and more consistent. Further, consumers will be protected by communitywide minimum
safeguards.

In the area of financial services, the EC has four primary goals:

1. To establish minimum essential standards for a prudential supervision that will protect investors, consumers, and depositors.
2. To establish mutual recognition of firms that meet these minimum
   standards among all EC countries.
3. To establish home country control of financial institutions operating in other member states.
4. To provide non-EC firms access to the EC-wide market only so
   long as EC firms are granted similar opportunities in those firms'
   home countries.

Essentially, provided that it meets the minimum essential standards established by the EC, an EC-based firm will be able to operate anywhere
in the EC (referred to as having a single license or passport), and third-
country firms will be able to do so as well provided EC firms are granted
the same treatment. There has, of course, been some controversy in
working out the details, most of it concerning the role of the home country versus that of the host country in overseeing operations.

Banking

General Areas to Watch: Reciprocity, deregulation, taxation.

The most important legislation in the banking sector is the Second
Banking Directive. Among its features is the single EC banking license,
which enables any credit institution incorporated or chartered under the
laws of one member state to operate, through branches or through cross-
border transactions (but not through subsidiaries, which are not covered
by the directive), in other member states without obtaining prior approval from each. It must, however, adhere to the host country's policies
governing margin and reserve requirements, the latter particularly because they can have an effect on monetary policy, which remains the pre-
serve of member states. Further, branches in other member states would
not need separate endowment capital. Basically, each member state
would agree to recognize the standards established by other member
states and to accept their prudential supervision of financial institutions.
This "passport" would also apply to a subsidiary of a third-country bank
operating in a member state; it too could then operate (through branches
or cross-border transactions—but not through yet other subsidiaries) in
other member states without further approval. There are some condi-

tions, of course; the major ones are "a minimum initial capital requirement of ECU 5 million (about \$5.5 million) and provisions relating to the identity, extent of holdings, and suitability of major shareholders." [14] Introduction of the directive is set for no later than January 1993.

Under the Second Banking Directive, banking activities encompass not only the deposit and lending functions that Americans associate with commercial banks, but also securities-related activities such as trading, underwriting, and portfolio management that in the United States are engaged in by investment banks and stockbrokers. Other than West Germany's and the United Kingdom's "universal" banks, few banks in the EC currently provide all these services. Yet, under the directive, if a bank provides one or more of these services and meets its home country regulations as well as the directive's minimum standards, it can provide the same service(s) in another member state, even if domestic banks in that country are not allowed to. This is likely to cause member states to lift restrictions on allowable banking activities so that their own banks won't be at a disadvantage vis-à-vis other EC banks. Figure 5-1 lists activities covered by the directive.

Figure 5-1. Banking activities covered by the Second Banking Directive.

1. Deposit taking and other forms of borrowing
2. Lending [including consumer credit, mortgage lending, factoring and invoice discounting, and trade finance (including forfeiting)]
3. Financial leasing
4. Money transmission services
5. Issuing and administering means of payment (credit cards, travelers' checks, and bankers' drafts)
6. Guarantees and commitments
7. Trading for bank's own account or for customers' accounts in:

   a. Money market instruments (e.g., checks, bills, and CDs)
   b. Foreign exchange
   c. Financial futures and options
   d. Exchange and interest rate instruments
   e. Securities

8. Participation in share issues and the provision of services related to such issues
9. Money brokering
10. Portfolio management and advice
11. Safekeeping of securities
12. Credit reference services
13. Safe custody services

Source: Panorama of European Industry, Publication of the European Community, 1988, pp. 29–34.

What This Means to U.S. Businesses.   As of the end of 1987, branches of U.S. banks located in the EC had assets of $140 billion, their subsidiaries assets of nearly $75 billion.[15]

The first draft of the Second Banking Directive became controversial outside the EC because its reciprocity provisions were deemed unclear, particularly by the United States, which was concerned lest the term "similar opportunities" be interpreted so strictly as to preclude U.S. banks from gaining fair treatment. Specifically, concern centered around the Glass-Steagall Act (which prohibits banks from engaging in both investment and commercial banking) and the banking laws unique to each of the fifty states. The U.S. government feared that the EC might determine that EC banks were not granted the same opportunities in the United States (for example, they couldn't do business in the United States without meeting the regulations of each state they wanted to operate in) that U.S. banks would be accorded in the EC (e.g., the ability to operate in all member states via the single EC license). The United States wanted the language changed from "reciprocity" to "national treatment," which would reflect the fact that EC banks wanting to operate in the United States would be granted treatment no less favorable than that granted U.S. banks operating in the United States.

The EC did indeed change the language to "national treatment" in its second draft of the directive, much in accordance with U.S. wishes. Further, while requests by non-EC banks for authorization in a member state will cause that state to notify the Commission, it will no longer result in the application's automatically being suspended during the Commission's review (as was the case under the first draft of the directive). However, the Commission did specify that when national treatment fails to provide "effective market access and competitive opportunities comparable to those accorded by the Community," the Commission could make this a negotiating point, and even seek to limit or suspend new authorizations from the country concerned. This concept could be activated if things get nasty. In February 1990, Sir Leon Brittan, EC Commissioner for Financial Institutions, said that the EC opposes the Glass-Steagall Act and the practice by some U.S. states of restricting the expansion of foreign-owned banks. He made it clear that he wanted both eliminated.

Although it is all but certain that existing subsidiaries of non-EC banks operating in the EC will have access to the single license, and although such access appears reasonably safe for those wishing to establish subsidiaries in the future, the Second Banking Directive does specify that such access would be subject to reciprocity and to periodic review of the home country's practices regarding EC-based banks operating there. The Commission would conduct the reviews and make recommendations to the Council, which will decide on any action.

The EC banking industry has already made known that it questions how effective the access is that EC banks have in other countries, including the United States and Japan. A list of offending countries was "drawn up by the EC's Banking Federation, a Brussels-based trade group representing the interests of banks in the Community."[16] Although this list was said to be a survey, and is not an official EC document, it isn't particularly good news. The questioned U.S. restrictions were those mentioned above—the Glass-Steagall Act and varying state regulations.

There are other possible complications as well. To gain access to the single license, a non-EC bank would, of course, have to meet its host EC-country's licensing requirements. In the case of a merger or acquisition, "it appears that member states would not be required to remove any barriers to non-EC direct investment that are now in effect."[17] But then, so long as even one member state imposes few barriers (e.g., Luxembourg and the United Kingdom), this may not be a major concern. However, a merger or acquisition of an EC bank involving more than ECU 5 billion in total revenues could be subject to review under the EC's cross-border mergers directive.

Other directives that affect banks include the following:

- *Solvency Ratios Directive.* To take effect in January, 1993, it establishes a minimum requirement of 8 percent of capital to risk adjusted assets. This figure is the same as that adopted by the Basel Committee on Banking Regulations and Supervisory Practices, under the auspices of the Bank for International Settlements (BIS).

- *First Banking Directive.* Adopted in 1977, this establishes minimum legal requirements for credit institutions.

- *Directive on Consolidated Supervision.* Adopted in 1983, this specifies that when one institution owns more than 25 percent of another, they will be supervised on a consolidated basis.

- *Directive on the Annual Accounts of Banks.* Adopted in 1986, this establishes the format and contents of the annual consolidated accounts of banks that have their head offices within the EC.

- *Bank Accounts Directive.* To take effect in 1993, it requires disclosure of hidden reserves.

- *Commission Recommendation on Monitoring and Controlling Large Exposures.* Calls for reporting exposures in excess of 15 percent of a bank's own funds, and prohibiting exposures in excess of 40 percent.

- *Deposit Insurance Programs.* These would be the responsibility of the host country.

- *Code of Conduct for Electronic Payment.* Would establish minimum protection for users of electronic card systems, e.g., by placing the burden of proof on card issuers when conflicts arise between issuers and users.

• *Mortgage Credit Directive.* Would grant the right to provide mortgage credit throughout the EC and provide for mutual recognition of funding and lending standards.

Another EC proposal affecting banks would impose a 15 percent withholding tax on depositors' earnings; this would be uniform throughout the EC in order to prevent tax dodging. France considered this particularly important because of the potential impact of the removal of exchange controls (in the eight largest EC countries) that occurred in July 1990. However, critics point out that even if such a tax were imposed, those wishing to avoid taxes, or just to get their deposits' earnings first and pay taxes only later, could simply go outside the EC, to the Channel Islands, for example. The United Kingdom and Luxembourg opposed the proposal because their status as international financial centers might be jeopardized if such a diversion of deposits were to occur. France has eased off and the proposal remains in limbo, where it will probably remain because, like all fiscal proposals, this one would require a unanimous vote by the Council.

The liberalization of short-term capital movements that officially took effect in July 1990 could have a profound impact on banks. EC citizens and institutions are now able to open bank accounts and engage in other banking activities in any country they like. As its consequences unfold, this ability to seek out better rates or services will undoubtedly make EC banking far more competitive than it has been. " 'The first casualties,' a German banker theorizes, 'will be the banks that are big in national terms but not big in international or even intra-European terms. When the shakedown is over, there will be fewer big banks, and those will be bigger. The rest will have to downsize and concentrate on local markets.' "[18] Banks in the southern EC countries and specialized institutions like British building societies (roughly similar to American S&Ls, but owned by depositors rather than shareholders) are considered prime candidates for takeovers.[19]

Whereas competition for commercial and investment banking markets will most likely intensify, that for consumer credit may remain unaffected for some time, except in the area of credit cards. In the United Kingdom, for instance, "Since even the building societies, with their new powers, have barely yet begun to challenge the clearing banks on unsecured consumer credit, it may be some time before foreign banks do so, even though most of them are legally free to do so already."[20] And in the credit card area (where Visa, Master Charge, and Eurocheque are the main competitors), the real competition "will be to acquire retail outlets in which to install single terminals capable of processing all the main types of card. Such competition will be mainly between domestic banks. . . ."[21]

Further, throughout the banking industry—investment, commercial, and retail—many believe that, in light of the local and highly personal nature of the business, 1992 will result not so much in offensive takeovers as in defensive measures. Even banks buying across borders have tended to keep on local management so as not to lose the local knowledge and relationships that make the acquisition worthwhile in the first place.

Note the following developments in EC banking:

- Citicorp is conducting a major campaign to become an EC-wide consumer bank. Other American banks, having tried similar strategies, are moving in the opposite direction: "Chase Manhattan Corp. has retrenched, selling its Belgian bank earlier this year. BankAmerica Corp., Chemical Banking Corp. and Manufacturers Hanover Corp. have largely quit trying to serve consumers overseas."[22]

- West German banks might soon be limited to owning no more than 15 percent of nonbank firms, a move that would significantly reduce the strong influence of these universal banks, which cross-own much of German industry. The move is being pushed by the Free Democratic Party, the junior partner in the coalition government.

- West German banks have been particularly aggressive in expanding activities (e.g., into investment management and insurance) and buying up other banks throughout the EC.

- Although the United Kingdom and Luxembourg both host a large number of foreign banks, they do so differently. Foreign branches predominate in the United Kingdom, while foreign-owned subsidiaries are more common in Luxembourg.

- Banks accounting for more than 90 percent of bank assets in the Netherlands abandoned restrictive agreements after the EC Commission ruled them in violation of the Treaty of Rome, which prohibits the restriction of competition. The agreements included minimum fees of banking services and uniform commissions.

- The Bank of Spain has been campaigning against *autocartera*, the practice of Spanish banks (and other firms) of owning their own shares. The Bank of Spain's opposition is "based on the potential it has to limit the central bank's policy of encouraging consolidation in the Spanish banking sector. It could also discourage the build-up of sufficient capital to meet new international standards. . . ."[23]

• Italian banks, which are highly protected and regulated, are deemed "too small, too numerous, lacking in international presence, overstaffed and, in some important cases, undercapitalised."[24] They are being encouraged to merge to prepare for 1992, especially for competition with the West German and British universal banks.

Investment Services

General Areas to Watch: Reciprocity, deregulation, taxation.

EC citizens have been able to make direct investments in other EC countries since 1962, and have been able to invest in long-term instruments across EC borders since February 1988. Further, the Capital Movements Directive of June 24, 1988, provides for the liberalization of all remaining intra-EC transactions, including short-term instruments such as financial loans and credits, current and deposit accounts, and short-term securities. This took effect on July 1, 1990, except in Spain, Portugal, Greece, and Ireland, which have been granted extensions until 1992. (Such full liberalization was already in effect in the United Kingdom, West Germany, the Netherlands, Italy, and Denmark.) Europeans will be able to seek out the highest returns on any financial instruments they desire anywhere in the EC. Free movement of capital will also place member states' financial markets in direct competition with one another. Monetary and exchange rate policies will be most affected because medium- and long-term capital movements have already been liberalized.

Full liberalization of capital movements will apply to non-EC countries as well, so EC citizens will be able to invest in the United States via any instruments they choose. Investors, however, will still face the risks of currency conversion. An Italian buying shares in a company on the French bourse, for example, will have to convert lire into francs to make the purchase and accept the possibility of the franc's decreasing in value versus the lira. But, then too, the success of the European Monetary System (EMS) has reduced this risk. Further, there are safeguard clauses that will enable a member state to restrict capital movements when its capital markets suffer dislocations, especially balance of payments problems, though the EC intends to establish a lending facility to help member states that develop such problems.

Free movement of capital could have profound effects on an industry which, in many EC countries, has been overprotected, overregulated, operating with a lack of information on listed companies, and subject to insider trading.

The proposed Directive on Investment Services is similar to the Second Banking Directive in that it would enable EC-based investment firms to operate throughout the Community, "based on home country autho rization and home-country prudential supervision. . . ."[25] Prudential supervision would address such matters as capital adequacy, segregation of customer accounts from those of the firm, protection of investors against bankruptcy or default, and establishing the "good repute and experience" of the principals. The single license provided by the directive would enable investment firms to join stock and other exchanges (financial futures and options) and to enjoy the same trading privileges as host-country firms if they are authorized to do so by their home country. However, the directive does not address access to host-country clearing facilities. Though a host country would not have to admit a bank to its exchange(s) if it normally does not do so, it would have to admit a subsidiary investment firm established by a bank.

The directive specifically lists the activities of investment firms; these include "brokerage, dealing as principal, market making, portfolio management, underwriting, investment advice, and safekeeping services."[26]

EC standards for capital adequacy will be addressed in a separate directive. (Capital adequacy will most likely be the responsibility of the home country; this is in contrast to the banking sector, where it will be the responsibility of the host country). Progress may be hard to come by because there is no equivalent to the Basel Accord in banking, and member states have much more diverse standards in investment services than they do in banking. There is concern that because member states would be free to establish their own capital adequacy standards, those with more lenient ones might gain a competitive advantage. The United Kingdom is particularly concerned that its high standards might even lead British firms to move elsewhere. The current draft allows for a reduction in the capital required if the investment company has reduced its risk by hedging or diversification. Companies offering only advice would be exempt, and those taking no positions would have a capital requirement of 100,000 ECU. Bank trading subsidiaries would be covered by this directive rather than by the more stringent banking solvency ratios.

The Investment Services Directive also contains "reciprocity" language that the United States and others are concerned about for the same reasons they were concerned about its use in the first draft of the Second Banking Directive. But, unlike the Second Banking Directive, the reciprocity provisions in the Investment Services Directive have not been modified, though many believe that the revisions of the reciprocity provisions of the Second Banking Directive will become the model for those in the other financial services directives. Unless such revisions are made, subsidiaries of non-EC firms would have to be authorized and regulated separately by each host state, though this would not apply to existing subsidiaries of non-EC financial services firms provided they have a registered office and their central administration or principal place of business within the EC. Direct branches of non-EC investment firms would not enjoy the access granted by the directive.

Because the Second Banking Directive would enable banks as well as investment firms to engage in investment activities, the timing of the implementation of these two directives could have competitive consequences. If one were adopted before the other, firms covered by it would have a head start. As a result, the Commission intends to implement the two directives simultaneously.

Other directives and developments affecting investment services include the following:

- *The Mutual Recognition of Prospectuses Directive.* Adopted in December 1988, avoids the need for separate sets of information for each member state, although host exchanges can require additional information if they deem it necessary to protect investors.

- *The Admission of Securities Directive.* Adopted in March 1979, this harmonized minimum standards that securities must meet to be listed on EC stock exchanges. It applies to both EC and non-EC securities. Member states remain free to impose more stringent standards and to require that non-EC securities be already listed on an exchange.

- *The Listing Particulars Directive.* Adopted in 1980, this specifies what information must be provided when securities are admitted to listing.

- *Interim Reports Directive.* Adopted in 1982, this specifies the information that must be provided on an ongoing basis by listed companies.

- *The Insider Trading Directive.* To be implemented in June 1992, this will harmonize restrictions on insider trading, which heretofore has been legal in Italy, West Germany, and other EC member states.

- *Development of an Interbourse Data Information System (IDIS).* Would create a real-time information exchange system among all EC bourses. The goal is an EC-wide securities market.

UCITS

> *General Areas to Watch:*   Reciprocity, deregulation, taxation.

Sales of UCITS (Undertakings for Collective Investment in Transferable Securities), roughly equivalent to American open-ended mutual funds, were liberalized under the UCITS Directive that came into effect in October 1989 (except in Spain and Portugal, which have until April 1992). It enables UCITS managers to market throughout the EC subject to home country supervision, except for marketing practices, which will be subject to host country rules. "It also deals with their structure, their investment and borrowing policy, information to be published, and general obligations."[27] Basically, the directive provides an EC-wide passport to funds managers who meet minimum requirements in areas such as asset mix and disclosure, both in their prospectuses and semiannual accounting. As with the other financial services sectors covered in this section, a host state can apply more stringent controls on domestic funds managers, but not on those from other EC countries (or from third countries meeting "reciprocity" standards).

Even with such a passport, marketers of UCITS might find the going hard largely because of different national attitudes and practices. For instance, whereas United Kingdom residents are used to buying UCITS in response to media and direct mail advertising, the French are not. That is why Fidelity Investment Services, Ltd, a United Kingdom UCITS manager, is selling UCITS in France through the Pelloux Group, which is experienced in selling real estate investment funds in France.

The UCITS Directive does not apply to money market funds, "investment trusts and funds investing mainly in unquoted securities,"[28] nor to those that invest even in part in anything but transferable securities, e.g., gold or property. Note the following:

• Luxembourg passed legislation meeting the UCITS rules within three months of the directive's publication. This, combined with its low annual fee (.06 percent of asset value), no income or capital gains taxes on funds, and no withholding tax on dividends distributed to investors, has resulted in numerous funds locating there, even if it is only their administrative headquarters as required to gain the EC passport. From 1980 to 1988 the number of investment companies in Luxembourg grew from seventy-six to more than 400.[29]

• Although an attractive target with its 18 percent savings rate, Germany will be a tough market in which to sell UCITS; authorities and much of the public alike remember only too well the disaster that accompanied Bernie Cornfeld's Investors Overseas Services,* which did half its sales in Germany.

• Marketing channels and distribution that follow local customs will be key. The United Kingdom is used to an American style of selling through advertising, whereas in Italy and Germany big banks and insurance companies are the normal channels. As a result, many British UCITS firms are seeking to develop relationships with such firms in these countries.

---

*Investors Overseas Services was a mutual fund organization that was long on selling and short on investments. Its bankruptcy resulted in many buyers not being able to get their money back.

- To avoid the possibility of a UCITS taking advantage of the passport, a UCITS firm is prohibited "from converting itself into an undertaking not covered by the directive."[30]

Insurance

> *General Area to Watch:*   Reciprocity.

Of all financial services in Europe, the insurance industry has been the most regulated, and is proving more difficult to harmonize than banking. Although most member states allow branches or subsidiaries of foreign firms to market locally, many also "impose extensive regulatory measures such as individual solvency ratios independent of the firm's parent office."[31] Reinsurance is an exception.

The liberalization of insurance throughout the Community will make it far easier for firms, particularly those operating in more than one member state, to get the coverage they need at competitive prices.

EC initiatives affecting insurance have included the First Non-Life Insurance Directive, implemented in 1975, which harmonized requirements in areas such as legal forms and solvency ratios. It also enabled insurers with a head office in one member state to establish branches in another. Directive 77/92/EEC, implemented in 1978, liberalized the freedom of establishment for agents and brokers and called for mutual recognition of their training and experience.

As in other areas, the European Court of Justice has played a significant role in determining EC policy in insurance. In December 1986, it found in favor of the Commission, which in 1983 and 1984 had brought suit against West Germany, France, Denmark, and Ireland. The Court upheld the principles of mutual recognition and national treatment, which, basically, enabled companies to sell insurance in another member state without setting up an establishment there. The Court ruled that whereas member states could impose regulations to protect their citizens, they could not:

1. Impose regulations that merely duplicate those met by the companies in their home countries
2. Impose regulations solely on nondomestic firms. Any restrictions designed for the general good must be "applied to all persons or companies in the host state (including domestic companies). . . ."[32]

In addressing the issue of consumer protection, the Court established a usage that would affect future EC actions: It ruled that more protection was required for private individuals ("mass" risks) than for corporate or commercial customers ("large" risks).

In June 1988, the Council approved the Second Non-Life Insurance Services Directive, which allows insurance firms to conduct transactions in other member states without establishing branches or other forms of physical presence. They are, of course, subject to home country supervision. The directive does not cover branches, which will continue to be authorized and supervised by host countries. Implementation occurred on December 31, 1989 (except in Spain, Greece, Portugal, and Ireland; Spain has until 1997 to be in accord, the other three until 1999).

This liberalization applies to nonlife insurance for "large" commercial and industrial risks, including those in the marine, aviation, and transport industries. To be considered "large" for purposes of this directive, a client must meet at least two of the following three requirements:

1. Total assets of 12.4 million ECU (approximately $13.6 million)
2. Net sales of 24 million ECU (approximately $26.4 million)
3. An average of 500 employees during the financial year

These numerical criteria will be reduced by 50 percent as of January 1, 1993.[33]

The above directive does not apply to "mass" risks; insurors selling nonlife insurance to individuals would remain under host country control, "effectively discouraging cross-border services in this area."[34]

There is also a distinction made between branches and subsidiaries of non-EC insurers. Non-EC-owned branches and agencies would be subject to the host country's rulings on the extent to which they could provide cross-border services. However, non-EC subsidiaries legally incorporated within a member state would have to be treated by host countries in the same way that subsidiaries of EC companies are.

In the life insurance area, many member states prohibit individuals from purchasing life insurance outside their own country. The Commission's Second Directive on Direct Life Insurance (February 1989) would remove such prohibitions on the condition that the prospective client took the initiative in entering into the contract; he or she would even have to sign a statement to that effect. Solicitation and advertising would not be allowed, by either a company or its broker, except through published notices indicating a company's address and the types of insurance it is authorized to transact in its home country. Companies that canvass for such prospects across borders may be required to seek authorization and meet host countries' regulations concerning reserves and conditions of insurance.

Cross-border canvassing may be allowed under a planned directive, but would require more harmonization of supervisory rules. The directive would enable EC insurance companies, including subsidiaries of U.S. insurers located within an EC member state, to provide individual life insurance policies across borders without first establishing a branch or other physical presence in the member state where the customer resides. (The directive would not entitle direct *branches* of non-EC insurance companies to operate under the liberalized rules.) This proposed directive also includes a reciprocity provision like that in the original Second Banking Directive. Third countries like the United States would have to provide reciprocal access, a potential problem for U.S. insurers because all insurers in the United States, including foreign insurers, must be licensed in each state in which they write policies. Further, about half the states have laws that enable them to deny licenses to insurance companies owned or controlled by foreign governments (and many EC insurance companies are fully or partly state-owned).

The Commission plans to address pollution liability, group health and disability, and medical product liability insurance in the future; liberalization of group insurance, for instance, might prove particularly complex because it would overlap the policies of many member states on social security and welfare.

Other insurance directives include the following:

- *Credit Insurance Directive*. Implemented July 1, 1990, it amends the First Non-Life Insurance Directive and requires an equalization reserve when credit insurance premiums are over 2.5 million ECU or 4 percent of total premiums.

- *Annual Accounts of Insurance Undertakings Directive*. Implemented January 1, 1989, this specifies what information must be included in financial statements and valuation rules. Requirements are similar to those in the United States, and harmonized standards will make it easier to operate in more than one member state.

- *Winding up of Insurance Undertakings Directive*. With an implementation date to be announced, this harmonizes the disposition of insurance contracts upon the liquidation of insurance firms.

- *A Coinsurance Directive*. Adopted in 1978, this enables companies to engage in coinsurance subject only to the rules in the directive and those of the leading company's home state. The 1986 decisions by the European Court of Justice prohibited requiring that the lead insurer be established in the member state where the risk is located.

- *A Motor Vehicle Liability Insurance Directive*. Proposed by the Commission in December 1988. This area had not been covered by the other nonlife directives, and would receive similar treatment.

• *A Directive on the Coordination of Laws, Regulations, and Administrative Provisions Relating to Insurance Contracts.* Currently under consideration by the Council, this would establish standards for nonlife insurance contracts, including policy documentation, nondisclosure of information by the policyholder, filing claims, and renewal and termination of contracts. The information required is similar to that in the U.S. industry.

Although insurance remains highly regulated by member states, liberalization, either accomplished or anticipated, has set off a rash of merger and acquisition activity, some of it conventional, some of it highly creative:

• In 1989, nine insurance companies from across Europe (Belgium, France, Spain, Italy, Denmark, the United Kingdom, West Germany, and Finland) signed an agreement to exchange information and develop products.

• Since 1986, Allianz, Europe's largest insurance group, has "paid a total of Dm 2.3bn for RAS of Italy and Cornhill of the UK."[35] Allianz is actively looking for a U.S. acquisition, "looking at about one U.S. insurer a month now."[36]

• "In 1986–1987, no fewer than seventeen Spanish insurers were bought out—wholly or in part—by their larger neighbors. Over the same period, two dozen British firms passed to new owners, only seven of which were based outside the EC."[37]

• Although reinsurance companies have not been subject to the trade restrictions being addressed by 1992, they will be affected. Primary insurers, facing a soft market and 1992-induced competition, are often assuming insurance risks they used to allocate to reinsurers. They are also buying or merging with reinsurance companies. Some reinsurers are playing the same game. "The most important of these is Munich Re's 25 per cent reciprocal stake in Allianz."[38]

The long-held borders between insurance and banking are also eroding as indicated by several actions:

• Shareholdings amounting to 15 percent have been exchanged between Verenidge Spaarbank, the Netherlands' biggest savings bank, and Amev, its third-largest insurer, and an eventual merger is possible.

• Marketing agreements have been signed between Allianz and the Dresdner Bank in West Germany, and between the Banque Nationale de Paris and Union des Assurances in Paris in France.[39]

• "After 20 months of research and planning, Deutsche Bank AG on September 1, 1989, will begin selling its own life insurance products over

The 1992 Analysis Matrix
Financial Services
Major Areas of the 1992 Process

Areas of Competitive Advantage	Harmonized Standards (Chapter 3)	Opened Government Procurement (Chapter 3)	Industry Deregulation (Chapter 5)	Fiscal Harmony (Chapter 7)	Community R&D Policy (Directory C)	Reduction of Physical Barriers (Chapters 2, 5)	Content-Quota/Tariff Reform (Chapter 3)	Social Dimension (Chapter 3)
Supplier relations	H		H	M				M
Manufacturing								
Scale								
Location								
Product								
R&D	H		H	H				
Products	H		H	H				M
Marketing								
Sales	H	M	H	H			M–H	
Distribution	H		H	H			M–H	
Price	H		H	H				
Customer service	H		H	H			M–H	
Organization								
Info tech	H		H	H			M–H	
HRM	H		H	H				M
Linkages	H		H	H				
Finance	H		H	H				

the counters of its 1,300 domestic branches."[40] Allianz, the EC's largest insurance company, didn't like this and "struck back by forming a coop-eration agreement with Dresdner Bank AG, West Germany's second-largest bank."[41]

The 1992 Analysis Matrix shows the dramatic impact of EC develop-ments on financial services.

Information Technology

General Areas to Watch: Standards, R&D policy, local content, quotas, intel-lectual property, government procurement.

The information technology (IT) sector has been identified as the cor-nerstone of Community R&D efforts, an indispensable element in overall European competitiveness. Information technology comprises several areas that share a sophisticated electronics foundation. These distinct sectors, however, appear to be merging as technology advances. The bor-der blurs between such areas as data processing and telecommunica-tions, consumer electronics and personal computers.

We've broken IT into three segments: electronics, computers, and telecommunications. We begin by identifying 1992 developments that might affect all three, and then discuss those unique to the individual areas.

For years Europeans have been in the forefront of technology development, but have failed to capitalize on the market potential of their discoveries. European efforts to create competitiveness in mainframe computers, for example, failed as infighting among French, British, and German scientists sabotaged the technological advances developed in the labs. Fragmentation, the rising costs and complexities of R&D, the shortening of product life cycles, and the prominent role IT now plays in most sectors of an industrial economy, forced the Community to reassess its efforts. It was clear that Europe had to improve its IT capability or be relegated to second-class status in the industrial world.

With the help of European industrialists, the Community created a framework to coordinate R&D in 1984. ESPRIT (European Strategies Program for Research and Development in Information Technology) laid the groundwork for comprehensive R&D programs, encompassing sectors from biotechnology to alternative energy. Nationalistic desires for technological dominance, however, make coordination of these programs a challenge, and there are claims that some are fraught with waste.

Many of the more general thrusts of the 1992 program will benefit the entire IT sector, from reduction of border barriers, to deregulation of transportation, harmonization of value-added taxes (VAT) and the establishment of common standards. All this will result in lower production costs, more efficient distribution, and lower prices for consumers. This means that companies will have greater opportunities to capitalize on scale economies, something Europeans have had difficulty doing in the past. Rationalization of manufacturing, advanced production and design ability, and sophisticated labor relations will be key factors for success in a more competitive European information technology market.

To acquire these skills and gain local market access, companies have been scrambling to forge alliances, purchase firms, or develop in-house strategic capability. Siemens's acquisition of Rolm, IBM's flat-screen television development deal with Toshiba, and AT&T's venture with Italtel to establish a beachhead in Europe are just a few of the more visible examples of such activities. The increasing numbers of such R&D ventures indicate that single companies, regardless of size, can no longer keep pace with the rapid changes in technology.

Electronics

Semiconductors, important building blocks for all information technology sectors, are critical components for such industries as consumer electronics, computers, and automobiles. The chip business is fiercely competitive and highly cyclical. U.S. firms have recently fallen behind the

Japanese in key commodity segments, an area considered by many scientists to be a technology driver, that is, a provider of valuable experience that can be applied to other more sophisticated semiconductors. Without the knowledge gained from producing commodity chips, companies can easily become vulnerable in the higher-end product areas.

European firms are even farther behind. Besides lacking the latest chip capability, Europeans use fewer semiconductors in products than do the United States and Japan. As a result, European chip producers like Philips, Siemens, and Thomson-SGS have an inferior local customer base. This also puts other European sectors at risk; whereas many foreign competitors have incorporated chip technology into their products, European companies often have not.

Although 1992 does not directly address these problems, the possibility of their resolution is enhanced by the internal market process. Several R&D programs are designed to improve chip technology and use throughout the Community. ESPRIT and the Joint European Submicron Silicon Initiative (JESSI) are the most important of these. JESSI is a $4 billion program that excludes all non-EC companies (see Directory C), indicating Europe's intention to become a world IT leader.

Another part of the Community's IT strategy is to use protection to provide European companies with the time necessary to improve their technology and manufacturing capability. Although tariffs (14 percent for semiconductors) are the main tool used to date, the imposition of rules of origin, voluntary restraint agreements, and restrictive procurement practices could also come into play.

The consumer electronics markets are dominated by Japanese firms. American companies are practically non-existent in this important sector. This could have defense ramifications for the United States because consumer electronics can also act as a technology driver. In 1988, the U.S. Department of Defense (DOD) claimed that the experience with lasers gained from producing compact disc (CD) players could be valuable in advanced military laser applications and that because no American companies make CD players, the United States' national security could be compromised.

While the Department of Defense is examining ways to encourage U.S. firms to reenter the consumer electronics market, Europe is in the process of challenging the Japanese. Philips and Thomson, two European consumer electronics giants, have formed a variety of alliances with firms around the world and are positioning themselves to take advantage of 1992 by rationalizing production, maximizing Community R&D opportunities, and revamping product management and sales organizations.

High definition TV, an emerging segment, has sparked controversy as Japan, the United States, and Europe embark separately to establish a world standard. Each believes that HDTV will be an important technology base because it will consume large numbers of commodity semiconductors and because the sets will not be mere TVs but instead develop into personal computers with interactive capabilities of performing home shopping, banking, and visual communications. The Department of Defense has already pledged assistance to U.S. industry, which is several years behind European and Japanese HDTV efforts.

Although HDTV activity is tangential to 1992, improved European competitiveness makes it likely that Europe will have the ability to control its own destiny by establishing an EC standard and by developing the ability to supply the product to the market. Although the United States has rejected the Japanese standard, which would make all existing sets obsolete, in favor of the European concept under which current television sets could still receive the HDTV signal (similar to the way black and white sets could still be used when color was introduced), the United States still lacks HD television manufacturing capability.

How all this might affect the U.S. market is still uncertain, but it is clear that the United States has inadequate clout to order the Europeans to conform to its wishes. HDTV ramifications go far beyond manufacturing; they will also have profound effects on broadcasting, programming, and production, the latter two being strong American exports. An isolated U.S. HDTV standard could adversely affect the dominant position of the United States in programming exports.

Computers

The United States dominates the mainframe, minicomputer, and personal computer (PC) European markets. Five of the top seven PC sellers in Europe are American.[42] IBM, Digital Equipment Corporation, Hewlett-Packard, and even Apple and Compaq have been successful because they not only have the technology and products the market desires; they also operate as European companies. Rationalized manufacturing, state-of-the-art products, and local sales and service are key U.S. strengths. U.S. companies have an added strength over such firms as Bull, Thomson, or SGS, because these so-called European firms have traditionally operated from a single country and have only recently begun to branch out. Smaller firms are being gobbled up by the likes of Philips, Siemens, and Olivetti in their effort to combat U.S. success and to increase market share.

Europe lags behind in computer use, but, perhaps largely because of 1992, companies are issuing purchase orders in record numbers; the EC market is now the fastest-growing in the world. The PC market alone is expanding nearly twice as fast there as in the United States.[43] This growth is attracting new Asian competitors like Taiwan's Acer, in addition to the traditional stable of Japanese firms like Toshiba. Prices should tumble, forcing those who fail to produce efficiently or keep up with technology to withdraw.

1992 strengthens the EC's ability to improve European competitiveness in computers. Standards and local content/tariffs appear to be the key areas that could affect computer companies. The recent lifting of U.S. export restrictions on computers should bolster American efforts. Although the Europeans desire their own computer capability, they have allowed U.S. firms within the Community to participate in most joint R&D projects.

Telecommunications

The importance of this sector can be summed up in this quotation from the EC's DGXIII (Telecommunications, Information Industries and Innovation): "Strengthening the telecommunications sector in the Community is one of the most important preconditions for the promotion of a harmonic development of the economic activity in the Community and for the completion of the EC-wide market for goods and services by 1992."[44]

Several technical barriers must be harmonized before Europe can reap the benefits of an internal market in the telecommunications sector. These include harmonized equipment and network standards, harmonized certification requirements, and an open procurement process. Telecommunications can be broken down into the following segments: transmission and switching equipment, terminal equipment (at the junction of the network and the customer), customer premises equipment (CPE), and value-added services (e.g., the manipulation of data being transmitted). 1992 will affect these areas differently, so it is important to understand the dynamics of each segment.

Several factors are driving the need for improved telecommunications in Europe, including increased globalization of the world's economies, the emergence of high-speed global financial transactions, and an increasing number of international travelers. Because it is essential for European business to have cost-competitive, state-of-the-art telecommunication capability, the forces impeding telecommunications integration, though formidable, will eventually be worn down.

Telecommunication fragmentation has been costly. It is estimated that Europe has spent $10 billion to develop ten telephone switching systems to meet different national standards, compared with just $3 billion spent by three U.S. companies to develop a common system in America and $1.5 billion to do the same in Japan.[45] The table shown in Figure 5-2 indicates the savings that would result from a more rationalized EC market in telecommunications equipment.

Until now, telecommunications companies have served several pur-

Figure 5-2. Telecommunications equipment: gains from EC market integration.

Product	Effects of Standardization	Effects of Procurement 40%	100%
Central office switching	0.45–.07	0.8	1.3
Transmission	0.2	0.4	0.5
Terminal equipment (CPE)	0.1	0.4	1.0
Other	0.1	0.4	0.9
Total	0.85–1.1	2.0	3.7

Source: Paolo Cecchini, *The Benefits of a Single Market* (Hampshire, England: Wildwood House, 1988).

poses for the member state governments that finance them. They are large employers, and labor considerations have been more important than productivity gains. Because consumer policy has also played a role, pricing has not been based on costs. For example, the cost of long-distance calls, which are made primarily by business, has been kept high so as to subsidize losses incurred on local calls and other services (like connections and equipment rental) that are used primarily by consumers. These distortions have affected demand and made it more difficult for companies offering new services to enter the market.

In that all member states except the United Kingdom have only one telecommunications network each, substantial savings from economies of scale are unlikely to materialize from the completion of the internal market. Domestic economies of scale have been maximized, and it would be too costly to replace national systems with an EC-wide one. It's also highly improbable that network competition will take place the way it has in the U.S. long-distance market, though recent developments in the United Kingdom may encourage the Community to examine such possibilities at some point in the future.

The Community will instead begin to limit the number of services in which national companies retain monopoly power. In late 1989, the EC decided to open up electronic mail and access to data bases by mid-1990, and data communications services by 1993. These moves should spark improved efficiencies and prices that more accurately reflect costs in a process similar to that which accompanied deregulation in the United States. Under the Article 90 directive (liberalization of telecommunications services), member states will be obliged to permit competition in all value added services. The monopoly on switched data transmission services will also be abolished. Although Article 90 comes into force in 1990, transitional arrangements will delay this process in some member states until December 31, 1992, and in Greece, Spain, and Portugal, perhaps even later. Also in late 1989, the EC agreed to the Open Network Provision (ONP) Framework Directive, which strives to harmonize services across the EC, and will enable private operators to gain member state licenses (subject to Commission review). The framework directive is voluntary and precedes specific directives to be drafted on individual services that private operators will be able to provide, starting with phone service and leased lines. The Commission hopes to have directives addressing all services drafted and adopted by 1992.

Other segments of the industry may evolve differently. Switching, for example, could achieve scale economies by improving coordination and harmonization among member state systems. The 28 percent stake that Telecom (of Canada) has in the United Kingdom's Standard Telephones and Cable (STC) indicates that more cross-border alliances may develop. Transmission equipment, on the other hand, is subject to international standards, so competition has already created scale advantages.

1992 is not the only force affecting the European telecommunications landscape. Technology improvements have occasionally caused structural changes in the industry, forcing regulators to adapt. For example, private branch exchanges (PABX) represent a recent advance that enables the customer to control the switching part of the telecom network. This development sparked new services and products that enhance the capability of PABXs, like local area networks and other data services, forcing member states to allow competition in areas once controlled by the national post, telegraph, and telephone authorities (PTTs).

Another way telecommunications companies can achieve cost reduction is via an open procurement process. Historically, contracts have been awarded for political rather than economic reasons, as indicated by the little intra-EC trade that exists across the industry. Open procurement could result in cost reductions in phone service; the Cecchini Report estimated from 2 to 8 percent.

Telecommunications, however is one of the areas specifically exempted from EC regulations on public procurement. Although many American companies operate within the Community, they have not fared well vis-à-vis national champions. As the process opens up, however, restructuring should eliminate many of the grossly inefficient producers, thus making room for competitive U.S. products.

A phased approach to contract notification whereby greater percentages of contract solicitation must be opened has been approved by the EC. Whether this will amount to anything, however, depends on how member states implement the ruling. They could use it to continue protecting national companies by allowing only contracts that national firms were not interested in to become public. If, on the other hand, the ruling prompts national telecommunication companies to make decisions based solely on economic reasons, substantial savings and increased competition could emerge. The Cecchini Report estimated savings from 3 to 5 billion ECU. There are indications that procurement decisions will indeed be based on economics. A $25 million contract was awarded to Fujitsu in 1989 for an undersea fiber-optic cable between West Germany and the United Kingdom. This has encouraged many non-EC firms.

The creation of the European Telecommunication Standards Institute (ETSI) in 1988 as a stand-alone entity (it was formerly part of CEPT, the European Post and Telecommunication Administrations), as called for in the EC Green Paper, has elevated the importance of European telecommunications standards not only for the network, transmission, and switching segments, but also for end uses such as videotex, teletex, and facsimile services. Consistent standards would have the greatest impact on central office equipment, with savings estimated for the total EC market at up to 5 billion ECU.[46]

Compatibility in these areas would help to contain costs and ease use; however, market forces may discourage cooperation among competitors. In any event, ETSI is available to serve as an important forum for encouraging this cooperation.

Through ETSI working groups, technical experts from academia, the corporate world, and government explore and debate the issues. The American National Standards Institute (ANSI), the only internationally recognized U.S. standards group, is a special guest at ETSI's technical assembly. Although ANSI doesn't have direct access to working groups, U.S. companies operating within the Community do. ETSI cooperates with such organizations as the International Standardization Organization (ISO) and the International Telecommunications Union (ITU), a UN agency that reconciles the often divergent interests of its members.

These efforts are quite important in telecommunications because the sector provides a technological foundation that is essential for European competitiveness. Therefore, as part of the R&D framework, several programs have been created to foster greater European coordination in telecommunications. Research and Development in Advanced Communications Technology for Europe (RACE) is dedicated to creating a coherent European telecommunications network that will enable one digital network to carry voice, data, text, and image messages (known as an integrated service digital network, or ISDN). Other noteworthy efforts include the APPOLO project, aimed at satellite transmission of high-volume digital information, and Euronet-DIANE, an economic and financial information network that connects 600 data bases and banks to computers and telephones.

Although American firms are competitive in telecommunications, their success is directly linked to how open the government procurement process really becomes, to the process of standards formulation and certification, and to how the EC applies reciprocity to non-EC companies. As Europe liberalizes, competition will become fierce, and only those companies that maintain a technological and services lead will survive.

Under Article 58 of the Treaty of Rome, American companies operating within the Community will be treated like European firms. Short of establishing an EC subsidiary, U.S. firms not already in the EC can gain these benefits through joint ventures with EC companies. AT&T, which was free to operate overseas only after its breakup in 1984, has recently joined up with Italtel, the Italian state-owned telecommunication company, to give itself a solid footing within the EC.

The 1992 Analysis Matrix shows the degree to which EC developments impinge on information technology.

For Further Reading. The EC Green Paper (COM (87) 290): "A common market for telecommunication services and equipment" identifies those telecommunication areas that require harmonization if Europe is to reap the benefits of a truly unified market. This was not part of the original White Paper.

The EC Committee of the American Chamber of Commerce: "Comments on the EC Green Paper on the development of the common market for telecommunications services and equipment," November 1987.

The 1992 Analysis Matrix
Information Technology
Major Areas of the 1992 Process

Areas of Competitive Advantage	Harmonized Standards (Chapter 3)	Opened Government Procurement (Chapter 3)	Industry Deregulation (Chapter 5)	Fiscal Harmony (Chapter 7)	Community R&D Policy (Directory C)	Reduction of Physical Barriers (Chapters 2, 5)	Content-Quota/Tariff Reform (Chapter 3)	Social Dimension (Chapter 3)
Supplier relations	M–H	M				M	M	
Manufacturing								
Scale	H	M				M		
Location	L–M					M–H	M–H	M
Product								
R&D	M–H	M–H		M–H	H			
Products	H	M–H		M–H	M–H		M–H	
Marketing								
Sales	H	M–H			H		H	M–L
Distribution	H				H		H	
Price	H	M			H		H	
Customer service	M–H	M				M–H		M
Organization								
Info tech	M	M	M					
HRM	M							M
Linkages	M							
Finance	M	M		M				

Pharmaceuticals and Medical Devices

General Areas to Watch: Standards, intellectual property.

The 1992 process should have considerable impact on the pharmaceutical industry because several aspects of the program are designed to liberalize this heavily regulated industry. Strict legislation regarding market approval, registration, pricing, and insurance reimbursement now exists in each country. Many of these regulatory activities lack transparency and are subject to governmental discretion, resulting at times in more favorable decisions for domestic companies. The EC hopes that market forces will increase competition and innovation and reduce prices to consumers.

The benefits of deregulation and restructuring should accrue to all companies, regardless of national origin. American companies dominate pharmaceutical sales globally, and have done well in Europe, garnering about 25 percent of the market.[47] Improved European performance, however, will naturally make U.S. efforts more difficult.

The industry has rapidly become a global one because the costs of developing new drugs have risen dramatically, and product life cycles have shortened. Companies now require international scale to recover these enormous up-front costs. The recent mergers of Smith Kline with the United Kingdom's Beecham, and Bristol-Myers with Squibb make it clear that bigness counts. Small firms can carve a niche for themselves through having unique technical skills and by forging alliances.

EC pharmaceutical sales are fairly international, with 34 percent coming from firms located outside the Community, 23 percent from intra-EC trade, and about 45 percent supplied by indigenous companies to their national markets.[48] Most companies produce locally, though in Denmark, Ireland, and the Netherlands imports are more prominent. Only 12 percent of European drugs are purchased over the counter, making doctors the key decision maker in buying.[49]

Consumption and attitudes toward pharmaceuticals vary across the member states. Those with a drug industry tend to be supportive of corporate activity, whereas those lacking a pharmaceutical infrastructure, like Greece, Portugal, and Spain, favor consumer interests, thus encouraging lower prices and stricter safety regulations.

Since 1965, the EC has attempted to harmonize this regulatory activity; however, it has fallen short of substantially reducing European vendor costs. Further complications arise because different member states use different governmental agencies—from economic ministries to social and health ministries—to regulate pharmaceuticals, thus making coordination that much more difficult.

Communitywide registration procedures do exist but are haphazardly administered. They include a time limit of 120 days on the approval process, guidelines for mutually acceptable data, and harmonized standards. Member states on average, however, take from eighteen to twenty-four months to approve a product.[50] According to the Commission, only France comes close to meeting the 120-day deadline.

Because the U.S. Food and Drug Administration (FDA) is considered the most stringent pharmaceutical regulatory agency in the world, American companies normally need make only slight modifications to data that are presented to each member state. Although the direct financial cost of accommodating twelve different regulatory processes is not terribly high, the cost of losing time can be substantial. In addition, no patent-term restoration, that is, reinstatement of time lost during the regulatory review process, exists in the Community. Thus, patents, which last twenty years in most EC countries, take effect from their date of invention, not from their date of approval. The Community has proposed extending patents beyond their current expiration date so that their effective life would normally be sixteen years.

Mutual recognition of member state approval would certainly shorten delays; however, there are considerable differences between northern and southern European medical cultures, making such a proposal controversial. A more palatable alternative is a European Registration Agency that would be recognized by all member states. How high European standards would be, and the political acceptability of such an option, remain unknown. In addition, American firms fear that European companies would receive more favorable treatment and that FDA data would not be acceptable to a European Registration Agency.

Pricing is another area that has been regulated by the member states (except in West Germany, where companies are free to set their own prices), resulting in price variations among the member states for similar products. Because member states administer price controls differently, harmonization is that much more difficult to achieve. The Commission will most likely prohibit the current practice of member states' allowing drug companies to set prices based on how much investment they have in individual countries: The higher the local investment, the higher the prices that a company can charge. This pricing practice would be replaced by one based on how much companies spend throughout the EC.

National health care systems and insurance reimbursement coverage schemes also differ significantly among member states. Opportunity for discrimination creates concerns among non-EC companies because governmental decisions on whether a new product is eligible for insurance reimbursement (plus the timing of that decision) and on how much a company can receive for a product provide regulators with an easy way to favor domestic firms.

On the other hand, the elimination of cross-border tariffs and import restrictions and uniform patent protection within the Community are factors favoring harmonization.

R&D, the bulk of a product's cost, is already centralized in most EC drug companies, so little economy of scale is expected from the completion of the internal market. In addition, local development work is essential to establishing local credibility, so companies will continue these operations.

Manufacturing, however, could benefit from rationalization. U.S. multinationals report that their plants often operate at one-third to one-half of capacity.[51] Unfortunately, it is doubtful that many of these operations will be eliminated because both customers and regulators prefer local production.

Marketing costs will not be much affected by 1992 because pan-European expenditures are comparatively insignificant. The most effective part of the marketing mix appears to be the local salesperson, whose job it is to convince doctors to prescribe the product.

Medical devices cover a broad range of products, from pacemakers to bandages. Rapid advancements in technology make this an important field for human health care.

U.S. efforts in this sector have been strong, but rapid changes in technology have forced most American manufacturers to centralize R&D and production at home. As a result, most sales to Europe are via exports. Because Europe is weak in this sector and U.S. products are considered the best in the world, this strategy has worked. Improved European efforts may change this cozy arrangement for U.S. companies.

The primary effects of 1992 will be positive for all medical device companies that operate in Europe. Two specific areas of 1992 will have an impact on this sector: standards and regulatory procedures. Although current rules for registration and product approval are slightly different from those applying to pharmaceuticals, the concept is the same: Companies must subject their products to each member state's approval process.

Although standards are being formulated through CENELEC, mutually acceptable testing and certification are contentious issues still to be resolved. Because American exporters can't participate directly in establishing these standards, groups such as ANSI and the Health Industry Manufacturers Association (HIMA) are working with CENELEC to present the U.S. position. HIMA is pushing for U.S. labs to be recognized as legitimate testers and certifiers of EC standards; otherwise, U.S. companies will be forced to submit their products to each member state for approval.

As with pharmaceuticals, insurance payment approval is an area where U.S. companies could be placed at a disadvantage vis-à-vis their European competitors.

Some manufacturers complain that U.S. controls on the export of

The 1992 Analysis Matrix
Pharmaceuticals and Medical Delvices
Major Areas of the 1992 Process

Areas of Competitive Advantage	Harmonized Standards (Chapter 3)	Opened Government Procurement (Chapter 3)	Industry Deregulation (Chapter 5)	Fiscal Harmony (Chapter 7)	Community R&D Policy (Directory C)	Reduction of Physical Barriers (Chapters 2, 5)	Content-Quota/Tariff Reform (Chapter 3)	Social Dimension (Chapter 3)
Supplier relations	M		M					
Manufacturing								
Scale	H		M–H					
Location	M		M–H			M	M–H	M
Product								
R&D					H			
Products	H		M–H		M–H			
Marketing								
Sales			H			M		
Distribution	M–H		H			M		
Price	H		M	M		M		
Customer service	M–H		M					
Organization								
Info tech	M			M				
HRM	M					M		M
Linkages	M							
Finance	M–H			M	M–L			

high technology products for defense reasons unfairly limit sales abroad. Coupled with increased European competitiveness, this limitation could mean tougher times for U.S. companies. Current negotiations between the U.S. Department of Commerce and the Department of Defense may loosen export restrictions.

Consult the 1992 Analysis Matrix for the areas in which pharmaceuticals and medical devices are affected by EC developments.

Service Industries and the Professions

General Areas to Watch: Intellectual property rights.

Although freedom to work anywhere in the EC is one of the main goals of the Treaty of Rome, professionals have encountered difficulties primarily because member states often do not recognize each other's admission standards and qualifications. This situation is addressed by a general directive that will take effect on January 4, 1991. It "will apply to any profession regulated in some way by the state and for which at least three year's education and training of university equivalent level is required. . . . It will cover lawyers, accountants, engineers, physiotherapists and many others.[52]

Professional qualifications will be recognized by member states in one of two ways:

1. When a professional's education and training have been substantially the same as those required by a member state he or she wants to practice in, the qualifications will be recognized.

2. When education and training have been substantially different, the professional will be able either to take a test that assesses his or her ability to practice, or to practice under supervision for up to three years before being deemed qualified. In the case of lawyers, the member state, not the professional, will make the choice of which applies. Under either option, a test or supervised practice, a professional would not be required to requalify and retrain in subjects he or she has already studied.

This directive applies to individuals, not to firms.

Whatever industry sector your company is in (or if you are a professional yourself), you will most likely encounter EC professionals if you export to or operate in Europe. Because practices often differ substantially from those in the United States, we provide the following overview of the EC professions.

Legal Services

In all EC states, access to the legal profession and the conditions under which it functions are controlled by organizations either recognized by the state (as in the United Kingdom and Ireland) or created by it (as in the other ten member states).

> When a person either does not wish to be or cannot be present in person before a court, he must be legally represented. In Belgium, Denmark, Greece, Italy and the United Kingdom this is undertaken by lawyers. In the other member states, other persons also undertake this task, notably the 'avoués à la Cour d'appel' in France; the solicitadores for the smaller cases in Portugal; the 'procuradores' in Spain; fiscal advisers before fiscal jurisdictions in Germany and the Netherlands; the legal advisers in Germany; 'huissiers' and legal advisers before lower jurisdictions in the Netherlands; chartered accountants and patent agents before administrative tribunals in Ireland; and those exercising power of attorney of 'agréés judiciares' before lower jurisdictions in Luxembourg, although this profession is in the process of extinction.[53]

Legal advice is provided not only by lawyers but by many professionals, ranging from fiscal advisers in Germany and the Netherlands to notaries public in Belgium, Greece, France, Luxembourg, and the Netherlands.

Lawyers may be hired under employment contracts only in the United Kingdom and Ireland (barristers and solicitors), Germany (Syndikusanwalte), Spain, Italy, the Netherlands, and Portugal.

Eurolink for Lawyers is a data base that lists lawyers, and their specialties, throughout the EC; it is available through Ian Cooper Communications of Leeds, England.

Accounting

In January 1990, the Commission announced plans to establish a European Accounting Forum, which will bring together representatives of the member states and coordinate with international accounting organizations. It will play no regulatory role. As in the United States, accountants in the EC have moved beyond simply auditing to financial and management consulting as well. However, in Belgium, France and Italy, government regulations prohibit auditors from rendering nonauditing services to their clients, thus obliging accountants to create separate legal entities if they wish to engage in consultancy services.

All member states impose audit requirements and many also require that preparation of opinions and some reports involve qualified accountants.

Management Consulting

Management consultants are having a field day with 1992 as an increasing number of companies seek advice on how best to approach it. In the United Kingdom, for instance, fee income in 1987 was almost 425 million ECU, nearly a fourfold increase over the 1981 figure of 112 million ECU.

The field is mainly national, but many larger firms, like the Big Six accounting firms, have EC-wide operations. Further, 1992 and the globalization of markets are prompting management consultants to expand into areas such as recruiting, out-placement, public relations, communication, advertising, and market research. Some may even move into the legal field.

Architecture

Architects are subject to different operating environments within the EC, depending primarily on three factors:

1. The existing legislation applicable to construction
2. The qualifying professional training required of architects

3. Especially within built-up areas, the effect of factors such as builders' capabilities and business structure, climate, and population density

Training, both in its technical and artistic dimensions, varies considerably, as do regulations governing practice, which range from rigid to virtually nonexistent. The constraints on building also vary widely. Some of the more important are:

- A ten-year liability period in countries whose legal systems derive from the Napoleonic Code (France, Belgium, Luxembourg, Italy)
- The legal requirement to purchase insurance (France, Belgium)
- Legislation and regulations relating to specific local conditions (e.g., earthquakes in Greece) or customs (e.g., maintaining the traditional village look in the Cotswolds)
- The procedures required for obtaining a building license
- Limitations on and specifications of building methods and/or materials

Architects should be particularly concerned over the growing tendency to take even minor questions of law to court and the apparent eagerness of the courts to abet this process. This has increased insurance

The 1992 Analysis Matrix
Service Industries and the Professions
Major Areas of the 1992 Process

Areas of Competitive Advantage	Harmonized Standards (Chapter 3)	Opened Government Procurement (Chapter 3)	Industry Deregulation (Chapter 5)	Fiscal Harmony (Chapter 7)	Community R&D Policy (Directory C)	Reduction of Physical Barriers (Chapters 2, 5)	Content-Quota/ Tariff Reform (Chapter 3)	Social Dimension (Chapter 3)
Supplier relations								
Manufacturing								
Scale								
Location								
Product								
R&D	M		M					
Products								
Marketing								
Sales	M–H	M	M–H					
Distribution	M–H		M–H					
Price	M		M	M–H				
Customer service	H		H					
Organization								
Info tech	M		M					
HRM	M–H		M–H					M
Linkages	H		H					
Finance				M				

costs and contributed to making insurance coverage mandatory for architects in France and Belgium.

Consult the 1992 Analysis Matrix for the effect of the EC process on service industries and the professions.

Shipping and Transportation

General Areas to Watch: Government procurement, subsidies, quotas, local content.

Although the transportation industry (road, rail, air, marine, and inland waterways) accounts for more than 7 percent of the EC's gross domestic product (GDP), it remains one of the most highly regulated and protected sectors of the economy. Member states' attitudes to national involvement in transport range from a total noninterventionist, free market approach in the Netherlands to the interventionist practices of West Germany, France, and Italy. Another complication is the "clear differences of interest between the various modes of transport. The widely dispersed road and inland waterway transport firms looked somewhat askance at tariff deregulation, which did not go hand in hand with measures to improve financial management of the railway monoliths."[54]

A sticky issue that directly affects transportation is that of value-added taxes (VAT). The Commission's efforts to harmonize the differing VAT rates (which range from a standard rate of 22 percent in Denmark to 12 percent in Spain and Luxembourg) have proved difficult. The Commission would like to impose Communitywide rates in two bands: a standard rate of between 14 percent and 20 percent and a reduced one of between 4 percent and 9 percent for essentials like food. This goal is based on observing the effect of different sales tax rates in the United States, where differences of up to 6 percent between contiguous states don't seem to matter. This would be accompanied by a clearing system through which member states would tally their net position vis-à-vis each other.

At the end of 1989, however, the Council was able to agree only to not increasing the divergence in member states' VAT rates at least until the end of 1991, at which time it would again address the problem of fixing ranges.

VAT harmonization faces member state opposition for varying reasons. Britain, for instance, imposes no VAT on children's clothing and has no desire to, whereas member states with higher VAT rates have no desire to lose this source of income, which, for example, accounts for nearly 10 percent of Denmark's GDP. As long as this issue remains unresolved, and it requires an unanimous vote in the Council, border stations (with their associated delays and costs) will remain because they are where VAT is levied by importing countries. And, though member states impose no VAT on exports, border controls help ensure that exporters do in fact export the products for which they claim zero tax status.

In May 1990, the Commission proposed eliminating border checks by 1993, replacing them with reports submitted by companies on their exports and imports. This would be a major step toward the goal of a borderless EC.

Air

As in many places of the world, a cartel that reduces competition also operates within the EC. This has come about primarily because of government ownership of the larger airlines. Airfares are fixed between national governments, thereby preventing competition and making EC air travel expensive. It can cost as much to fly from London to Athens as from London to New York. Problems are compounded by a shortage of airspace and runways and by incompatibility among the numerous air traffic control centers.

Proposals adopted by the Transport Council at the end of 1987 were aimed at introducing price competition, liberalizing flight allocation, and increasing flexibility in passenger-sharing arrangements. Member states have been slow to accept the proposals and convert them into corresponding national law, however. These proposals included:

- Permitting airlines to offer lower fares, subject to restrictions on minimum length of stay and time of ticket purchase. (Fewer restrictions would apply to off-peak times.) Non-EC carriers would not be allowed to initiate such fare changes.
- Permitting airlines to add capacity.
- Opening all major routes to competition.
- Permitting two or more routes to be combined into a single multi-stop service.
- Establishing a mechanism for reviewing potentially anticompetitive interairline agreements and for granting exemptions where justified.

At the end of 1989, the Council agreed to implement the so-called second aviation package by January 1993. This would:

- Reduce member states' ability to block changes in fares. Whereas new fares on flights between two member states must currently be approved by both, a "double disapproval" stipulation would henceforth require that new fares take effect unless both governments are opposed.

▪ Curtail the ability of member states to limit bilateral flights from another member state. (The current ratio of 40/60 was already set to be reduced to 25/75 by 1992. That is, in future a government will be able to limit another member state's share of bilateral flights only when it exceeds 75 percent.)

▪ Prohibit governments from discriminating against airlines that meet safety standards. (For example, France discriminated against UTA, the country's second-biggest airline, when it denied it access to routes served by Air France.)

The Commission also plans to enable member state airlines to offer services between airports in other member states.

As for the United States, "EC intervention in the intra-European market may change the complexion of bilateral agreements which the United States negotiated with any one EC Member."[55] The United States currently prohibits foreign carriers from flying within U.S. airspace, "but that is expected to change eventually. Once the EC starts negotiating traffic rights for its airlines as a group, it is likely that the Europeans won't allow U.S. carriers to fly around Europe as they have been since the war without something in return. . . ."[56]

In August 1989, the Commission ruled that member states cannot limit ownership in their airlines by investors from other member states. This ruling would not apply to non-EC investors, whom member states currently allow ownership percentages ranging from 25 percent to 49 percent. To date, the United States has allowed no more than 25 percent ownership by foreign investors.

Anticipating both the changes of 1992 and the increasing internationalization of airlines in general, EC-based carriers have started buying into U.S. airlines as well as consolidating within their own countries and buying stakes in other EC airlines. Some fear that these consolidations, such as the purchase of UTA, France's largest private airline, by Air France, its national airline, will create cartels able to block the EC's goal of liberalizing air transport. In fact, the Commission opened formal proceedings against this takeover in February 1990, one month after it occurred.

Road Haulage

A major symbol of 1992 has been the Single Administrative Document (SAD), which took effect on January 1, 1988, and relieved truckers of the need to deal with each member state's unique dispatch and entry documents. SAD replaced approximately seventy different forms.

However, all member states except Denmark, the Benelux countries, and Greece limit trucking by non-nationals via quotas and permits.

Trucks account for a majority of intra-EC trade, but much of their activity is regulated by bilateral permits that are valid for only one trip between two countries. Permits are checked at borders. The EC Transport Ministers agreed in June 1988 to liberalize road haulage by the end of 1992, by which time all permits and quotas will be eliminated. Further, until then, "the quota of Community multilateral permits (which allow transport between all twelve Member States) was increased by 40 percent in 1988"[57] and 40 percent in 1989. (Under a 1974 directive, however, non-EC carriers would not be able to operate under the liberalized rules.) To circumvent the restrictions that remain in place, some "manufacturers and retailers put their transport requirements into the hands of specialised transport companies, thus blurring the distinction between private lorry fleets (which are not restricted in their rights to make one-way journeys to collect or deliver goods) and transport companies carrying goods for a fee, whose trips are clearly regulated."[58]

Directives affecting road haulage include:

• *Simplification of Community Transit Procedure Directive.* Adopted July 1, 1988, this enables transport operators established in one member state to obtain a guarantee waiver (similar to a bond used for the transit of goods through a third country) when traveling through another member state. This directive should contribute to reducing transportation costs. Member states being traveled through can charge fees (e.g., for fuel use), as American states do.

• *Gaseous Emissions, Commercial Cars (Diesel Engines) Directive.* Adopted July 1, 1988, this establishes pollution control requirements for all diesel-powered road vehicles except automobiles. Vehicles meeting the U.S. Environmental Protection Agency standards would meet the ones established by this directive. However, American-produced vehicles may have to undergo both EPA and EC tests.

• *Weights, Dimensions, and Characteristics of Certain Road Vehicles Directive.* Implemented January 1, 1989, this establishes maximum weights and dimensions for commercial vehicles, using refrigerated vehicles as the standard because they are the widest in use. Maximum width is set at 102.36 inches, the same as in the United States, so it should not affect U.S. products.

Allowing for some cabotage, the trucking or shipping of freight entirely within the borders of a country, by truckers of one member state within another, was finally agreed to in December 1989. The EC will issue 15,000 permits as of July 1990. They will be issued to individual companies by national authorities and their number will increase by 10 percent each year through 1992. What happens after that has yet to be decided.

Another Commission proposal would abolish the transit notice that truckers must present each time they cross an EC border. The purpose of these transit notices is to "track where and when consignments go astray—usually to avoid tax—and levy the right rate of VAT regardless."[59] The proposal would establish the presumption that cargo that disappeared did so in the country it was shipped from; this country would not only get the tax "but, as a new penalty for dishonest shippers, at the highest rate applicable to the goods anywhere in the EC."[60] Combined with the Single Administrative Document, this proposal would further reduce lines of trucks at borders and contribute to reducing trucking costs.

Road Passenger Transport

Draft regulations would liberalize rules governing international road passenger transport, and also permit cabotage, but freedom to provide services has yet to be addressed. Bus companies would have to be majority-owned by EC nationals. A Council directive on package travel, to be implemented December 31, 1990, provides for increased consumer protection, requiring tour operators to provide accurate information and to honor contract terms. Different procedures in member states have made these consumer rights hard to protect. It is of concern to American tour operators in the EC because it requires insurance additional to that required by the United States. The EC also would like to impose uniform speed limits.

Shipping

Four major regulations applying to shipping were adopted in 1986:

- *Freedom to Provide Services Regulation:* Ensures the freedom to provide shipping services between member states and between member states and third countries by 1993. Further, the regulation calls for phasing out bilateral cargo sharing arrangements with third countries by 1993, or transforming them into EC arrangements.
- *Coordinated Action Regulation:* Enables the EC to act as an entity to deal with moves by non-EC countries to restrict EC carriers' competitive access to ocean trade.
- *Unfair Pricing Practices Regulation:* Provides for imposing duties on non-EC shipowners who engage in unfair pricing. This has already been applied to the Hyundai Merchant Marine of South Korea, which had to raise its container rates on EC-Australia routes.

▪ *Competition Regulation:* Prohibits agreements and concerted practices that restrict competition and any abuse of a dominant position within the EC or any substantial part of it.

Proposals being considered address liberalizing cabotage (six member states now allow cabotage only to ships flying their own flag) and harmonizing state subsidies. To reverse the decline "in the number of ships registered in EC countries," the Commission advocates EC registration. Only ships flying the EC flag "would be eligible for government subsidies and gain free access to intra-community shipping."[61] The plan is opposed by shipowners. The United States would not be affected because its shippers are not active within the EC.

Railways

Given the costs in time and money of air traffic congestion, many observers expect railroads to make a comeback in Europe. "Plans are already laid for a superrail system that will stretch south from Edinburgh to Marseilles, and most of the way east from Lisbon to Belgrade. . . ."[62] Many of the trains on this network will reach speeds of 180 miles per hour. The Chunnel between France and England, scheduled for completion in 1993, will enable rail passengers to ride under the English Channel at 100 miles per hour. Further, because economies of scale make rail travel more competitive at distances over 500 miles, the Chunnel will make railways that much stronger a competitor in transportation.

However, railroads present unique problems, largely budgetary, that not only pose harmonization problems (e.g., in the area of subsidies) but also affect overall transport policy. Railroad deficits have been "on the point of becoming an uncontrollable financial liability. . . . [T]he problem of the railways eventually became so acute that it affected virtually all transport policy decisions and acceptance of policies regarding the other modes of transport was governed by potential effects on the railways."[63] This problem was especially hard on road transport. Part of the problem lies with what governments see as their obligations to their citizens, and part of it lies with mismanagement and higher pay scales for rail workers than for those in other transport sectors.

Different member states have developed different approaches to the rail industry. Those whose policy can be called interventionist see the rail system as important to other policy goals, e.g., subsidizing transportation used mostly by lower-income workers, whereas noninterventionists look upon it as a self-contained sector, which must function on a laissez faire basis. The former include West Germany, France, and Italy; the latter include the Netherlands, Belgium, and Luxembourg.

The 1992 Analysis Matrix
Shipping and Transportation
Major Areas of the 1992 Process

Areas of Competitive Advantage	Harmonized Standards (Chapter 3)	Opened Government Procurement (Chapter 3)	Industry Deregulation (Chapter 5)	Fiscal Harmony (Chapter 7)	Community R&D Policy (Directory C)	Reduction of Physical Barriers (Chapters 2, 5)	Content-Quota/Tariff Reform (Chapter 3)	Social Dimension (Chapter 3)
Supplier relations			M–H			M		
Manufacturing								
Scale			M–H			M–H		
Location ·			M–H			H		
Product								
R&D	M–H		M–H		M–H			
Products	M–H		M–H		M–H		H	
Marketing								
Sales			H			M–H	H	
Distribution			H			M–H	H	
Price			H	M–H		M–H	M–H	
Customer service			H			M	M	
Organization								
Info tech			M	M		H	M–H	
HRM			M			M–H	M–H	M
Linkages			M			M–H	M–H	
Finance		M–H	M–H	M		M–H	M–H	

In November 1989, the Commission advocated two major policy changes concerning railroads:

1. Separate accounting systems for member state railroad infrastructure and for the services that use it.
2. Guaranteed transit rights for international companies, e.g., joint ventures between companies in two member states.

The former is aimed at making subsidies and other financing arrangements more transparent, while both strive to rationalize the operation of railroads throughout the EC.

The effect of 1992 on the shipping and transport industry can be grasped from the 1992 Analysis Matrix.

Notes

1. Paolo Cecchini, *The Benefits of a Single Market* (Hampshire, England: Wildwood House, 1988), p. 55.
2. Ibid., p. 57.
3. European Community, *Panorama of European Industry* (Brussels: Publications of the European Community, 1988), p. 7-1.
4. United Kingdom Department of Trade and Industry, "The Single Market, The Facts," February 1989, p. 66.

5. Ibid.
6. Eamonn Lawlor, "Individual Choice and Higher Growth: The task of European consumer policy" (Luxembourg: Office for Official Publications of the European Communities, 1988), p. 35.
7. Ibid., p. 37.
8. Ibid., p. 39.
9. Ibid., p. 40.
10. Ibid., p. 36.
11. Ibid., p. 30.
12. Ibid., p. 45.
13. See B. J. Phillips, "Gearing up for the New Europe," *Institutional Investor,* July 1988, p. 54.
14. Sydney J. Key, "International Finance Discussion Papers," Board of Governors of the Federal Reserve System, April 1989, p. 88.
15. Ibid, p. 103.
16. "EC Bankers identify possible targets for reciprocal action," *Financial Times,* August 17, 1989, p. 1.
17. Key, "International Finance Discussion Papers," p. 101–102.
18. Phillips, "Gearing up for the New Europe," p. 54.
19. Ibid.
20. Christopher Johnson, "Banking Services After 1992—A Prosperous Future for the Consumer?" (edited) talk before the Consumers' Association Conference,"1992 and the Consumer," Park Lane Hotel, London, May 11, 1989, p. 7.
21. Ibid., p. 8.
22. "Global Reach: Citicorp Strives to Be McDonald's and Coke of Consumer Banking," *Wall Street Journal Europe,* August 10, 1989, p. 1.
23. Stephen Fidler, "Spanish bank raises $25m via international placing," *Financial Times,* June 28, 1989, p. 22.
24. "Italian bankers given 1990 lecture," *Financial Times,* June 28, 1989, p. 18.
25. United States Department of State, "Financial Services and the European Community's Single Market Program," January 1989, p. 5.
26. Key, "International Finance Discussion Papers," p. 105.
27. "Financial Services and the European Community's Single Market Program," p. 5.
28. Matthew Barrett, "One for All," *Euromoney,* Special Supplement, 1988, p. 11.
29. Claire Making, "Luxembourg picks its niche," *Institutional Investor,* July 1988, p. 62.
30. Commission of the European Communities, *Toward a European Market for the Undertakings for Collective Investment in Transferable Securities* (Luxembourg, 1988), p. 16.
31. "Financial Services and the European Community's Single Market Program," p. 5.
32. Ibid., p. 6.
33. S. Cassin Muir, "Facilitation of freedom to provide services in insurance other than life insurance," U.S. Department of Commerce, p. 1.
34. Ibid., p. 6.

35. Jeffrey Brown, "Big Players will not be unscathed," *Financial Times*, September 4, 1989, p. III.
36. "Allianz maintains a premium pace," *Financial Times*, July 25, 1989, p. 18.
37. Phillips, "Gearing up for the New Europe," p. 54.
38. "Reinsurance: A shifting perspective," *Financial Times*, Spetember 4, 1989, p. 1.
39. "Competitive edge sharpened," *Financial Times Survey*, June 1989, p. 4.
40. "Deutsche Bank's Insurance Arm Reflects Sector's Diversification," *Wall Street Journal Europe*, August 22, 1989, p. 9.
41. Ibid.
42. Richard I. Kirkland, Jr., "Europe Goes Wild for Yankee PCs," *Fortune*, June 5, 1989, p. 257.
43. Ibid.
44. Alfred L. Thimm, "Europe 1992—Opportunity or threat for US business: The case of telecommunications," *California Management Review*, Winter 1989, p. 59.
45. "Making Europe a Mighty Market," *New York Times*, May 22, 1988.
46. Ibid., p. 346.
47. Michael Calingaert, *The 1992 Challenge from Europe* (Washington, D.C.: National Planning Association, 1988) p. 110.
48. "The Cost of Non-Europe," p. 515.
49. Ibid.
50. Ibid., p. 521.
51. Ibid., p. 529.
52. United Kingdom Department of Trade and Industry, "The Single Market; The Facts," February 1989, p. 41.
53. *Panorama of European Industry* (Brussels: Publications of the European Community, 1988), pp. 30–32.
54. Carlo degli Abbati, *Transport and European Integration* (Luxembourg: Office for Official Publications of the European Communities, 1987), p. 52.
55. "Business America," U.S. Department of Commerce, August, 1, 1988, p. 1.
56. "Buying Binge: European Airlines Join Bidding for Holdings in American Carriers," *Wall Street Journal Europe*, September 1–2, 1989, p. 2.
57. "The Single Market," p. 38.
58. "Europe's Internal Market," *The Economist*, July 9, 1988, p. 36.
59. "Brussels wants red tape cut for trucks at borders," *Financial Times*, July 6, 1989, p. 3.
60. Ibid.
51. "A Ship-Registration Plan aims to hoist EC flag on the high seas," *Wall Street Journal Europe*, August 31, 1989, p. 1.
62. "The New Supertrains," *Newsweek*, July 31, 1989, p. 46.
63. Abbati, *Transport and European Integration*, p. 114.

Chapter 6

A Short Course in the Basics of Doing Business Abroad

The sector analysis in Chapter 5 was designed to help you think about 1992 and your business. But those of you who have never ventured abroad may need to take a step back and consider some fundamentals of international business. Most U.S. players in 1992 will either export to Europe or establish some overseas operations. This chapter outlines the basics of exporting, moving abroad, and running a pan-European organization. It is not meant to be a definitive examination, because that would be beyond the scope of this book. But if you're a newcomer to the international business scene, it will help you to get started. Even if you're more experienced, this overview may refresh your understanding of the issues and offer a few new insights.

Export Strategies

With all the excitement in Europe and the inviting prospect of plugging into a rationalized market of 325 million, it is naturally tempting to take precipitous action (farsighted, if it works out): Buy something; form a joint venture; set up a subsidiary; anything! The impulse is to just do it quickly so you don't get locked out. Alluring, yes—a prudent business move, probably not. Ignoring Europe isn't the answer either. Even if you decide your company isn't ready for an export drive, you'll eventually be competing with European companies that try to penetrate the U.S. market (from the EC point of view, the 1992 process will have failed if they don't). You can also expect increased import competition from non-EC countries, which, finding the EC more competitive (or, perhaps, more barrier-ridden), will find even more reasons to look to the U.S. market.

Exporting: Obstacles and Opportunities

Here are two statistics about exporting that you may find interesting:

1. U.S. exports to the EC in 1988 totaled $75 billion, representing 23 percent of all U.S. exports.
2. Of these exports, 34% go directly to affiliates of U.S. companies with direct investments in Europe.[1]

The Commerce Department estimates that there are more than 30,000 companies in the United States with products that could compete abroad. These companies either aren't aware of the opportunities or choose not to take advantage of them. Their reasons for inaction are numerous, the most common being:[2]

- Lack of time, expertise, or resources
- Lack of information on European markets, customs regulations, local laws
- Warranty and service support problems
- Foreign exchange complications
- Accounts receivable problems
- Added shipping and packaging expenses
- Long-distance communications
- Language differences
- Restrictive distribution channels
- Government protection of domestic industry

On the other hand, successful exporters cite many reasons why they export:

- For growth
- To balance domestic business cycles
- To smooth production runs
- To broaden or vary market bases
- To extend product life cycles
- To discover new market and product strategy ideas
- And, most important, for profits

Experts on exporting identify CEO commitment as critical to the success of an export effort. In addition, organizational flexibility, planning, and a positive attitude are necessary. Many companies will bump an export sale in favor of a domestic one simply because it's easier, or for more provincial reasons: They consider U.S. sales more important. You have to be dedicated enough to treat a sale in Frankfurt with the same care and sense of urgency as one that goes next door.

There are a number of excellent "how to export" books on the market, some of which are listed at the end of this chapter. However, a quick overview may help get you started. Export planning means that you must:

1. Identify target markets.
2. Identify structural changes that may occur in your market (and among likely competitors) because of 1992 or other developments.
3. Determine your market objectives.
4. Decide on a market entry strategy.
5. Monitor and support company efforts.
6. Develop a long-term global strategy.

In addition to your business analysis, you must become familiar with the unique legal and governmental structures and cultural practices of each country you export to. You will need to gather information about the following:

- Economic conditions
- Government regulations
- Local technical expertise
- Tax and accounting laws
- Labor laws
- Intellectual property rights
- Agent/distributor agreements
- Customs regulations
- Banking regulations
- Competitive forces
- Licensing
- Language

1992 should harmonize each of these areas (except, of course, language) so that conditions in one EC country will be the same as in the others. But this harmonization process will take time, and in some areas may not be complete until the next century.

Although economic conditions and business practices are converging in Europe, many people still hope to keep their separate national cultural heritages intact. There may be an EC-wide trend toward an acceptance of fast food, but in other product areas, like beer, this isn't the case. When the European Court of Justice outlawed Germany's sixteenth-century beer purity laws, the ruling didn't result in a flood of foreign beer into West Germany despite expectations to that effect.

Export Entry Strategies

Export entry decisions involve trade-offs mostly having to do with investment costs and risks versus level of control and return.

Indirect Methods

Indirect methods involve few up-front costs, but tend to produce lesser results. Most methods involve importer commissions ranging from 7 to 20 percent depending on the difficulty of the sale. Control of the exporting effort is lost when you delegate to third parties, but the investment and risk are lower, and indirect methods provide flexibility. This is important in the early stages of exporting because most firms are unsure of the market, and because the cost of changing strategy is not high, indirect methods enable you to try different entry strategies until the right one emerges.

Indirect options include:

- *Third-Party Agents.* Third parties can be individuals, companies, or governments; they generally don't take title.

- *Export Management Companies (EMCs).* EMCs serve as an export department for several manufacturers of noncompetitive products. They normally specialize by geography or industry, don't take title, and usually handle only easy selling items.

- *Export Trading Companies (ETCs).* ETCs purchase a variety of items from U.S. firms for resale in foreign markets, or provide complete exporting services to clients. ETCs usually take title.[3] The Export Trading Act passed in the early 1980s makes it easier for American companies to band together to conduct international business. Contact your regional Commerce Department office for information, or use your trade association as a catalyst to get an ETC going.

- *Listings in Overseas Directories.* Consult, for instance, *Thomas Register,* the *American Export Register,* the Commerce Department's *Commercial News Magazine,* or product lists at U.S. embassies. (Refer to Directory A for more on government export assistance.)

If being first in a market is not critical to your company's strategy, indirect methods are good ways to test the water. If, however, you are forced to move faster, then other export methods are more appropriate.

Indirect-Involved Methods

These methods go halfway between indirect and direct options. The arrangements are more complex than indirect methods, requiring greater time and investment, but the benefits can be greater.

Options include:

- *Distributors:* Most helpful when your customers are geographically fragmented and your product requires parts and service.
- *License Agreements.*
- *Joint Ventures.*

Whenever you deal with third parties under the indirect or indirect-involved methods, ask for references and determine the following:

- Do they understand your product?
- Have they a successful track record with similar products?
- Do they know your market and potential customers?
- Will they represent you the way you are represented in the states— in quality, style, and ethical practices?

Also, you will want to do the following four things:

1. Protect your inventory (see the discussion under "Getting Paid" later in this chapter).
2. Set up measurable performance goals so that both parties go in with the same expectations and so that you can monitor progress.
3. Make sure the deal is good for both parties: If there isn't any money in it for the distributor, he won't push your product.
4. Avoid exclusive agreements when possible.

Direct Methods

Naturally there's greater risk involved here. The tasks are more complex and the investment and exit costs are higher. But in return you gain greater control and opportunity to reap rewards.

Direct method options include:

- Direct sales force
- Franchises
- Wholly owned direct foreign investment

As you can see, these options present some of the greatest challenges in all of business. The latter two basically involve overseeing or starting entirely new enterprises.

Advantages and Disadvantages of Entry Methods

Method	Advantages	Disadvantages
Indirect	Flexible Low risk Low cost	No control Low returns No real overseas experience gained
Indirect-involved	Assurance of some service and support Better commitment from third parties	Quality varies Low returns
Direct	Total control Most experience gained Best return	Highest cost Highest risk

Pricing Strategies

Different market conditions, a wide range of value-added tax (VAT) rates, and selective price controls have created considerable price differentials across Europe for many products. As border controls diminish and if VAT rates become harmonized, pricing will stabilize. Until this occurs, however, expect cross-border shopping. A visual example of this can be seen at Luxembourg's border with Belgium, where twelve gas stations are lined up, pump to pump, in the town of Martelange, Luxembourg, because of the differences in VAT and excise duties. Because Luxembourg's gas prices are 30 percent lower than Belgium's, numerous gas stations have cropped up on the Luxembourg side of the border.

Setting Your Price

U.S. exporters often set international prices based on cost or to skim for extra profits. Both methods ignore market conditions, a hazardous practice in rapidly changing markets like the EC. Whereas these approaches involve simply taking the U.S. list price and adding the additional costs of exporting (plus, perhaps, an extra profit margin) to determine an overseas selling price, the market approach factors in such variables as competition, market conditions, and currency fluctuations.

1985 Community Average Before-Tax Price Variations

All consumer goods	15.2%
All capital equipment	12.4%
Tea	27.0%
Ladies linen and hosiery	31.0%
Glass and crockery	21.0%
Books	49.0%
Telephone service (incl. tax)	50.0%
Electrical repairs (incl. tax)	42.0%

Source: Paolo Cecchini, *The Benefits of a Single Market* (Hampshire, England: Wildwood House, 1988), p. 79.

To incorporate these changing conditions into a selling price, but still maintain corporate profit objectives, you must make price a function of volume. The market approach requires first establishing a local market price, and then working backwards, subtracting all costs to determine gross margin. This margin multiplied by expected volume then gives you a return that can be used to determine whether the investment meets corporate objectives. Or the margin can be divided into the amount of incremental investment required, enabling you to determine a break-even volume, which you can then subject to a reality check.

Other Pricing Issues

Deciding on what currency to quote a price in can become an issue, often reflecting your relationship with the importer. If you quote in dollars, then the buyer accepts the currency exchange risk; if you quote in local currency, you assume the risk. An increasingly acceptable way of sharing the risk is to quote in ECU. You could also establish a range, or a forward contract that guarantees a specific exchange rate at a specified time. Or, of course, you can buy currency futures that would counterbalance any decrease in the local currency's exchange value versus the dollar.

Getting Paid

Many U.S. companies have enough difficulties getting paid in the same state let alone overseas. But there are several options to reduce the risk of getting burned on your receivables.

- *The Letter of Credit (LoC).* The most common method used by U.S. firms to establish an EC buyer's credit. It substitutes the credit of the buyer's bank for that of the buyer. Normally your bank receives payment from the buyer's bank once the buyer's bank has seen the appropriate documents stating that the transaction is complete (e.g., bill of lading and other appropriate shipping documents).

- *A Sight Letter of Credit.* The most common LoC. It simply means that the buyer's bank transfers payment to your bank (into your account) when the buyer's bank has all the documents indicating that the product transaction has occurred.

- *The Confirmed Letter of Risk or Credit Insurance.* Offers protection from political and commercial payment risk. Your bank assumes the risk for a fee.

- *Time Draft.* Less expensive for the buyer than a letter of credit. It contains some elements of the LoC, but not all of its protection. Therefore it is best to use time drafts only after you've established a relationship with the customer.

- *Open Account.* Naturally the most attractive to the buyer but affording you little protection. Put only those customers with whom you have a successful track record on open account.

Another way to insure your receivables is through the Foreign Credit Insurance Association (FCIA). This group is associated with the Export/Import Bank in Washington. To obtain details on the programs they offer, refer to the Export/Import Bank section located in Directory A.

Export Logistics

Trying to figure out the best way to get a product from San Francisco to Wichita is tough enough for many firms; consequently, many companies figure that shipping overseas is just too complicated and expensive to be worthwhile. Yet today's advances in transportation and communication make overseas logistics almost as easy as going cross-country.

Don't be alarmed if you don't have the expertise to answer such questions as, What are the local customs regulations? What export documents are required? What tariffs will I be forced to pay? There are plenty of sources out there to help you. Besides government advice, consider the following sources:

- *Banker and Lawyer.* If your current banker and lawyer lack international experience, you might have to get others.

• *Freight Forwarder.* A good freight forwarder could make or break your exporting effort. They provide extensive shipping services. Full-service FFs provide the following services:

— Reserve shipping space.
— Prepare all documents.
— Arrange routing and scheduling.
— Quote rates, tariffs, and fees in advance.
— Arrange for insurance.
— Provide labeling instructions.
— Complete arrival arrangements.

FFs can be invaluable partners, especially for smaller firms. Contact your regional Commerce Department or state export assistance agency for a list of local freight forwarders.

• *Independent Export Consultant.* Your regional Commerce Department office or state export bureau can provide you with a list. When checking references you can pick up additional information as well.

Always remember that the tiniest detail can trip up the most carefully thought-out export plan. So don't forget the basics of any sales deal:

1. Execute a sales contract that clearly specifies quality, grade, quantity, and product model.
2. Specify the terms of delivery; when, how, and who pays for it; who takes title when (i.e., who bears the risk?); and the amount of insurance.
3. Clearly establish the method of payment, the payment date, and the currency you are to be paid in.

While exporting can range in intensity from simply using a foreign distributor to buying a foreign company, deciding to operate in Europe invariably entails a full commitment; there's no parallel to testing the waters as in indirect exporting methods. It's a decision to be made only after asking all the pertinent questions.

Moving Overseas: Is 1992 a Good Reason?

Taking that first investment plunge overseas can be intimidating. But more and more companies are making the move abroad, establishing a sales office in an important export market or setting up a small manufacturing facility to be closer to their customers. Most are pleasantly surprised to find that the move is easier than they expected. But that doesn't mean it's a breeze. Choosing a location, for instance, can require patience and the ability to sort through several highly optimistic presentations by economic development agencies.

American business has invested more in Europe than in any other area—close to $125 billion in Common Market countries (see Figure 6-1).[4] The bulk of this investment is concentrated in Britain, West Germany, the Netherlands, and France.

According to the Commerce Department, U.S. foreign direct investment (FDI) in Europe has increased 70 percent between 1984 and 1987. Further, U.S. companies nearly tripled their takeover activity in the Community in one year alone, from $1.3 billion in 1987 to $3.6 billion in 1988.[5] Companies aren't waiting for the jury on 1992; they're taking action now and in big ways.

Whether this is because of 1992 or, as many economists claim, because of economic fundamentals such as exchange rate movement and the strategies of individual companies really doesn't matter. What does matter is what it means to you.

To assist in your analysis, we present a few checklists to help you identify areas worth thinking through. In addition, Directory B provides individual country profiles and valuable information on Community and member state relocation incentives and assistance that will help make the move overseas easier.

But first, ask yourself: *Why move to Europe?* In general, companies find that it makes sense to make an overseas investment for reasons coming under the following heads:

Improved Market Access

- To avoid import duties and tariffs
- To reduce shipping costs
- To establish closer ties with customers (e.g., via flexible manufacturing, servicing, product development, and marketing mix adjustments)
- To produce locally in order to be eligible to sell the product (e.g., because of local content requirements)

Manufacturing Advantages

- Lower wage rates
- Reduced or nonexistent union activity
- Quality of work force (productivity and skill sets)
- Availability of labor
- Ability to establish better ties with suppliers and/or customers (via just-in-time manufacturing)

Figure 6-1. U.S. direct investment abroad at year-end 1988.

	All Industries	Petroleum	Manufacturing	Wholesale Trade	Banking	Finance Insurance	Services	Other Industries
	($Billions)							
World	$326.9	$59.7	$133.8	$34.4	$16.1	$60.6	$7.1	$15.2
EC-12	**$126.5**	**$15.7**	**$65.4**	**$12.8**	**$5.8**	**$21.6**	**$2.9**	**$2.2**
Belgium	7.2	0.6	3.9	1.5	0.4	0.8	*	*
Denmark	1.2	—	0.3	0.5	*	0.2	—	*
France	12.5	0.9	8.0	2.4	0.2	0.5	0.2	0.3
Germany	21.7	2.0	14.2	1.0	1.7	1.9	*	0.7
Greece	0.2	*	0.1	*	*	—	—	*
Ireland	5.7	*	4.1	*	*	1.7	*	—
Italy	9.0	0.4	6.6	1.2	0.3	0.5	0.2	0.1
Luxembourg	0.8	*	0.5	*	0.2	*	0	0
Netherlands	15.4	2.2	6.1	2.4	0.2	3.2	0.9	0.4
Portugal	0.4	—	0.2	0.1	0.1	—	*	0.1
Spain	4.4	0.1	2.6	0.8	0.5	*	0.3	0.1
United Kingdom	48.0	9.3	18.9	2.8	2.3	12.9	1.3	0.6
Japan	$16.9	$3.5	$7.9	$3.5	$0.3	$1.3	$0.2	$0.3
Canada	$61.2	$11.7	$28.1	$3.8	$0.8	$10.4	$1.3	$5.1

*Less than $500,000.

Source: U.S. Department of Commerce, *Survey of Current Business,* June 1989.

Organizational Improvements

- To rationalize organizational relationships among functions

Financial Advantages

- To reduce exchange rate volatility

The issues just mentioned of course represent the most basic strategic considerations facing any company. 1992 simply introduces another level of complexity. Further, if you do decide to make the jump, or if you're reassessing current operations, you will confront still more decisions. In selecting the location of your overseas business, you will have to consider the following:

- *Local infrastructure.* Roads and communications, banking, accounting, and legal services.
- *Transportation.* Railroads, ports, airports (for goods transport and employee travel).
- *Quality of life for employees.* The environment, educational opportunities, recreational and cultural facilities, civic activities.
- *Political stability.* Local and national.
- *Availability of research facilities in universities and institutes.*
- *Tax structure.*
- *Labor laws.*
- *Government incentives.* Grants or tax breaks (see Directory B).

In addition, there are questions specific to the 1992 process you'll want to ask yourself:

- Will emerging local content rules reclassify your product so that it is subject to additional tariffs and/or quotas?
- Will it be necessary to operate in Europe through a subsidiary to avoid possibly onerous reciprocity provisions?
- Will the standards formulation, testing, and certification process cause exported products to be treated differently from European-produced goods?
- Will government procurement still favor locally produced goods?

How does it work in practice? One company that considered many of the issues we've been discussing was Aritech Corporation, a Massachusetts-based manufacturer of electronic detectors and other communications and security devices. In the late 1970s, Aritech decided to supplement its successful European exporting operations by making a move into the Community.

Aritech purchased a company in Holland that not only gave it local manufacturing capability but provided distribution and contact with customers throughout northern Europe. The Dutch government sweetened the deal by offering a combination of grants, loans, and training assistance. But according to Aritech's vice-president of finance, Michael O'Donnell, "We bought the company because it made sense strategically. The government incentives were a bonus."[6]

Moving to Europe meant that Aritech no longer had to pay tariffs. It was also able to avoid the vagaries suffered by the dollar in the currency market in the mid-1980s, in addition to being able to shorten supply lines. "This made us that much more competitive," claims O'Donnell.

Aritech's moves have put the company in a position to take advantage of 1992. "We have worked hard at making Aritech a European company," says O'Donnell. "Most of our employees are locals, including the CEO of the European operation. Although standards formulation is frustrating, we participate in the process, and are considered European."

Aritech is now looking at Ireland. The reason, according to O'Donnell: "Besides offering very attractive incentives, their corporate tax rate is the lowest in Europe."

Managing a Pan-European Operation

Managing a pan-European operation presents management challenges similar to those of managing any multinational enterprise. The same dilemma lurks at the core of both European and truly global businesses: How can the organization be structured so that it is sufficiently integrated to be globally competitive while at the same time retaining enough local flexibility to be nationally responsive?

The approach to pan-European organizational structure must begin with the acknowledgement that the pan-European company is a federation of different constituencies and interests, all of which are legitimate and necessary. Linkages between local-country organizations and the vertical business organizations (usually located at European headquarters) should be created at several levels. Achieving this requires a long-term management commitment to fostering multicountry and multifunctional careers throughout the company. Improved information flow through the resulting linkages ensures that top managers are not sheltered from the pressures and demands felt by front-line managers, especially from those concerning local market preferences.

It is equally important that subsidiary managers have access to and involvement in the companywide decision-making process. Without this input and involvement, those developing new products or strategies will not understand market needs and those implementing new directions will not be committed to them.

One company that has been particularly successful in building multiple organizational linkages is Matsushita, whose explicit strategy is to employ "market mechanisms" to direct centrally located activities. For example, senior marketing managers from Matsushita's worldwide sales companies attend an annual internal "trade show." Proposed product lines for the new model year are put on display, and the sales managers, relying on their understanding of their country markets, pick and choose among the proposed products. As a result, individual products and even entire product lines may be modified, or simply dropped altogether. This process ensures that Matsushita continues to offer the right products to the right customers.

An issue that will increase in importance has to do with the split that often exists between the subsidiary of a U.S. company and its U.S. parent. The European subsidiaries of American corporations are often treated as the poor relations of the parent company, resulting in inequality in resource allocation and subsequent performance. In a more competitive Europe, this organizational myopia will become an unaffordable luxury.

Once organizational structure and procedures are determined, management procedures should reinforce the choices you have made. Three common issues are:

- *Incentive Systems.* Performance reviews, together with salary and bonus awards, should be structured to support the company's European objectives rather than single-country performance.

- *Coordination.* A business-focused organization should be supported by the appointment of managers with responsibilities for the coordination of business activities across countries.

- *Planning and Budgeting.* Strategic planning, reflecting the company's European competitive position, should initially be conducted on a pan-European basis, and not country by country. Individual country strategies that are consistent with the overall European strategy can then be developed. Similarly, the annual budgeting process should be consolidated at the European level, allowing an efficient allocation of resources.

People

One of the most important tasks in managing a pan-European operation is planning the development of a cadre of superior "Euro-managers." Creating such managers requires a commitment to:

- *Multicountry Careers.* Work experience in different countries should be a requirement for career progression. Philips's formal management development system, for example, has always required considerable overseas experience as a prerequisite for top corporate positions. By contrast, tenure overseas traditionally has not been the route to the executive suite in many U.S.-based companies.

- *Frequent Travel.* Senior managers should acquire the habit of spending a large amount of time out of the country. This keeps managers current on developments in other countries, and demonstrates the organization's commitment to a pan-European operation.

- *Foreign Nationals.* High-potential foreign managers must gain experience not only in their own countries but at company headquarters. This practice broadens the talent pool and also shows commitment to the pan-European business.

Culture

Organizational culture can make or break a pan-European strategy. Don't take a laissez-faire approach. Your decisions send messages that can shape and influence your company's culture.

Strive to minimize cultural differences within the company. Break down the home country versus subsidiary "them and us" mentality. Emphasize the company's pan-European identity.

Demonstrate the same level of commitment to all employees. Don't make employees in any one country "more equal" than those in another. When making tough decisions, such as to shut down a plant, for example, don't irrationally protect employment in the "home" country at the expense of employees in another country.

In sum, to create a successful pan-European operation, you must:

- Create a strategy that your company is capable of carrying out. Ignore the quick fixes of "standardization, rationalization, and centralization." Take a gradual approach that protects and builds upon your company's strengths and heritage.
- Demonstrate commitment to your strategy with consistent actions.
- Support your strategy with the right organizational structure and management practices. Build flexible and local-management capabilities, then link them to create an adaptive organization with true transnational capabilities.
- Develop the people and culture that will make your strategy successful.

Notes

1. Quoted from a report by the Subcommittee on International Economic Policy and Trade of the Committee on Foreign Affairs, U.S. House of Representatives, May 31, 1989, p. 1.
2. "Exporting: Creating an International Market," *Small Business Report*, February 1987, p. 20.
3. Ibid., p. 24.
4. Congressional Research Service, "European Community: Issues Raised by 1992 Integration," by Glennon J. Harrison, *CRS Report for Congress*, May 31, 1989, p. 23.
5. John B. Goodman and David Palmer, "Europe 1992," Harvard Business School Case no. N9-389-206, 1989, p. 12.
6. This and the following quotations from O'Donnell are taken from an interview conducted September 1989.

Further Readings

Exporting

Brownstone, David M., and Gorton Carruth. *Where to Find Business Information: A Worldwide Guide for Everyone Who Needs Answers to Business Questions.* New York: Wiley, 1979. Lists more than forty general sources on exporting, including books and periodicals, and also offers a listing of business publications by country.

Walvoord, Wayne. *Ten Steps to Successful Exporting.* New York: American Management Association, 1981. An AMA briefing, this features a concise step-by-step approach to exporting.

A Basic Guide to Exporting. Department of Commerce no. 003-009-00487-0. Washington, D.C.: U.S. Government Printing Office. Order by calling 202 783-3238, or through your regional office. A good guide to export fundamentals, it provides an excellent listing of government sources of export assistance.

The International Trade Reporter. Published by the Bureau of National Affairs, Washington, D.C. (*phone* 1-800-372-1033). A weekly newsletter on world developments that affect U.S. exports and imports.

Managing a Pan-European Organization

Bartlett, Christopher A., and Sumantra Ghoshal. "Organizing for Worldwide Effectiveness: The Transnational Solution," *California Management Review,* Fall 1988.

Drucker, Peter F. "Strategies for Survival in 1993," *The McKinsey Quarterly,* Autumn 1988.

Friberg, Eric G. "The Challenge of 1992," *The McKinsey Quarterly,* Autumn 1988.

van Dijck, Jules. "Towards Transnationalization of Economic and Social Life in Europe," *European Affairs,* Spring 1989.

Strategy Help

Dudley, James W. *1992 Strategies for the Single Market.* London: Kogan Page, 1989. Dudley does a good job of bringing together the best business thinking of the past several years, from Kotter to Porter, to the BCG matrixes and the like. Only about 20 percent of the book is geared to 1992 issues. It's primarily a general business text.

Euromonitor. *The 1992 Single Market Handbook,* and the annual *European Marketing Data and Statistics.* Euromonitor is a comprehensive research group that publishes numerous valuable publications on market information, consumer data, and company information. Ask for the *Euromonitor Index,* which lists its offerings.

> Euromonitor
> 87-88 Turnmill Street
> London EC1M 5QU
> *Phone:* 44-1-251-8024
> *Fax:* 44-1-608-3149

Porter, Michael. *Competitive Strategy: Techniques for Analyzing Industries and Their Competitors.* New York: The Free Press, 1980.

———. *Competitive Advantage: Creating and Sustaining Superior Performance.* New York: The Free Press, 1985.

Consultants

There are several types of consultants who can help you. Most of the big-name firms are beyond a small company's budget, but there are many consultants who specialize in small businesses. Consult your regional Commerce Department for a list of local sources.

Advice can also be obtained from bankers, ad agencies, and law firms. Seminars abound; but be careful! Most are simply ploys to generate business leads. Examine the agenda closely; much of the discussion is shallow, and many of the topics are covered in this book.

Chapter 7 | Save Your ECU? What You Need to Know About the European Monetary System

The European Monetary System (EMS) has enjoyed considerable success on the bond markets and in banking circles, but has played a less significant role in commercial transactions. This chapter describes what the EMS is, its major components, and the debate on the Delors Committee Report, which advocates eventual full monetary union, including a single currency. This report and the decisions made on its recommendations will most likely determine the course of future EC monetary policy, because unlike other areas discussed in this book (e.g., industrial sectors and social and environmental policy), the EMS is not the subject of proposed directives.

For U.S. executives, it is important simply to know about the EMS; you cannot claim to be conversant with 1992 matters unless you do. Further, though EMS has yet to play an important role in commerce, its increasing success may cause many Americans to hear prices and contracts quoted in European Currency Units (ECUs). It's always advisable to know something about the currency the other guy proposes to do business in.

Background

The purpose of the European Monetary System, established on March 13, 1979, was to increase monetary stability within the EC and to reduce inflation. Most observers believe it has been successful in meeting the second of these objectives; inflation rates in the participating countries have converged toward Germany's low rate. However, there has been a slight increase in interest rate volatility because EMS relies on semifixed exchange rates (see below), leaving interest rates as the major tool for addressing discrepancies in national budgetary policies and trade balances. This interest rate volatility has had little impact within the EC largely because the impact of freeing up all capital movements on July 1, 1990 has yet to be felt. On balance, the EMS is widely viewed as successful; many credit its success with being a major impetus behind the 1992 program.

The ECU

Central to the EMS is the European Currency Unit (ECU), which is a basket containing specified amounts of all twelve European currencies weighted on the basis of gross national product, intra-Community trade, and "quotas applied under the short-term monetary support arrangements."* Further, nine of these member states are members of the Exchange Rate Mechanism (ERM), which ties every currency to every other currency at agreed-to exchange rates. The exceptions are the United Kingdom, Greece, and Portugal whose currencies, though not part of the ERM, are weighted into the ECU. Members of ERM agree to maintain their exchange rates within +/− 2.25 percent versus each other's currency (with the exception of Spain, which is allowed +/− 6 percent). An example of the resulting parity grid can be seen in Figure 7-1. They also agree to prevent too much deviation from the ECU itself,[1] but it is usually bilateral rates that necessitate action. When the currencies of ERM participants reach these bilateral limits, their respective monetary authorities are expected to intervene. As a result, membership in the ERM means relinquishing some national authority because member states cannot unilaterally adjust central rates, but must negotiate adjustments with all the other participants. Realignments of the underlying parity grid used to occur quite often; although realignments have occurred twelve times in just over ten years (most recently in September 1989) only four have occurred during the past five years. The resulting currency stability has made business easier to conduct within the EC. In fact, some companies like Philips have demonstrated faith in this stability by no longer covering some forward transactions in the futures markets. During realignment discussions, the member states first fix bilateral rates and only then establish the new ECU-related central rates.

The ECU is also reexamined every five years, or on request if any currency's weight has changed by 25 percent or more, for possible reconstitution. So far, these reviews have occurred twice, both at the five-year mark. Both resulted in reconstitution, and the one in September 1989 was accompanied by the inclusion of the Spanish peseta and the Portuguese escudo.

A major goal is that realignments and reconstitutions, even those that include the addition of a new currency, will not change the ECU's

---

*Currencies are not permitted to exceed a "divergence threshold," which is a deviation of 75 percent from the weighted average movement of the other currencies.

Figure 7-1. Central rates of EMS currencies (parity grid effective September 19, 1989).

	Band	Belgian Franc	Danish Kroner	German Mark	Spanish Peseta	French Franc	Irish Pound	Italian Lira	Dutch Florin
100	+2.25%		18.9143	4.959	334.619	16.6310	1.8510	3,710.2	5.5870
BFr		100	18.4938	4.84837	315.143	16.2608	1.80981	3,494.21	5.46286
	−2.25%		18.0831	4.740	296.802	15.8990	1.7695	3,290.9	5.3415
100	+2.25%	553.0		26.810	1,809.4	89.925	10.0087	20,062.0	30.21
Dkr		540.723	100	26.2162	1,704.05	87.9257	9.78604	18,894.0	29.5389
	−2.25%	528.70		25.630	1,604.9	85.97	9.56830	17,794.0	28.8825
100	+2.25%	2,109.50	390.16		6,901.7	343.05	38.1825	76,540.0	115.235
Marks		2,062.55	381.443	100	6,500.00	335.386	37.3821	72,069.9	112.673
	−2.25%	2,016.55	373.00		6,121.7	327.92	36.4964	67,865.0	110.1675
100	+6%	33.6930	6.23100	1.63300		5.47850	0.609772	1,177.30	1.84050
Peseta		31.7316	5.86837	1.53847	100	5.15981	0.574281	1,108.77	1.73345
	−6%	29.8850	5.52600	1.44900		4.85950	0.540858	1,044.20	1.63250
100	+2.25%	628.97	116.32	30.495	2,057.8		11.3830	22,817.0	34.36
FFr		614.977	113.732	29.8164	1,938.06	100	11.1299	21,488.6	33.5953
	−2.25%	601.295	111.20	29.150	1,825.3		10.8825	20,238.0	32.8475
1 Irish	+2.25%	56.5115	10.4511	2.740	184.892	9.1890		2,050.03	3.0870
Pound		55.2545	10.2186	2.67894	174.131	8.98480	1	1,930.71	3.01848
	−2.25%	54.025	9.9913	2.619	163.997	8.7850		1,818.34	2.9510
1,000	+6%*	30.387	5.620	1.4735	95.76	4.9410	0.549952		1.660
Lire		28.6187	5.29268	1.38754	90.1899	4.65362	0.517943	1,000	1.56340
	−6%	26.953	4.985	1.3065	84.994	4.3830	0.487799		1.4725
100	+2.25%	1,872.15	346.24	90.770	6,125.3	304.44	33.8868	67,912.0	
DF1		1,830.54	338.537	88.7526	5,768.83	297.661	33.1293	63,963.1	100
	−2.25%	1,789.85	331.02	86.780	5,433.1	291.04	32.3939	60,241.0	
1 ECU		42.4582	7.85212	2.05853	133.804	6.90403	0.768411	1,483.58	2.31943

*As of January 1990, Italy's band was reduced to the standard 2.25 percent range and the lire was devalued by 3 percent.
Source: National Westminster Bank PLC, London.

external value on the day of the change; otherwise, each realignment would create a separate instrument, e.g., the 12 January 1987 ECU and the 19 September 1989 ECU. The commitment among ERM member states on this point is critical to ensuring smooth market responses because all ECU assets and liabilities in the private sector become reevaluated in terms of the new basket. Although most observers believe that the ECU has maintained equal value through its various realignments, some skeptics claim that it has not and that the value of the new ECU has indeed been different. However, rapidly changing foreign exchange markets make it difficult to isolate the causes of the fluctuations that occur during realignments. The wide acceptance of the ECU indicates agreement with those who claim that such fluctuations simply reflect the ongoing workings of the market, which are no different from the fluctuations that occur all the time.

Note the following:

- The English pound, the Greek drachma, and the Portuguese escudo, though weighted in ECU, are not part of the ERM. This creates the anomaly of the ECU's being based partly on a semifixed system, which the parity grid represents, and partly on a free float of three currencies, one being as important as the pound, which currently constitutes about 13 percent of the ECU's value (based on the realignment of September 19, 1989).
- After realignments, investors often buy currencies that yield the highest rates in the belief that another realignment (and possible devaluation) won't occur for some time. However, these weaker currencies often move up, thus decreasing yield, because so many buy them.
- The Soviet Union has been using ECU to finance foreign transactions.
- There are ECU traveler's checks, ECU-denominated Eurochecks, and credit cards linked to ECU accounts. Further, both the Belgian and Spanish governments issue gold and silver ECU coins.

The amount of each currency in the ECU basket, its central exchange rate, and its resulting "weight" in the ECU are shown in Figure 7-2. You can calculate the bilateral rate of any two currencies by dividing the central rates of each against the ECU. For example, the bilateral rate of the French franc versus the West German deutsche mark (DM) is obtained by dividing 6.90403 by 2.05853, resulting in 3.3539 francs per deutsche mark.

If, for example, the mark appreciates against the other currencies, it also appreciates versus the ECU and becomes more weighted in the basket. The mark's weight in the ECU is currently just over 30 percent, a fact decided by the markets, not by Germany. The result is that the mark and

Figure 7-2. The ECU basket.

Currency	Weighting (in percent)	Central Rate
Belgian franc*	7.6%	42.4582
Luxembourg franc	0.3	42.4582
Danish kroner	2.45	7.85212
German mark	30.1	2.05853
Spanish peseta	5.3	133.804
French franc	19.0	6.90403
Irish pound	1.1	0.768411
Italian lira	10.15	1,483.58
Dutch florin	9.4	2.31943
UK Pound	13.0	.739615
Greek drachma	0.8	150.792
Portuguese escudo	0.8	149.5

*Luxembourg and Belgium share a monetary unit.

Source: National Westminster Bank PLC, London.

the German central bank (the Bundesbank) play a central role in the functioning of the ECU. Many observers believe that EMS's success to date in containing inflation has resulted from the Bundesbank's consistent conservative policies, and from the other ERM states aligning their monetary policies in the direction of Germany's. The ECU has even been referred to as a deutsche mark bloc.

The value of the ECU versus the dollar can be calculated by translating each constituent currency into dollars (at the prevailing exchange rate). But, rather than perform this laborious calculation, you can always find the ECU's value in *The Wall Street Journal*.

Public vs. Private ECU

In addition to the anomalies and exceptions noted above, there are two types of ECU, the public and the private, and neither is fungible with the other, that is, neither can be substituted or exchanged for the other. Official ECU are created when EC central banks convert gold and dollar reserves into equivalent ECU (at the prevailing exchange rates and value of gold). This is done via the European Monetary Cooperation Fund (EMCF), which administers the EMS's official accounting. These swaps are temporary (three months), and official ECU have little use other than in central bank accounting.

There would be rather dramatic consequences if the two types of

ECU were fungible. If the public ECU were able to be converted into private ECU, the conversion would represent creation of money denominated in ECU by central banks and EC institutions. The conservative Bundesbank, for one, is not ready for this because control over ECU-denominated money supply would weaken, which, given the large weighting of the deutschemark in the ECU, would in turn result in loosening German money supply without the Bundesbank's say-so.

This contrasts with the private creation of ECU, which relies on converting constituent currencies into ECU; as a result, the value of the ECU is "controlled by the 'average' monetary policies of the central banks concerned."[2]

ECU bank deposits are created by commercial banks "bundling" and "unbundling" the ECU from its component currencies. If a borrower wants an ECU-denominated loan and if the bank does not have ECU deposits, it must (1) attract ECU deposits, (2) borrow ECU in the interbank market, or (3) bundle the component currencies into the amount of the loan.[3] Item 3 creates ECU based on which the bank credit multiplier creates even more.

Although there are many banks engaged in arbitrage between the ECU and its component currencies, there can be divergences between the interest rate on ECU and that on its appropriately weighted component currencies, largely because the laws of supply and demand affect the ECU as well as the currencies. If investors believe, for example, that the demand for ECU is going up enough so that the ECU interest rate will increase more than on the underlying currencies, they can borrow the currencies, create ECU, and take the interest rate differential as profit. If investors believe that demand for ECU is going down, they can do the opposite. These operations are called making and breaking the basket.

The ECU Bond Market

Private ECU are widely used in both primary and secondary bond markets and other commercial activity. Although not used as legal tender, ECU are recognized as foreign currency in all EC countries, and they are used in bond issues and in bank deposits and checks. In fact, in 1988, ECU-denominated bond issues accounted for 5.5 percent of all international bond issues, placing the ECU sixth among global currencies. A common feature of bond issues is a swap provision, whereby the issuer can borrow in ECU and convert into the currency he or she want to use the proceeds in, thereby lending ECU bond issues additional flexibility.

Initially, those issuing bonds were primarily governments and international organizations within the EC, but in recent years private business has more than doubled its percentage of EC-based issues (from 19 percent in 1982 to the 40 percent range in the late 1980s), probably because of increased secondary-market activity in ECU bonds and because the weighted nature of the ECU makes it less risky than an individual country's currency (see Figure 7-3). Many EC companies now use ECU in the financial section of their annual reports. Further, governments, international organizations, and corporations outside the EC have increased their borrowings in ECU by four to six times since 1982.

The ECU is always weaker than the strongest currency constituting it but stronger than the weakest. As a result, borrowers tend to be from soft-currency countries where interest rates are higher than on ECU issues, and buyers tend to be from hard-currency countries where interest rates are lower than on ECU issues.

Borrowers have been mostly nonbanks in France and Italy, not only because of these countries' soft currencies but also because of prohibitions against holding foreign exchange balances before July 1990. Buyers have been mostly from within the EC, predominantly from Belgium (both the legendary Belgian dentist who is presumed to have ample funds available for investment and, increasingly, institutions) and Luxembourg. The establishment of an ECU Treasury Bill market in the United Kingdom in 1988 created a liquidity that significantly increased the number of issues. In fact, secondary bond trading in ECU bonds has sometimes exceeded that of all other currencies, including dollars.

Given that the ECU has existed only since 1979, this record is remarkable, and bespeaks significant confidence in the EMS despite its many drawbacks (e.g., Britain's refusal to join the ERM and the uncertain future of European Monetary Union or EMU). Again, the success of the Euro-

Figure 7-3.   ECU bond issuers.

	1982	1985	1987
EEC Borrowers			
Business	340	3,454	2,103
Government	1,230	3,540	2,000
Institutions	202	1,140	1,345
Non-EEC Borrowers			
Business	65	3,401	1,930
Government	0	200	453
Institutions	55	560	350
Total	1,892	12,995	8,186

Numbers in ECU millions.

Source: Gavyn Davies, "A Plan for European Monetary Union," Goldman-Sachs, November 23, 1988, p. S.9.

pean Monetary System in containing inflation and the risk-hedge represented by ECU issues have much to do with this success.

The ECU in Commercial Markets

Even though there is no central bank that can create ECU and function as the guarantor of last resort, the "volume of ECU bank deposits rose at an annual rate of over 50 per cent between December 1983 and June 1988"[4] despite a slowdown in international bank credit during part of this period. However, there has been a paucity of ECU deposits from nonbank sectors, especially since 1985, "suggesting that the ECU's appeal as a near money substitute and store of liquidity is modest."[5] It is used very little in financing trade flows, "covering at present only about 1% of the Community countries' external trade."[6] However, the recent development of a true interbank clearing system for the ECU has already facilitated market growth.

But use of ECU enables banks "from smaller member states whose currencies are of lesser international significance, or banks from countries which restrict the international use of their currencies, to play a more active role on international financial markets."[7] These banks can conduct business in a currency that enjoys wide acceptance by banks and bond markets. Total ECU bank liabilities as of December 1988 were ECU 88.1 billion; total assets, 100.6B. There were also approximately 600 banking offices around the world conducting operations in ECU.[8]

The ECU is likely to play a larger role in financial services once the impact of the complete freedom of capital movements that came into effect in July 1990 is fully felt. Insurance and mortgage loans, for instance, will be far easier to sell across Europe in ECU because the problems of contract currency, exchange rate risk, and internal accounting will be simplified. (Think, for instance, of the arithmetical nightmare presented by determining the present value of an income stream of French francs expressed in pounds, taking into account projected currency fluctuations.)

Perhaps even more important to increasing commercial use of the ECU will be its facilitating integration of financial markets by enabling importers and exporters to share currency risks, and by making pricing policies easier to compare. However, there are two caveats: (1) More widespread and rationalized futures markets will significantly reduce currency risks, and (2) full liberalization of capital flows may result in large flows out of some countries and into others, which could threaten the stability essential to the ERM.

Great Britain and the EMS

The absence of the pound from the EMS is a painful subject in Britain that arouses fierce differences in opinion. Prime Minister Thatcher's attitude toward entry into the EMS seems to range from "Not until the time is right" to "Not in my lifetime." *The Economist* believes that the Tory leader's fears are mostly political (British governments have had miserable luck changing the pound's exchange rate, usually through "humiliating devaluations"[9]), but points out that incumbent governments within the EMS have won twice as many elections as they have lost. The editorial also points out that although the City of London remains for the time being Europe's financial capital, this position in the future could be assumed by Frankfurt, home of the Bundesbank. Despite the United Kingdom's GNP being barely half that of Germany's, the City has retained its predominance because of its liberal rules and the presumption that the United Kingdom's membership in the EC implied that "Britain's backyard" would be the whole EC, "from the Mountains of Mourne to the Peloponnese. . . ."[10]

Both these advantages could vanish. A major component of "1992" is liberalization, including that of financial services and capital movement, so London's advantage here will erode. And the longer the United Kingdom stays outside the EMS, any claim that the whole EC is its financial backyard becomes less convincing. *The Economist* concludes that "the British debate over the EMS grows quainter by the day." As London becomes "a less convenient place to do Europe's business in," the United Kingdom will lose its chance to play a central role in the EMS (and therefore in Europe), even to the point of forgoing the possibility of being the home of a European central bank. This, of course, would be a blow to London's prestige as a financial center. It might also inconvenience Americans who would have to forgo the ease of doing central bank business in a capital that is nearer and that uses the same language.

While the debate goes on, many observers believe that Britain will join the EMS when, and for the same reasons that, the ECU becomes a common currency—in other words, when and if the market, significantly affected by other aspects of "1992," dictates it.

The EMS and the United States

It is widely agreed that in the future, more European companies will want to conduct transactions with U.S. businesses in ECU. Some will prefer ECU to dollars simply out of pride (they don't like being forced to use the dollar), and others so as to diversify exchange rate risk (when the dollar or the company's national currency is volatile) or to lower costs (when U.S. or home country interest rates are high). U.S. exporters can use ECU (rather than dollars) to keep buyers happy if the dollar is falling versus the buyer's currency.

From a purely economic point of view, whether American companies trading with EC countries should denominate transactions in ECU will depend largely on how a currency's strength via both the dollar and the ECU is assessed, and the probability of a realignment's occurring during the period the transaction is financed.

For American business, the EMS is a positive development. It lends stability and can provide exchange rate risk diversification. Use of the ECU, for example, can prevent what happened to IBM in the late 1970s when it floated an issue in low-interest Swiss francs only to have to repay in francs that had appreciated 51 percent!

Further, some large U.S. companies have swapped dollar-based issues for ECU-based issues to reduce costs. The scenario works as follows: A small EC-based manufacturer, lacking the credit to issue fixed-rate ECU bonds, will, instead, float a variable rate dollar issue. A large U.S. company, able to issue fixed-rate ECU bonds, does so. The two companies swap issues, the EC company providing the U.S. company a discount on the dollar-based issue. The U.S. company gets the lower rate and the EC company gets the stability of a fixed rate.

Several U.S. multinationals are using ECU for inter-EC transactions; it simplifies accounting and financial comparisons, and lends them an EC panache. Even small firms can benefit because computer programs now available can automate ECU calculations. However, they might face higher transaction charges on a percentage basis. U.S. exporters will most likely want to work through a bank that has experience in conducting business in ECU.

To give you perspective on ECU, you might wish to note the following:

- U.S. investors might buy ECU instruments to diversify exchange risks or when U.S. rates are low.
- ECU options have been traded on the Philadelphia Stock Exchange since February 1986, while ECU futures have been traded on the Financial Instrument Exchange since January 1986.
- Since 1985, a reference interest rate, or commercial interest reference rate (CIRR), has been set for the ECU as for other currencies under the Office of Economic Cooperation and Development's export credit agreement.

Finally, until the ECU is more widely used and EC monetary policy more tightly coordinated, there will probably be little effect on the United

States in terms of its negotiating position in international monetary meetings. To date, the German position has tended to predominate as the EC position. However, the further the EC progresses toward monetary union, the more say it will have in such negotiations, especially in G7 meetings;* this increase in influence is certainly a goal of many supporters of EMS, including the Delors Committee, whose important report of April 1989 concerning monetary union we shall now discuss.

The Delors Committee Report

The Delors Report advocates full monetary union, to be brought about in three stages. Perhaps the most important feature of the overall plan is that it contains no deadline for implementation; this, as the report acknowledges, will be a political decision. Certainly the most important feature of Stage One is its stipulation that agreement to it implies agreement to the other two, more difficult, stages. Mrs. Thatcher disagrees that participating in Stage One represents any such commitment.

Stage One

Stage One, as the report states, "would aim at a greater convergence of economic performance through the strengthening of economic and monetary policy co-ordination within the existing institutional framework."[11] In the economic area, this goal would comprise "action in three directions":

1. Complete removal of physical, technical, and fiscal barriers "in line with the internal market programme."
2. Doubling structural funds "in order to enhance the ability of Community policies to promote regional development and to correct economic imbalances."
3. Strengthening "economic and fiscal policy co-ordination," which would be "the primary responsibility of the Council of Economic and Finance Ministers (ECOFIN)."

Item 3 would entail increased surveillance of national policies, and consultations for "promoting the necessary corrections in national policies."
The monetary area would comprise four action points:

---

*That is, meetings of leaders of the world's seven largest economies (the United States, Canada, Japan, the United Kingdom, France, West Germany, and Italy).

1. Attaining free movement of capital.
2. Inclusion of all EC currencies in EMS, all observing the same rules.
3. Removal of "all impediments to the private use of the ECU."
4. Granting the existing Committee of Central Bank Governors new authority, including the right to be "consulted in advance of national decisions on the course of monetary policy, such as the setting of annual domestic monetary and credit targets." The Committee could express majority opinions, but they would not be binding.

Stage Two

The most significant fact about Stage Two is that it would require a new treaty among EC members and "consequent changes in national legislations" because the Single European Act "does not suffice for the creation of an economic and monetary union."

In the economic field, previous activities (e.g., progress toward the single market, in structural and regional policies, and in economic convergence) would be extended to include "precise—although not yet binding—rules relating to the size of annual budget deficits."

The monetary field would entail more dramatic action, the most important being "that the European System of Central Banks would be set up and would absorb the previously existing institutional monetary arrangements (the EMCF, the Committee of Central Bank Governors, the sub-committees for monetary policy analysis, foreign exchange policy and banking supervision, and the permanent secretariat."

This European System of Central Banks (ESCB) would "begin the transition from the co-ordination of independent national monetary policies by the Committee of Central Bank Governors in stage one to the formulation and implementation of a common monetary policy by the ESCB itself scheduled to take place in the final stage."

While acknowledging the difficulties inherent in transferring "decision-making power from national authorities to a Community institution," the report does not propose a detailed action plan. However, it does make clear that "general monetary orientations would be set for the Community as a whole, with an understanding that national monetary policy would be executed in accordance with these global guidelines."

Stage Three

During the final stage, "the rules and procedures of the Community in the macro-economic and budgetary field would become binding." This would include "directly enforceable decisions," such as the imposition of constraints on national budgets and making discretionary changes in Community resources.

In the monetary field "the irrevocable locking of exchange rates would come into effect and the transition to a single monetary policy would be made. . . ." Further, the "change-over to the single currency would take place during this stage."

Will It Work?

The Delors Committee Report was reviewed at the Madrid summit of June 1989. Advocates of its findings, including President Mitterand of France, expressed their desire to initiate Stage One commencing July 1, 1990. At the Strasbourg summit of December 1989, the Council decided that the Community's readiness to start Stage One in July 1990 would be evaluated at the Dublin summit of June 1990. The Strasbourg summit also decided to initiate the Inter-Governmental Conference, which will formally discuss implementing Stage Two, in December 1990.

Mrs. Thatcher would like to go more slowly, and has presented an alternative plan for attaining a form of monetary union through competing currencies. But even those countries, like Germany, that favor early formal discussions do not necessarily agree that the Delors Committee Report will become the blueprint for monetary union. Rather, it will form the basis for discussion.

There is much debate in Europe as to whether monetary integration is essential to the 1992 concept of a unified market. Even those who believe that it is disagree on the sequence of events. Some believe that the EC must develop monetary union via the Exchange Rate Mechanism, either as a parallel currency to the existing national ones, or as *the* currency of the EC. Others believe that even this implies a central bank's assuming monetary authority that the member states, especially Great Britain, simply will not give up, no matter how compelling the arguments for it. Still others believe that monetary union, though not essential to creating many of the benefits of the unified market, would certainly magnify them, but that this union will not occur until there is greater convergence of the monetary policies of the member states. These people argue that the progress made in other areas of European integration—the free movement of people, goods, and (especially) capital—will, over time, help create the convergence in macroeconomic policies necessary for full monetary union to occur; once it does, even more progress will take place. Essentially, full monetary union at this time would seem to be an imposition for which the member states' political and economic systems are not prepared, whereas full monetary union down the road may well become perceived as a necessity. The markets will speak.

Others believe that the full freedom of capital movements that took full effect in July 1990 in the eight largest economies could destroy what success the EMS has had; they believe that only if the governments cooperate in setting interest rates will the EMS, with its semifixed currency exchange rates, be able to survive. For instance, weaker economies risk massive capital outflows to stronger ones; the tactic of increasing interest rates to counteract such a flow would no longer be available.

In any event, virtually no one believes that full EMU will occur by 1992, nor that it will occur as a single event. Even the English and Germans, who disagree on many things in this area, agree that full EMU cannot be imposed and that further convergence of monetary policies must first take place.

Notes

1. *The ECU*, Luxembourg: Office for Official Publications of the European Communities, 1987, p. 10.
2. Gavyn Davies, "A Plan for European Monetary Union," Goldman Sachs, November 23, 1988, p. S.12.
3. Ibid., p. 5.8.
4. Christopher Johnson, "The European Monetary System," talk sponsored by the European Business and Politics Programme at The City (London) University Business School, July 7, 1989, p. 8.
5. "Report on Economic and Monetary Union in the European Community," Committee for the Study of Economic and Monetary Union, chaired by Jacques Delors, April 12, 1989, p. 3.
6. Ibid.
7. Ibid., p. 29.
8. Christopher Johnson, "The European Monetary System," p. 8.
9. "If sterling stays parochial," *The Economist*, May 21, 1988, p. 13.
10. Ibid.
11. "Report on Economic and Monetary Union in the European Community" (Delors Committee Report). The remaining quotations in this section are from the same report.

Further Readings

The Economist, Financial Times, Wall Street Journal, Euromoney. Periodicals and newspapers that keep you up to the minute on European economic and monetary developments.

"The ECU." An excellent booklet on the EMS's history and status, published by the Office for Official Publications of the European Communities. Available free from that office in Luxembourg, and from the European Community Information Service in Washington, D.C. (see Directory E).

"Report on Economic and Monetary Union in the European Community." Published by the Committee for the Study of Economic and Monetary Union on April 12, 1989, this is the complete Delors Committee Report, which will be the basis for further discussions and decisions. Available from the offices listed above.

New Kid on the Economic Block: The EC and COMECON, EFTA, and Japan

Imagine that capitalism is an aquarium and socialism is fish soup. You can easily make fish soup with the contents of an aquarium, but it is very difficult to transform a bowl of fish soup back into an aquarium.

Lech Walesa, Polish Solidarity leader

Even alongside the stunning developments in Eastern Europe and the increasingly likely reunification of Germany, the 1992 project is playing a prominent role in the most important changes to occur in Europe since World War II. Its possible hazards and its intriguing possibilities alike are of vital interest to major trade partners like EFTA, Japan, and the United States as well as to the East European countries that look to the EC to help them revitalize their economies. While the new freedom of Eastern Europe is certainly of political interest, it is unlikely that the economies there will soon produce anything nearly so exciting as what 1992 could bring to Western Europe. Even if you are interested primarily in the new Eastern Europe, a thorough understanding of the 1992 process will enable you to address issues of concern to Eastern European business decision makers. The following sections discuss how COMECON, EFTA, and Japan view 1992.

The EC and COMECON

COMECON, the Council for Mutual Economic Assistance, was established in 1949 as Stalin's response to the Marshall Plan. It is the East bloc trading system, originally comprising the Soviet Union, Poland, East Germany, Bulgaria, Czechoslovakia, Hungary, and Romania. Vietnam, Cuba, and Mongolia have since become members.

For many years after the creation of the European Community in 1957, Eastern European countries, and particularly the Soviet Union, remained hostile to it, claiming that it was the economic arm of the North

Atlantic Treaty Organization (NATO). But during the 1970s, despite Soviet hostility, Bulgaria, Czechoslovakia, Hungary, Poland, and Romania
found it useful to conclude agreements with the EC in such sectors as
textiles (based on the Multi-Fibre Agreement linked with GATT), steel,
and sheep and goat meat.

General negotiations between the EC and the COMECON powers
were first made possible by Secretary-General Gorbachev, who in 1985
stated that it was time to increase cooperation in economic and international matters. A formal agreement could not be reached until three years
later, however, mainly because of legal problems related to West Berlin's
location in EC territory. A diplomatic solution was finally reached in June
1988 when the EC and COMECON recognized each other after ten years
of rocky talks. The Joint Declaration established official relations between
the EC and COMECON, and paved the way for normalizing bilateral relations between the EC and individual COMECON countries, except Romania.

Also in 1988, the EC approved requests for diplomatic relations from
the U.S.S.R., Poland, East Germany, Bulgaria, Czechoslovakia, and Hungary. This was followed by extensive trade and cooperation agreements
with Hungary and Czechoslovakia.

Then along came 1989. Communist governments gave way throughout COMECON, first in Poland and finally in Romania. Western business, already interested in markets totaling over 420 million people,
became even more interested as COMECON countries embraced at least
some form of free market economy and increasingly welcomed Western
aid, not only in the form of government grants and loans but also in the
form of business investment. And in March 1990, COMECON significantly weakened itself by eliminating its rules on multilateral cooperation
and coordination. These will be replaced by bilateral arrangements.

The EC's credibility as a political entity was increased during this
transitional period by its being appointed coordinator of Western aid to
the East. Further, the EC itself, rather than its individual member states,
embarked on reaching new trade and cooperation aggreements with the
COMECON nations, concluding a ten-year trade and cooperation agreement with the Soviet Union in December 1989. This and other trade
agreements under negotiation emphasize reducing or eliminating quotas; those with East Germany and Bulgaria will be the first such agreements reached. Agreements will also strive to make COMECON markets
more accessible to EC business.

Some economic and political writers have even advanced the idea of
an EC-COMECON free trade area similar to the one established between
the EC and EFTA (see the section "The EC and EFTA" later in this chapter). However, this idea is unlikely to become a reality until at least some
of the differences between the economic and trade policies of the two

areas have been ironed out. Perhaps the biggest stumbling block is the inconvertibility of East bloc currencies. The Soviets have announced the goal of achieving full convertibility by 1995. Progress will also depend on how much modernization and reform the East European economies achieve.

The dramatic changes in Eastern Europe have also caused much concern as to how West Germany would be affected. Many in the EC feared that West Germany might lose interest in the EC in favor of its relations, including increasingly likely reunification, with East Germany. West Germany made it a point to reassure its fellow EC member states that its relations with East Germany would evolve in the context of West Germany's place in the EC. To date, this has been the case. Given that just over one-half of West Germany's exports go to the EC, this stance would seem to be in its interests.

The new relationship between West and East Germany creates at least three issues of more than purely German concern:

1. Trade between the two is considered as trade within one country rather than as trade between one member state and a nonmember state. Therefore, it is not subject to any tariffs or other trade policies the Community has with nonmember nations. This creates the possibility of East European goods entering East Germany, then gaining tariff-free access to the whole EC through West Germany.

2. A similar possibility applies to people. Under West German law, East Germans and anyone of German descent, e.g., in Poland, have the right to West German citizenship. Those exercising this right would then have the right to freedom of movement throughout the EC if that goal is finally realized.

3. The cost of rebuilding East Germany could tie up several hundred billion dollars of West Geman capital, thereby placing upward pressure on interest rates not only in West Germany but throughout the EC and perhaps in the United States and Japan as well.

The complications surrounding the second point resulted in the postponement of the Schengen Agreement under which West Germany, Belgium, Luxembourg, the Netherlands, and France were to have created a border-free region in 1990. The sudden collapse of the Berlin Wall introduced enough uncertainty to make all five countries involved hesitant. France, for example, was concerned that East Germans might replace Turkish immigrant workers in West Germany, who might then enter France under the agreement. In that the Schengen Agreement had been viewed as a model for an open European Community, its postponement is considered a setback for the 1992 program.

The opening up of Eastern Europe has caused other problems as well. Southern European member states fear that it will divert the attention of their more prosperous EC neighbors from them to COMECON. In particular, Spain fears that its status as the "California of the New Europe" will be jeopardized, especially in that most of the increase in investment there has come from West Germany. Perhaps nations like West Germany will be increasingly likely to invest in Eastern Europe for the same reasons that countries like Spain and Portugal have been attractive: low labor costs and comparatively untapped markets. COMECON nations have the additional attraction of geographical proximity, and, in the case of the two Germanies, a common language.

Much of the private sector, however, is enthusiastic. Even before the events of late 1989, consortia of European banks from Germany, Italy, France, and Britain offered approximately $7 billion in trade financing to the Soviet Union. Companies as diverse as Siemens, Rank Xerox, French aluminum producer Pechiney and construction giant Bouygues, the Italian state oil and chemicals group ENI, as well as the engineering giant Asea Brown Boveri rushed to set up joint ventures with Soviet firms, hoping to gain access to sizable and relatively untapped new markets. COMECON countries also offer the inducement of a well-educated and inexpensive work force.

In 1989, Fiat expanded its already active role in the Soviet Union, Poland, and Yugoslavia (not a COMECON member) by entering the biggest joint-venture deal ever with the Soviet Union, under which it will be able to sell abroad one-third of the 300,000 cars it plans to produce. German interest was illustrated by Deutsche Bank's announcing that it would open offices in Warsaw and Budapest. In March 1990, Volkswagen, Daimler-Benz, and General Motors all announced deals in East Germany, and Lufthansa agreed to buy a minority stake in the East German carrier Interflug.

This activity will increase the importance of the EC as COMECON's biggest trading partner. Of its exports to the West, the Soviet Union sends more than 70 percent ($11.7 billion in 1988) to the EC, while about 45 percent of its imports from the West are from the EC. The numbers for other COMECON countries are of similar magnitude. However, COMECON represents only about 7 percent of the EC's trade, and COMECON is concerned about maintaining access to the EC's market, particularly at a time when prices for raw materials and fuel, its major exports, are falling.

For the Soviets and other COMECON states, a favorite way of getting Western help in revitalizing their economies is the joint venture, which can provide management expertise as well as technology. But, though the Soviets have allowed foreign investment since January 1987, after forbidding it for decades, progress remains slow and the deals tend to be small. By the end of 1989, it was reported "only 40 joint ventures are fully operational out of more than 1,000 registered over the past three years. Only three out of the first 250 registered involved investment of more than $20m."[1] Some observers even believe that "some firms are signing agreements that involve small amounts of investment in order to get their hands on scarce office space in Moscow."[2]

There was initial resistance in the West to the limits the Soviets placed on foreign ownership and the freedom of Westerners to run jointly held firms. Recognizing the problem, the Soviets liberalized their regulations in April 1989. Westerners can now own up to 99 percent of a Soviet business. Other provisions of the new joint-venture rules include the following:

- Ability of a foreign national to be chairman or general director
- Freedom for the foreign owners to decide issues of employment and firing, as well as rates of pay, bonuses, and incentive schemes
- Reduction of duties on goods imported for use in the venture's production
- Permission for foreigners to pay for housing and other services in rubles
- Reduction of the 20 percent tax on exported profits for enterprises in key economic sectors and in Asia[3]

Outside the Soviet Union, joint ventures are doing best in Hungary and Poland. In fact, in Hungary, nearly "200 joint ventures are operating, . . . the largest number in the Eastern bloc."[4] Most joint ventures enjoy a five-year tax exemption.[5]

The inconvertibility of COMECON currencies is a major hurdle because COMECON economies have had little experience in pricing according to market demands. In response to this problem, the Soviets and other COMECON countries have engaged extensively in countertrade, which entails such things as forcing their trading partners to use local materials or services in the product being imported, or to buy specified goods in the COMECON country for export abroad. Finding products that will stand the rigors of competitive Western markets has proved difficult, as has the transportation of products because of poor infrastructures. Poland and Hungary, anxious to attain convertibility and other signs of fully equal trading status, have frowned on countertrade. Starting in 1991, COMECON countries will phase in the use of dollars in trade.

Other roadblocks include determining just who can make a decision in a rapidly changing situation involving (often several) people in entirely new roles with access to few, and usually unreliable, statistics. Telephone directories are poor to nonexistent. The same can often be said of the phone service. Hungary is considered the most advanced in resolving these problems.

The United States and COMECON

Only the events of 1989 significantly reduced the U.S. government's latent skepticism about *perestroika* and its political consequences. The result is that the United States has been much slower than other countries to react to the new possibilities. Whereas a high percentage of EC exports to COMECON is represented by finished products, machinery, and other value-added goods, the United States has tended to concentrate on grain shipment. Although American exports to the Soviet Union rose 66 percent in 1988, a much higher increase than occurred in any EC country, most of it came from grain exports due to the Soviet's poor 1988 harvest. And despite this strong gain, overall U.S. shipments to the Soviets ran to $2.5 billion versus $13 billion from the EC.

Things are changing, however. American companies like Combustion Engineering have signed sizable joint venture deals, in Combustion's case with the Soviet Union to produce petrochemical products. And the U.S. government has expressed interest by strengthening agencies like the Overseas Private Investment Corporation (OPIC), which helps underwrite investments in developing countries, and the Export-Import Bank (Eximbank), which helps finance U.S. trade (see Directory A). The Bush administration is anxious that private business take the lead in any Western drive to help the East.

The United States remains particularly cautious concerning the transfer of any technology that could have defense uses. To this end, it uses the Coordination Committee for Multilateral Export Controls (CoCom), which is responsible for preventing just such exports. Other members, including West Germany, believe that the United States is too restrictive in areas where West Germany is strong (e.g., machine tools) and more liberal where the United States is strong (e.g., computers but only up to 16-bit models). West Germany also claims that the number of prohibited items should be fewer, but enforcement more rigid. The United States has said that it will relax exports to Poland, Czechoslovakia, and Hungary, but not yet to the Soviet Union. The U.S. Congress is also pushing for a more liberal policy, concerned that U.S. businesses might otherwise lose sales.

The EC and EFTA

While the European Free Trade Association (EFTA) and the EC have had a close relationship since the 1960s, sharing practices like the use of the Single Administrative Document (SAD), EFTA could soon become nearly integrated into the EC, thereby creating new advantages for firms with operations on the continent. Further, some observers believe that EFTA may become a gateway through which the nations of Eastern Europe will gain access to capital and markets in the West.

The European Free Trade Association was founded via the Stockholm Convention, which took effect on May 3, 1960, its impetus being the desire of non-EC nations "not to be left out of the Western European economic integration process"[6] represented by the newly formed EC. Its original members were Austria, Denmark, Norway, Portugal, Sweden, Switzerland, the United Kingdom, and, later that year, Finland. Denmark and the United Kingdom left EFTA to join the EC in January 1973; Portugal did so in January 1986; Iceland joined EFTA in March 1970. The Stockholm Convention also applies to Liechtenstein, which forms a customs union with Switzerland.

Whereas the EC represents a customs union, which, as defined by the General Agreement on Tariffs and Trade (GATT), has a common external tariff, EFTA is a free trade association, which, as defined by GATT, leaves each member free to define its own external tariff policy. (These are the two forms of economic integration allowed under GATT as exceptions to the most favored nation rule.) More important than the Stockholm Convention in the way EFTA operates "are the numerous informal and unbureaucratic ways of cooperation and coordination within a small organization consisting of small nations, all very dependent on foreign trade."[7] EFTA's small secretariat has no executive powers. This contrasts with the EC, which has "established supranational powers and a body of common legislation. . . ."[8] In fact, the Stockholm Convention "formally established only one institution, the Council, consisting of representatives of member Governments. . . ."[9]

EFTA nations eliminated all tariffs on industrial goods between members by 1966.

Founded largely in reaction to the EC, EFTA has since found that the EC constitutes its major concern; the subject currently consumes 80 to 90 percent of its agenda. This is not surprising considering that nearly two-thirds of EFTA's noninternal exports go to EC member states. By contrast, only about 10 percent of the EC's exports go to EFTA nations. Although the EC in no way wants to jeopardize this relationship (EFTA is its largest market, as EFTA representatives often point out), the EC is nevertheless far more important to EFTA than EFTA is to the EC, an "assymetry" that is of some concern to EFTA. The 1992 process has intensified this concern, some EFTA nations fearing a diversion of EC-EFTA trade to intra-EC trade because of the efficiencies that will result. The EC's growing interest in the new Eastern Europe compounds EFTA's concerns.

Further, the highly formal, relatively centralized decision-making apparatus in the EC enables it to move faster and more forcefully than can EFTA with its unstructured, noncentralized decision making. This difference could be of concern to the EC as well; some project that if EFTA retains its current approach, "the debate about whether the EFTA countries were carrying a 'fair' share of the burden of responsibility for economic adjustment would be likely to increase. . . ."[10] But the rapidity of the EC's progress and recent developments in Eastern Europe have prompted EFTA to act more decisively.

In fact, at their summit in Oslo in March 1989, EFTA heads of government expressed in their communiqué a desire to make the organization's decision making more forceful, both within EFTA and vis-à-vis the EC, and "to explore together with the EC ways and means to achieve a more structured partnership with common decision-making and administrative institutions."[11] Just such common decision making and institutions are a major subject of the European economic space negotiations started in 1990 (see below).

And, of course, there is always talk of some EFTA nations, like the United Kingdom, Denmark, and Portugal before them, joining the EC. In fact, Austria made its formal application in July 1989, but found opposition because it insisted on maintaining its neutrality,* a problem that is compounded by the fact that Austria's neutrality is not a free choice, but imposed on it by the Soviet Union as a price for restoring Austrian independence and removing Soviet troops in 1955. The Soviets have made it known that they have reservations about Austria's joining. Belgium has expressed fears that an explicitly neutral country could complicate the movement toward greater political union. Negotiations will most likely not start until after 1992.

Although Switzerland has not formally applied for membership, developing problems have made it increasingly possible. Erosion of its bank secrecy laws has led to outflows of foreign deposits and to a lower value for the Swiss franc. Its "per capita trade deficit—already bigger than the U.S.'s—is widening."[12] And 1992 represents a force that could make its insularity, a strength throughout the twentieth century, a liability. Still, Switzerland prizes its neutrality enough so that application for EC membership is unlikely any time soon.

The opening up of Eastern Europe has created a parallel and intriguing possibility, namely, that one or more of those nations will want to join EFTA as a means of becoming more integrated into Western Europe. The EC having expressed its desire to focus on internal development rather than enlargement, EFTA membership would be one way for Eastern European nations (Hungary is mentioned most often) to enjoy some of its benefits. However, some EFTA members are wary of this development for two reasons: They do not want to appear solely as an access route to

*Ireland is also neutral but did not make maintaining it a condition for entry (in 1973), as Austria has done.

the EC, and they do not want EFTA's focus on EC relations to be diverted East.

The primary basis of EC-EFTA relations remains the Free Trade Agreements (FTAs) signed in 1972-1973 between each EFTA country and the EC. These eliminated virtually all import duties on industrial products by July 1977, and are still "administered bilaterally through joint committees."[13] Quantitative import restrictions in EFTA-EC trade were also eliminated by the FTAs.

In 1989, the EC and EFTA agreed to start negotiations in 1990 to establish throughout their countries the same freedom of movement for goods, services, labor, and capital that is the goal of the 1992 program, thus creating a market of 350 million people. The most difficult issue to work out will be EFTA's role in the resulting European economic space when the EC insists that its decision making remain solely within the power of EC member states. One possible approach would be for EFTA to participate in discussions, but not in voting.

EFTA nations work with the EC in less spectacular ways than full negotiations. For instance, Switzerland and Austria are associate members of the Group of Twelve Railways of the European Community, founded in 1986. Both countries obviously play a role in traffic between EC countries (e.g., Germany and Italy).

Other areas in which the EC and EFTA cooperate include:

- Providing their insurance companies with equal access to each other's markets (agreed to in August 1989 after fifteen years of negotiations)
- Simplification of the requirements governing proof of origin for goods moving between countries in the two groups
- Dismantling export restrictions "(notably on non-ferrous waste) between the EC and EFTA by 1993."[14]
- Fuller exchange of information on state aid to industry
- Adherence to the Lugano Convention of 1988, which provides "common rules for the jurisdiction of the courts and for the mutual recognition of judgments in civil and commercial matters between the Member States of the EC and EFTA."[15]

EFTA's Importance to the United States

Upon implementation of the FTAs with the EC in 1972-1973, EFTA became part of the largest international tariff-free market for industrial goods in the world. Further, many EFTA companies have moved aggressively into the EC to take advantage of a European-wide market, EFTA investment in the EC having increased from $2.1 billion in 1985 to $10.1 billion in 1988. With a combined GDP roughly equal to that of France,

EFTA countries cannot be ignored. Their uniquely close ties to the EC may give EFTA-based competitors of U.S. companies an upper hand in gaining access to EC markets.

EFTA and Portugal

EFTA has a special relationship with Portugal, dating from April 1976, when it set up "an EFTA Industrial Development Fund for Portugal with a capital of 84.6 million Special Drawing Rights, equivalent at the time to 100 million US dollars." [16] The fund's purpose was to help develop Portuguese industry, especially small and medium-size businesses, and was to operate for twenty-five years, a commitment that is still honored despite Portugal's having left to join the EC. The funds were to be paid back starting after the eleventh year at a rate of 3 percent from the sixth year. In 1988, the EFTA Council decided to delay the start of payback until 1998.

The EC and Japan

No one doubts that a major impetus behind the 1992 program is to address the challenge presented by Japan, to counter both the aggressiveness of its companies in Europe and its numerous barriers to imports. In response to complaints from the United States and the EC, Japan has reduced some of its tariff and quota barriers, but others remain. The complexities of Japanese distribution and bothersome import regulations are proving just as onerous. If, as many suspect, there is a protectionist bias in the 1992 program, it is designed primarily to reverse the widening trade imbalance with Japan. Europe is no happier than the United States is about Japan's propensity to import raw materials and export high value-added manufactured goods.

Some numbers tell the story. The European Community's overall trade imbalance rose from $21.5 billion in 1986 to $28.4 billion in 1988, a year during which its trade deficit increased by over 12 percent with Japan. Although this gap with Japan decreased in 1989, because of an increase in EC exports to Japan, EC investments in Japan remain at less than one-tenth of those made by Japan in the EC.

Japanese investment activities in Europe alone outweigh total foreign investment in Japan. Although Japanese investment is still being viewed within the Community as an opportunity to create new jobs, many fear that an increased Japanese presence in the EC will lead to increased market share. In addition, the EC would like to see more Japanese investment in manufacturing industries, as opposed to services. As recently as 1987, 80 percent of Japan's investment in Europe was in nonmanufacturing activities, particularly in banking and insurance. And the EC would like more technology transfer, a major reason behind its rulings against "screwdriver plants," where foreign-made components are simply assembled.

The complex EC-Japanese relationship can be summarized by a look at three sectors in which the Japanese have been particularly successful and in which EC tactics have yielded some initial results: financial services, automobiles, and high technology.

Financial Services

The Community has openly stated that it will use reciprocity as a means to negotiate the opening of Japan's highly regulated markets to European financial services. Japanese inroads in the EC's profitable banking and insurance industries have only reinforced this attitude. In particular, the strict reciprocity provisions of the first draft of the Second Banking Directive, which specified that EC banks would have to be accorded the same opportunities in non-EC countries as non-EC banks would be accorded in the EC for these banks to be granted the single license to operate throughout the EC, were directed toward gaining a better negotiating position with Japan rather than toward creating a "Fortress Europe" against third countries in general. In accordance with strongly stated U.S. wishes, the reciprocity provisions were changed to "national treatment," which means that EC banks operating in non-EC countries will need to be provided only the same opportunities as domestic banks. However, the EC specified that national treatment would have to result in "effective market access," and reserves the right to limit or suspend single licenses to banks from countries that don't provide it.

Further, the reciprocity language concerning investment services and insurance has yet to be changed, providing the EC still more negotiating room.

Automobiles

The White Paper stated that all national import quotas would have to be replaced by a common EC quota. Because some EC countries, notably France and Italy, have strongly limited Japanese auto imports, it is unlikely that they would allow their national champions—Renault and Fiat—to be suddenly subject to more liberal quotas. Although these countries could try to push through a tough EC-wide quota, Japan and the Community have instead been negotiating a voluntary restraint agreement (VRA) for Japanese cars. This VRA will involve an EC commitment to phase out existing national quotas on Japanese car imports in return for a Japanese commitment to restrain its automobile exports during a transition period. The number of cars to be allowed and the length of the transition period have yet to be specified. Some fear that Japanese cars made in America (and perhaps even in the EC) will be included in the VRA.

A major dispute in this area involves the EC's demand for a minimum "European local content" for Japanese cars, a demand directed largely against Japanese screwdriver plants. Fiat's 1989 attempt to demonstrate that a British-made Bluebird had less European content than Nissan claimed it had was one example of the mixture of nationalism and protectionism that lies behind the issue. This places the Commission in a delicate position, because EC regulations that are too stringent could strain trade relations and hurt European firms depending on foreign supplies.

The Japanese response has been to raise the local-content level of the cars they sell in the EC and to diversify into joint ventures and takeovers.

High-Technology Products

An important part of the 1992 program is designed to lessen Europe's dependence on imports of high-technology products, particularly in view of Japan's increasing strength in developing these products in addition to its long-standing abilities in commercializing theme. The Joint European Submicron Silicon Initiative (JESSI) and MEGA microchips projects, the development of an EC technology policy based on broad industry-government R&D programs, and, in particular, the EC's efforts to secure future markets by defining worldwide standards for high definition television are but the most visible steps in this direction.

The EC's tactics in this area have shifted since the early 1980s, from the wide use of discriminatory import barriers to the use of an increasing number of antidumping actions via local content rulings. In early 1989, for instance, the EC ruled that the diffusion process involved in chip making had to be conducted in the Community for a chip to be considered European. In that this was an area in which Japan relied heavily on non-local sourcing for its European operations, the ruling was intended to curtail Japanese dumping of chips. Because plants required to conduct the diffusion process cost around $100 million, Japanese (and American) manufacturers must reexamine their investment plans and decide whether they should pay the 14 percent tariff or commit the funds necessary to avoid import status.

The EC's strategy in high technology is to pursue a middle course that would embrace more domestic R&D programs while not excluding cooperative ventures and technology transfer from Japan. Aware of this need and in response to the challenges posed by an improving European economy and increased trade friction, Japan is increasing its EC investments in production facilities and in research and development centers.

This process will help develop relationships with local suppliers, thereby improving business links between Japan and Europe. Investments will most likely be greatest in mass production industries, in which Japan tends most to outdistance Europe: in cars, consumer electronics, electronic parts, and office equipment.[17]

Europe has succeeded in gaining more leverage to reduce trade imbalances through coordinated adjustments like VRAs and Japanese local sourcing. In return, Tokyo wants reassurance that the EC's unified market priorities will not hinder multilateral trade negotiations within GATT. At the same time, Japan and the EC share many concerns: Both condemned unilateral U.S. trade actions stemming from the "Super 301" clause; both are concerned about the specter of competing trading blocs; and both are wary of the changes in the other's relationship with the United States. Both hope that the world of the 1990s will become one of *competitive interdependence* rather than of conflicting trading blocs.

Notes

1. "Business remains cautious over investment inflows," *Financial Times*, November 29, 1989, p. 8.
2. Sophie Quinn-Judge, "Joint Ventures: Around 400 Now Registered," *International Herald Tribune*, June 6, 1989, p. 10.
3. Ibid.
4. "Making Cooperative Deals Across Political Borders," *International Herald Tribune*, June 6, 1989, p. 10.
5. "Hungary Devises Foreign Investment Incentives," *International Herald Tribune*, June 6, 1989, p. 16.
6. EFTA Secretariat, *The European Free Trade Association*, June 1987, p. 11.
7. Ibid., p. 9.
8. Ibid., p. 10.
9. Ibid., p. 35.
10. Helen Wallace and Wolfgang Wessels, "Occasional Paper No. 28, Towards a New Partnership: The EC and EFTA in the Wider Western Europe," Economic Affairs Department, EFTA, March 1989, p. 15.
11. European Free Trade Association, "Two Tracks to Progress," *EFTA Bulletin* (Switzerland: EFTA, February 1989), p. 1.
12. "Idyllic Switzerland Discovers Its Idyll is Turning Prosaic," *Wall Street Journal*, July 26, 1989, p. 1.
13. *The European Free Trade Association*, p. 95.

14. United Kingdom Department of Trade and Industry, "The Single Market: The Facts," February 1989, p. 62.
15. Ibid., p. 63.
16. *The European Free Trade Association*, p. 29.
17. Stefan Wagstyl, "Japan will transfer technology to EC response to 1992," *Wall Street Journal*, August 4, 1989, p. 4.

Chapter 9 | Trade Law and GATT

While trade law may seem like stuff for overpaid people in Washington to ponder rather than for an executive who is trying to run a business, the increasing globalization of markets is making knowledge of trade law more and more important. Through gaining some understanding of how the United States manages its international trading relations, you'll discover how the government can help your company if it is embroiled in a trade dispute. Besides, most of the 1992 program refers to international agreements.

This chapter explains the fundamentals of U.S. trade law and the General Agreement on Tariffs and Trade (GATT), and provides an overview of the issues and of how they relate to the new Europe. It also discusses specific trade action suits you can file against foreign companies that have violated international agreements. Finally, we include a trade glossary and a list of additional information sources.

U.S. Trade Law Basics

Business depends on a coherent American trade policy and the U.S. negotiators' ability to get a level playing field in foreign markets for U.S. companies.

In the ongoing debate between free trade and protectionism, U.S. companies engaged in exporting have normally supported free trade, whereas those solely reliant on domestic markets have usually been in favor of protection. Although the United States has generally spoken in favor of free trade, it has often acted in a protectionist manner, the most noteworthy example being the Smoot-Hawley Act of 1930, which raised the average import levy to almost 60 percent, sparking an international reaction that resulted in a substantial reduction in world trade. It thus played a major role in casting the world into the Great Depression. In general, however, U.S. efforts have been directed at obtaining fair access

169

to foreign markets and promoting open competition within the United States.

Today's trading world is far too complex for it to be divided simply into those who support free trade and those who support protectionism. Increasing numbers of multinational firms that once supported free trade are now advocating a third type of trade policy called *strategic trade*. This calls for government to erect trade barriers to protect specific sectors of the home market if those same sectors are protected in a foreign market.[1] The U.S. semiconductor industry advocated such action against Japan, and wound up with the 1986 semiconductor accord. Japanese dumping on the U.S. market had caused most American companies to pull out of the market for DRAM (dynamic random access memory) chips because they could not earn a return at the price Japan was selling them in the United States. At the same time, the Japanese market provided limited access to U.S. DRAMs, enabling companies like Fujitsu and Hitachi to earn higher margins in Japan to subsidize their losses in the U.S. market.

The 1986 United States-Japan semiconductor agreement was designed to rectify this situation by limiting imports of Japanese DRAMs in the United States and placing a pricing floor for those sold in the United States to prevent further Japanese dumping. Another part of the accord, aimed at improving U.S. access to the Japanese market, specified an increase of from 9 percent of the market in 1986 to 20 percent by 1991. The results were mixed: U.S. companies did reenter the market, but not in the number expected, and an upswing in DRAM demand created a shortage (some say because of the agreement), causing makers of everything from talking dolls to personal computers to limit production because they all depended on DRAMs. Further, the Japanese received windfall profits from their chips because the shortage enabled them to get a higher price for them, while U.S. access to the Japanese market has only marginally improved. A similar semiconductor agreement was negotiated between Europe and Japan in 1989.

These bilateral arrangements also complicate the GATT process that requires signatories to negotiate multilaterally (so that all countries play by the same rules). Yet some trade experts claim that the world is moving more and more to these types of arrangements. Automobiles and steel are two other industries where such arrangements have developed.

U.S. Trade Policy Since the 1970s

Tariff reductions under the successful Kennedy round of GATT helped create a great increase in world trade in the 1960s, but the world trading scene changed dramatically during the 1970s as the oil crisis hit and inflation flared. Protectionism once again infected the world's trading system and the *Trade Act of 1974* reflected these changed circumstances. This legislation made it easier for American companies to appeal for protection from imports.

Later in the 1970s, the success of Japanese imports, raging inflation, and low national self-esteem propelled the protectionist-minded in Washington to the forefront of policy making. The *Trade Agreements Act of 1979* shifted authority for dumping and countervailing duty cases from the free-trade-oriented Treasury Department to the more protectionist-oriented Commerce Department.[2] By 1980, the United States had its first trade deficit since the end of World War II.

The *Trade and Tariff Act of 1984 (TTA)* continued the legislative trend toward a more protectionist-oriented trade policy. TTA enabled the President to negotiate bilateral free trade zones (the free trade agreement with Canada is an example) while not having to grant similar concessions to other countries enjoying a most favored nation (MFN) status.[3] The increasing trade deficits of the 1980s resulted in the *1985 Presidential Trade Initiative,* which reaffirmed President Reagan's commitment to free trade but also stated his intent to retaliate against unfair trading partners. The first dumping and unfair trading suits were brought against Japan, the EC, Korea, and Brazil.

The Treasury Department claimed that the U.S. trade deficit was a result of the overly high value of the dollar. Pressure to devalue the dollar led to its dramatic drop in the mid-1980s from being worth 240 yen in 1984 to being worth only 150 yen in 1987.

Although the dollar adjustment caused moderate changes in the trade deficit, it clearly wasn't enough, so the government moved on several other fronts. The *Omnibus Trade Act of 1988,* a lengthy 1,000-page document, was designed to improve America's overall competitiveness. A new Council on Competitiveness (led by Vice-President Quayle) was created; the Exon-Florio Amendment provided the President with the power to halt foreign takeovers when the national security was at stake; and the U.S. Trade Representative (USTR) was given a mandate to open up closed markets and to take action when barriers weren't removed.

Future U.S. Trade Policy

There is a growing awareness in the United States that trade policy must be coordinated with the other policies that affect industry (e.g., defense, monetary, and fiscal policies). The FSX fighter deal cut with Mitsubishi revealed the schizophrenia of U.S. policy: The Defense Department claimed that the deal helped the U.S. aircraft industry, while the Commerce Department argued that it was detrimental.

Clyde Prestowitz, a former U.S. trade negotiator, claims that Americans are inept in their efforts—poorly prepared, unable to speak foreign languages, and confused about objectives. Much of the problem is that trade policy gets tangled up in State Department political agendas and Defense Department military objectives, with the result that economic goals take a back seat and U.S. negotiating leverage is diluted. With the change in administration and a continuing U.S. trade problem, it will not be surprising to see the development of greater coordination among government agencies regarding policies that affect U.S. competitiveness. For example, a 1992 task force comprising twenty agencies and departments was formed in 1988 to identify and coordinate government policies that would be required to keep U.S. firms abreast of the changes in Europe.

U.S. Trade Law and 1992

A big part of the 1992 process involves centralizing and coordinating European efforts in such areas as trade negotiation. The Commission now represents the member states in these discussions. From the U.S. perspective, dealing with one entity rather than with twelve separate countries has both advantages and disadvantages. Once an agreement is hammered out, all EC countries will abide by the new rules. This should reduce the time required to monitor, adjust, and enforce new agreements. On the other hand, a united Europe represents a much stronger negotiating partner. Although most trade experts feel that Europe is not in a position quite yet to gain the upper hand, all agree that some power has shifted to the other side of the Atlantic. In fact, the United States has begun to tread lightly around subjects that it previously would have bullied for. The 1989 super 301 list, which put Japan, Brazil, and India on notice for unfair trading practices, conspicuously omitted mention of any European countries, even though several warranted being named.

U.S. Trade Weapons

When negotiations break down between countries or when foreign governments or companies violate trade agreements, there are a variety of tools the United States can use to address the situation. Most are under the jurisdiction of the United States Trade Representative. Companies that experience trade difficulties abroad can file complaints with the USTR under the following sections of U.S. trade law:

- *Section 201: Escape Clause.* Provides relief from injury caused by import competition by way of tariffs, quotas, voluntary restraint agreements, or adjustment assistance to the workers affected. Filings are made with the U.S. International Trade Commission (USITC) and are then subject to presidential approval. In 1986, the President granted a 35 percent tariff so that the western red cedar shakes and shingles industry could restore its competitiveness.

- *Section 232: Safeguarding National Security.* Provides the President with broad authority if the Commerce Department determines that imports threaten national security. Only three petitions were filed with the Department of Commerce between 1985 and 1988 (relating to the bearings, oil, and injection plastic molding machine industries).

- *Section 301: Retaliation.* Gives the President authority to take all appropriate action to obtain the removal of foreign trade barriers. *Super 301 status,* created in the 1988 trade bill, puts countries on notice for unfair trading practices and gives them eighteen months either to rectify the situation or to face U.S. retaliation (in 1989 Japan, India, and Brazil were put on notice).

- *Section 303: Countervailing Duty.* Designed to assess duties on imports that have benefited from a subsidy or grant from a foreign government. In 1988 there were seventy-one countervailing duty orders in effect.

- *Section 337: Unfair Trade Practices.* Enables the President to take action based on laws regarding the infringement of U.S. intellectual property rights (patent, copyright, or trademark). The EC maintains that applying Section 337, with its different procedural rules and practices, exclusively to imports is inconsistent with GATT's national treatment provisions.

- *Section 731: Antidumping.* Gives the Treasury Department authority to levy duties on imports sold below their fair market value in the United States. It is administered jointly by the Commerce Department and USITC; thirty-eight antidumping orders were made in 1987.

For more information on U.S. trade law and procedures, contact the United States Trade Representative's Office (USTR), the Department of Commerce, or the International Trade Commission (USITC) (refer to Directory A for addresses).

Trade Glossary

A few important trading terms with which you should be familiar appear in the following list:

ad valorem A type of tax or tariff in which the levy is set as a percentage of the price of the product. The European Community currently assesses a 14 percent *ad valorem* tax on all semiconductor imports.

comparative advantage   Manipulation of imports to create an artificial advantage. British economist David Ricardo stated in 1821 that if a country exports goods that it produces relatively more efficiently and imports goods that another country produces relatively more efficiently, the trade will benefit both countries. Although the Japanese were not the first to challenge Ricardo's theory, they are a modern-day example of how a country can create its own comparative advantage through an industrial policy that limits imports in selected areas such as steel, electronics, and autos, thereby enabling domestic companies to gain economies of scale and the benefits of going down the experience curve.

country accounting   Balance sheets and income statements, similar to those of corporations, maintained by countries to keep track of their activities. Although the terms are different, the principle is the same: Whereas a balance sheet reveals the fiscal health of a corporation, a country's benchmarks gauge the varying strengths of its economy. These include:

- *Balance on goods and services.* A country's exports of goods and services minus its imports of goods and services (items such as transportation and tourism).
- *Balance of payments (BOP).* A record of an economy's international economic transactions in goods, services, and liabilities. The BOP account should always equal zero; in this, it is similar to the accounting mechanism that balances the assets and liabilities sides of a balance sheet.
- *Balance on merchandise, or balance of trade (BOT).* A gauge of the strength of a country's manufacturing capability by subtracting merchandise imports from merchandise exports.
- *Capital account.* An account that keeps track of capital flows in and out of the country. Examples include foreign direct investment, securities, and portfolio investments.
- *Current account.* The net effect of exports and imports of goods and services plus net unilateral transfers (e.g., the money an immigrant sends back home). It shows the extent to which a country is sending its resources to the rest of the world, or is drawing on resources from abroad, to supply its own current consumption and investment demands.

dumping   Selling a product abroad at a price below what it is sold for in its home market or at a price that is lower than the cost of production. Although illegal under GATT, there have been many cases of dumping in the recent past. Companies dump to obtain market share, usually cross-subsidizing the losses in one market with the higher profits earned from a protected domestic market.

excise tax   A sales tax on certain commodities that is levied at either a fixed rate per unit or *ad valorem*.

tariff   A tax on merchandise imports that is usually levied on an *ad valorem* basis.

value-added tax (VAT)   A sales tax levied on the value added at each stage of processing. In 1989, VAT rates varied throughout the Community, creating price differentials among member states. The EC plans to harmonize these rates over the next decade.

GATT

Although there's a lot in the news about GATT rounds, negotiations, violations, and new treaties, many people have no idea how any of this translates into day-to-day business. Are these trade sessions held in exotic spots around the world simply junkets for trade negotiators, or does something really worthwhile come from all this talking? Some feel that these meetings are mainly good for generating arcane documents that will be honored primarily in the breach; others, that GATT provides a meaningful forum in which the world's trading partners can tackle their problems.

Because agreements hammered out in GATT negotiations are the international trading rules your business must operate under, it's important to know what they're about. You'll be required to abide by these laws, or to comply with any penalties dished out for violating GATT rules. If you come across a government and/or foreign company not playing according to GATT, you have the right, through your government, to file a complaint and to seek retribution.

The General Agreement on Tariffs and Trade (GATT) was negotiated after World War II to promote world trade and investment. Its purpose was to reignite the forces driving the exchange of goods and services that had been dormant since the Great Depression. Ninety-six countries adhere.

GATT's lofty ambitions included raising the world's standard of living, securing a growing volume of real income and demand by developing the world's resources, and expanding the production and exchange of goods. It set out to create reciprocal and mutually advantageous arrangements that would reduce tariffs and other barriers to trade and to eliminate discriminatory trade practices. It also provided a framework for settling trade disputes. GATT does not at present apply to services, investments, or intellectual property; however, discussions to expand GATT jurisdiction into these areas are taking place.

The GATT Framework

GATT's authority is derived from a series of articles that function as guidelines the signatories agree to abide by. Here are the ones to be familiar with—and their attendant problems.

• *Article I: General Most Favored Nation Treatment (MFN).* Countries recognizing each other under Article I agree to treat all MFN-status countries equally as regards custom duties, rules, and regulations governing trade. A tariff reduction granted to one nation has to be granted to all other MFN countries as well.

Problems: Although bilateral trade deals (arrangements between two countries) directly conflict with Article I, EC member states have many bilateral agreements with countries around the world, and across a variety of sectors. A free flow of goods across EC borders will substantially reduce the effectiveness of these member state agreements. Thus, in some areas, there will be a push for Community arrangements because most of these deals have been cut to provide European firms breathing room from foreign competition. Attempts to resolve these issues through GATT have been difficult because the driving force behind most of the agreements is political.

• *Article VI: Antidumping and Countervailing Duties.* Selling exports for less than a reasonable price (e.g., for less than the cost to produce and market) is condemned by all GATT members. Countries can take action against other countries that violate this article by means of a countervailing duty, which forces the offender to pay damages for the dumping action.

Problem: Because GATT's definition of dumping is vague, the potential for abusing antidumping action is great. The EC was accused of such practices in 1989, when new antidumping legislation was passed by the Council of Ministers without prior notification being given in the EC's *Official Journal.* The new legislation liberalizes the definition of dumping to such an extent that critics claim it is being used as a protectionist trade weapon, not as a control against dumping. Most actions taken have been against Japanese electronics manufacturers.

• *Article XI: General Elimination of Quantitative Restrictions.* This prohibits quotas on imported products.

Problem: EC member state quotas on such things as autos, agricultural products, and textiles are in violation of GATT. However, other countries, including the United States, have violated this article as well. Ongoing GATT negotiations attempt to reduce these infractions. One way in which countries circumvent this article is never formally to enact the quota, but rather to insist on voluntary reductions from the offending country. Technically speaking, because such agreements are voluntary, they don't constitute GATT violations.

- *Article XIX: Emergency Action on Imports of Particular Products.* When an imported product threatens serious injury to domestic producers, a country can take action to remedy the situation so long as it treats all exporters equally. An injured country is required to consult GATT members before taking action.

Problem: Because this procedure is time-consuming, however, many countries don't take action via this GATT article, but instead opt to implement a VRA that limits the amount of the product entering the injured country.

- *Article XXIV: Customs Unions and Free Trade Exemptions.* This article allows countries in certain regional trading blocs to give each other preferential treatment, exempting them from MFN obligations under certain conditions. These conditions state that duties and other restrictions on trade can be removed exclusively among members of the bloc, but that duties and restrictions placed on nonbloc countries must not, on the whole, be higher or more restrictive than before the bloc was formed. The United States-Canada free trade pact and the 1992 program are examples of agreements that are permitted under this GATT article.

The GATT Rounds

A GATT round is a series of multilateral trade negotiations that can last for several years. The first five GATT rounds encouraged exchanges among countries but produced little. The *Kennedy round (1963–1967)* is credited with GATT's first major accomplishments, which resulted in slashing tariffs and duties (by an average of 30 percent) and in substantially increasing world trade.

After the first oil crisis in the 1970s, barriers began to reappear as countries learned to circumvent GATT restrictions on protectionism by turning to voluntary restraint agreements, public subsidies, and nationalistic procurement policies.* The *Tokyo Round (1973–1979)*, also referred to as the *Multilateral Trade Negotiations (MTN)*, attempted to reduce these nontariff barriers to trade. Its results were mixed.

The *Uruguay round (1986–1990)*, begun in Punta del Este, Uruguay, has attempted to get the ninety-six GATT member countries to accept the notion of multilateral liberalization. Two major goals of this round are the overall reduction of agricultural subsidies and the development of a trade framework governing services. While agreement on general guidelines is

---

*Tariffs of any amount, however, are legal under GATT agreements. Tariffs average 5 percent in the EC, with some as high as 22 percent.

expected for services, details and implementation will take several years beyond the conclusion of the round to work out.

1992 and GATT

It is unclear how EC integration will affect the multilateral set of rules under GATT. A good sign, though, is that European negotiators have not delayed the current Uruguay round by claiming that they must wait until all the 1992 directives have been drafted.

The EC will implement regulations in some areas that are already covered by GATT, e.g., government procurement, standards, and dumping. Although agricultural trade is an important issue in the Uruguay round, the 1992 process will have little effect on this area; consequently, even if GATT agricultural agreements are reached, EC implementation will not be tied to the 1992 process.

In services, however, a strong link exists between the GATT negotiations and the 1992 process. One goal of the Uruguay round is to develop a framework governing services. At the same time, the EC is establishing directives to deregulate and coordinate banking and other services throughout the Community. Because there are no international agreements on service trade, the EC began creating its own rules, usually using reciprocity as the test for allowing other countries to conduct services business in the Community. This area is one of the major contributors to the fear of a "Fortress Europe."

Notes

1. Helen V. Milner and David B. Yoffie, "Between free trade and protectionism: strategic trade policy and a theory of corporate trade demands," *International Organization*, Spring 1989, p. 240.
2. David Yoffie, "United States Trade Law," Harvard Business School case no. 9-387-137, 1987, p. 5.
3. Ibid., p. 6.

Further Readings

Books

Dam, Kenneth. *The GATT: Law and International Organization.* Chicago: University of Chicago Press, 1970. Although this book is dated, it does provide an excellent history of GATT's development and an overview of its procedures.

Prestowitz, Clyde. *Trading Places*. New York: Basic Books, 1988. Explains in disturbing detail the inadequacies of the U.S. trade negotiators as they pit their skills against much better-prepared negotiators, the Japanese.

Winham, Gil. *International Trade and the Tokyo Round Negotiation*. Princeton, N.J.: Princeton University Press, 1986. Provides a blow-by-blow description of the Tokyo round and depicts the frustrations of multilateral negotiations.

Magazines, Newsletters, and Other Publications

Business America. A monthly magazine published by the Commerce Department that provides up-to-date reports on U.S. trade activity and changes in U.S. trade law.

Focus. The GATT newsletter, published ten times a year. Recaps GATT activities and lists upcoming negotiating sessions. Contact: Centre William Rappard, 154, rue de Lausanne, 1211 Geneva 21; *phone:* 39 51 11.

Foreign Trade Barriers. An Office of the United States Trade Representative publication that identifies trade activity and problems for each major country in the world. The 1989 edition provided an in-depth analysis of U.S. trade relations with thirty-six countries.

International Trade Reporter. A weekly newsletter published by the Bureau of National Affairs that provides recaps of trade activity and analysis around the globe. Contact: 1231 25th Street, N.W., Washington, D.C. 20037; *phone:* 1-800-372-1033.

Annual Report to the President of the United States on the Trade Agreements Program. An annual USTR publication that provides a recap of U.S. trade agreements and activity throughout the world. Excellent explanations of how the legal trade process works is included.

Conclusion | Is This the Start of Something Big?

Undoubtedly, 1992 is an exciting development. When visiting EC institutions in Brussels and Luxembourg, one gets a sense of being present at the creation of something truly momentous—perhaps the way a visitor to Philadelphia felt in 1776. Indeed, some envision a United States of Europe, a goal toward which 1992 would be but one, albeit an important, step. Full monetary union would perhaps be a more important one.

Those who know something about history and who believe it hasn't stopped quite yet might recall that in 1914, a mere seventy-eight years before 1992, Europe was capable of entering hostilities whose causes, conduct, and resolution make the current enmities in the Middle East seem an exercise in moderation. And that starting in 1939 Europe hosted the greater part of the most destructive war in history, largely because of the economic devastation brought on by the previous one. (In fact, some historians feel that the rapprochement between France and Germany is the single most important postwar development in Europe, including 1992.) Further, the impetus toward a true Common Market has been slowed and even halted before, specifically during the recessions of the 1970s. In the light of the numerous political compromises that will have to be made and sustained to achieve full integration of the European Community, it is evident that the goal can easily be sabotaged by misunderstandings and shortsightedness.

Of the major groupings in Europe, labor remains the most dubious about 1992, wondering if the process will benefit only top businessmen and other white-collar workers. As dislocations occur during the rationalization of industry, the resulting increase in unemployment, at least in some sectors and in some areas, will probably induce labor to exert political pressure against continuing the process.

These caveats aside, it is clear that 1992 is enthusiastically supported by an increasingly influential business community, that it is officially and fully supported by the member states (for that is what they said upon signing the Single European Act), and that it has captured the popular imagination.

Probably more important than any other issue, and an admitted goal of the EC, is addressing the threat posed by the domination of American and Japanese business, a threat that is certainly not going to go away. The proponents of 1992 say, and few argue with them on this, that to effectively counter that threat demands a European approach rather than several national ones. Like other threats to the common good, this one may induce the spirit of sacrifice that will be required to answer it.

On a more positive note, that the EC as an institution rather than its constituent member states was assigned responsibility for coordinating aid to Eastern Europe after the developments of late 1989 indicates that the EC has started to find a political as well as an economic role.

Trying to predict how successful 1992 will be is certainly an intriguing exercise. The geopolitical consequences could be of historic moment. But for the detached observer, which a business decision maker purports to be, it is probably not all that important to correctly forecast how successful the whole 1992 project is going to be; prudent business decision making will not require accurately forecasting the outcome of the whole exercise. But it will require an understanding of the forces working within your sector (and of others that impact on its value chain). For instance, in banking, it will be more important to know if the member states *really* are going to implement the Second Banking Directive on January 1, 1993, than to forecast how much of the 1992 program will be effected. The same sort of thinking applies to the issue of Fortress Europe. If one is erected at all, it is highly unlikely that it would be uniform across sectors. Again, tracking developments in your sector, e.g., how the issues of reciprocity and "effective access" will affect banking, will be key.

This book has provided information that will help you monitor such issues. The following presents some guidelines to help you get started (names and addresses are in the following directories):

1. Contact the European Community Information Service in Washington, D.C., or in New York City to request "Publications of the European Communities," which lists nearly a thousand publications and periodicals.
2. Upon receiving this booklet, order information pertaining to your sector or other areas in which you are interested.
3. Get an updated copy of the "List of European Community 1992 Directives and Proposals" from the Single Internal Market Information Service of the U.S. Department of Commerce or of "Business Guide to EC Initiatives" from the American Chamber of Commerce in Belgium. The United Kingdom Department of Trade and Industry (DTI) offers a similar publication. Use one of these to start or update your Directive Status Report from Chapter 4.
4. Refer to Chapter 4, Step 2, for other publications and data bases.

5. If you have questions that are not covered in these publications or data bases, write the Directorate-General most pertinent to your area of concern with specific questions.
6. If you have questions about specific industries or countries, contact the Department of Commerce desk officers listed in Directory A.
7. Also from the Department of Commerce, try to get newsletters like *Europe Now: A Report* and *Business America* to keep up with developments in the EC as they affect U.S. business. Other government agencies offering information are listed in Directory A.
8. If you are interested in loans, grants, or cooperative R&D programs in the EC, contact some of the many organizations mentioned in Directories A, B, and C.

It is often said that the devil is in the details. Analyzing the importance of 1992 is one of the few times this may be advantageous to the business decision maker. Because even if the 1992 concept falls short of fulfillment, many of the details are already in place, many others are sure to follow, and, most important, it's not that difficult to track a few individual developments. This book has focused on details because it is the microeconomic, the business, level that we presume interests you. As it turns out, the impact of numerous business decisions like yours will, in the end, determine how much of 1992 will become a reality.

Directories

U.S. Sources of Information and Assistance

This directory describes U.S. government and private sector sources that provide analysis of and information about the changes in Europe, general exporting, and how to secure financing for overseas selling.

Government Agencies and Services

The U.S. government provides a wealth of information and services for business. Offerings such as market research, trade show assistance, and tariff advice are either free or given for a nominal charge. In addition, we've found that the people involved are prompt, courteous, and knowledgeable about their subjects. U.S. government assistance, however, is available only to companies whose products have at least 50 percent U.S. content.

Beginning in 1987, the U.S. government has placed special emphasis on 1992. It mobilized a 1992 task force comprising twenty agencies and departments to identify challenges and priorities regarding the new Europe.

With the U.S. balance of trade deficit hovering at $100 billion, the government has also intensified its effort to aid U.S. company exports. The Commerce Department's 1992 efforts are particularly noteworthy. Federal deficit pressures, however, have affected government staffing and resources.

U.S. government aid is a supplemental resource and a tool to help your business; it is not a substitute sales force nor a direct extension of your strategy group.

Here's a list of agencies and a brief description of how each can be of service to your 1992 efforts:

The Department of Agriculture
U.S. Department of Agriculture
The Foreign Agricultural Service (FAS)

International Trade Policy-Western Europe (WEIA)
South Building, Room 5514
Washington, D.C. 20250
Phone: 202/382–9013

Export services include trade leads, importer lists, export market reports, trade negotiations, credit guarantees, market development, and efforts to counter unfair trade practices abroad.

Congressional Research Service

The Congressional Research Service (CRS) is the research arm of the Library of Congress. For the Senate and the House it provides analysis on a variety of issues from the Strategic Defense Initiative (SDI) to welfare. It has produced several excellent reports on 1992, some of which are available to the public. The best way to obtain them is to make a request through your local Congressional office (ask for an updated report list). The following reports are worth ordering:

The European Community, Its Structure and Development, August 31, 1988, 88–620 F.
The European Community: 1992 and Reciprocity, April 11, 1989, 89–227 E.
European Community: Issues Raised by 1992 Integration, May 31, 1989, 89–323 E.
European Community: 1992 Plan for Economic Integration, June 20, 1989, IBS 89043.
The European Community's 1992 Plan: Bibliography-in-Brief, 1986–1988, December 1988, 88–754 L.
Bibliography on Europe 1992, Joint Economic Committee, June 8, 1989.

The Department of Commerce
U.S. Department of Commerce
Single Internal Market: 1992 Information Service
Office of European Community Affairs, Room 3036
14 Street and Constitution Avenue, N.W.
Washington, D.C. 20230
Phone: 202/377–5276 or 202/377–5279

The Department of Commerce (DOC) encourages, serves, and promotes the nation's international trade, economic growth, and technological advancement. In mid-1988, the Department created a 1992 task force to keep U.S. firms abreast of developments in Europe. This group is referred to as the Single Internal Market Information Service (SIMIS). It is part of the Department's International Trade Administration (ITA) group, which has forty-eight district offices and nineteen branch offices through-out the United States.

SIMIS provides copies of the Single Internal Market regulations, background information on the European Community, and assistance re-garding specific opportunities or potential problems. We've spoken to most of the DOC groups and have been impressed with their knowledge and willingness to assist the private sector.

In addition to SIMIS, which is staffed by country-desk officers, Com-merce's trade development industry analysts, who have 1992 expertise, can be reached at the locations and telephone numbers listed below:

Office of Industrial Trade (coordinating office): Room 2800 A, 202/377-3703.
Textiles and Apparel: Room 3119, 202/377-2043.
Service Industries: Room 1128, 202/377-3575.
Information Technology, Instrumentation, and Electronics: Room 1001A, 202/377-4466.
Chemicals, Construction Industry Products, and Basic Industries: Room 4045, 202/377-0614.
Autos and Consumer Goods: Room 4324, 202/377-2762.
Construction Projects and Industrial Machinery: Room 2001B, 202/377-2474.
Aerospace: Room 6877, 202/377-8228.

Country-specific information is available at these numbers:

Belgium and Luxembourg	202/377-5401
Denmark	3254
France	8008
Germany, Federal Republic of	2434
Greece	3945
Ireland	4104
Italy	2177
Netherlands	5401
Portugal	3945
Spain	4508
United Kingdom	3748

Your regional DOC office can provide most of the information that omes out of Washington. Each office is staffed by trade specialists. Be-cause of the federal budget crunch, some offices may be understaffed, but there's one in almost every state; call 202/377-4767 for the office near-est you.

Regional offices also sponsor seminars on 1992 and exporting; con-tact them for a schedule. The DOC's international economists and trade experts are available for speeches and corporate seminars; they'll come to you free of charge, except for travel expenses. Call 202/377-5279 for more information.

Among the more important Department of Commerce publications relevant to 1992 are the following:

EC 1992: A Commerce Department Analysis of European Community Directives. Produced in three volumes, this provides an excellent analysis of the main EC directives. Using a combination of government and private sector input, the analysis is comprehensive and intelligent. The author of each directive analysis provides a phone number, so you can follow up if you have further questions. Each volume is available for $10 through the U.S. Government Printing Office; *phone:* 202/783-3238.

- Volume One: Manufactured products and services (66 directives), June 1989, GPO stock #003 009 00557 4.
- Volume Two: Processed foods, company law, and trademarks, October 1989.
- Volume Three: Standards and government procurement, more manufactured products and services, December 1989.

Europe Now: A Report. A free quarterly newsletter that gives an overview of current issues and provides 1992 anecdotes and sources of additional information. Ask to be put on the mailing list; phone: 202/377-5823.

Business America. A biweekly magazine on international trade issues. Contact your regional DOC office for subscription information.

Another service offered by the Department of Commerce is the *Commercial Information Management System (CIMS)*, which electronically links the information resources of all the Department's posts and offices worldwide to provide in-depth marketing data. It is excellent for market research, trade leads, market contacts, and competitive assessment reports. There is a reasonable user fee for this service. For more information, contact:

U.S. Department of Commerce
International Trade Administration
Room 1617, Code BR-188
Washington, D.C. 20230
Phone: 202/377-5823

In addition to *Commercial News USA,* an export promotion magazine sent to over 100,000 foreign agents, distributors, and end users around the world, the U.S. and Foreign Commercial Service of the International Trade Administration offers many export services:

- *Comparison shopping service.* Helps compare your products with those of foreign competitors.
- *Agent distributor service.* Locates a minimum of six agents/distributors to sell your product overseas.
- *Foreign buyer program.* Stages United States-based trade shows for overseas buyers.
- *Catalog and video catalog shows.* DOC personnel present your product overseas via these catalogs.
- *Trade fairs.* DOC sponsors U.S. trade fairs around the world.
- *Matchmaker program.* Trade delegations offer introductions to new markets through short overseas visits to match U.S. firms with possible international partners.

Contact your regional DOC office for more information on these programs.

The Export-Import Bank

Export-Import Bank of the United States (Eximbank)
811 Vermont Ave., N.W.
Washington, D.C. 20571
Phone: 1-800/424-5201; *Europe desk:* 202/566-8813

Eximbank facilitates the export financing of U.S. goods and services and helps U.S. exporters compete in overseas markets against foreign companies receiving government subsidies. Eximbank supported more than $6 billion worth of U.S. export loans in 1988. Although the Reagan administration favored eliminating the bank's loan program, President Bush sees Eximbank as a vehicle for narrowing the trade deficit.

Four major export finance programs are available:

1. *Lending program.* Extends loans to foreign buyers of U.S. exports and intermediary loans to finance responsible parties who extend loans to foreign buyers. These loans are made at low, fixed-interest rates according to arrangements with the Office of Economic Cooperation and Development (OECD).
2. *Guarantee program.* Provides repayment protection for private sector loans to credit-worthy foreign buyers of U.S. goods and services. Guarantees of up to 85 percent are available.
3. *Working capital guarantee program.* Offers guarantees to lenders to support pre-export financial needs.
4. *Insurance.* Protects U.S. exporters and banks against the political and commercial risk of nonpayment by foreign debtors.

The bank's insurance agent, the Foreign Credit Insurance Association (FCIA), offers a variety of policies for protecting U.S. exporters against the risk of nonpayment by foreign debtors. FCIA is an association of leading insurance companies, operating in cooperation with, and as agent for, Eximbank. Its main office is in New York City: 40 Rector Street, 11th floor, New York, N.Y. 10006; phone (212) 227-7020. Regional offices are located in Chicago, Houston, Los Angeles, and Miami.

Eximbank offers free one- and two-day briefings on the bank and its services that are held in Washington several times a year; call: (202) 566-4490.

Although many of the bank's loans are intended to counter foreign competitors who receive special financing grants from their governments, small business loans under $2.5 million don't require proof of a foreign competitive subsidy.

More than 27 percent of the money that Eximbank lent in 1988 went to small and medium-size businesses. Of the 1,395 loan guarantees authorized by the bank in 1988, 868 went to small firms; seventy had never used the program before.[1]

The U.S. Small Business Administration

The U.S. Small Business Administration (SBA)
1441 K Street, N.W.
Suite 501A
Washington, D.C. 20416
Phone: 202/653-7794
Fax: 202/254-6429

The Small Business Administration offers aid to current and potential small or minority companies through two major programs:

1. *Business Development Assistance.* Provides consulting services through a Service Corps of Retired Executives and/or additional referrals. Special emphasis is placed on 1992.

2. *Financial Assistance.* Provides guarantees of up to 85 percent of a private lending institution's loan to an eligible small business. The 1988 Omnibus Trade Act authorized a larger loan limit for the acquisition, construction, renovation, modernization, improvement, or expansion of productive facilities or equipment to be used in the United States in the production of goods or services involved in international trade. It is now possible to receive guarantees of up to $1.25 million (though certain restrictions apply). SBA's Export Revolving Line of Credit provides credit for up to eighteen months to develop new export markets. Other financing programs include the Eximbank-SBA joint program and small business investment financing for equity infusions.

The SBA also helps small businesses to take advantage of the Commerce Department's matchmaker program. SBA began a 1992 alert program in the summer of 1989 and now offers a small business 1992 fact sheet. SBA regional offices are also active and offer a variety of services and seminars relating to exporting and 1992.

Useful SBA publications that can be acquired through your SBA regional office include:

Is Exporting for You?, a free SBA publication on things to think about before exporting.
Market Overseas with US Government Help, which includes detailed information on federal programs. $1.
Exporters Guide to Federal Resources for Small Business, a guide to federal agencies, with Washington and regional office listings.

The Department of State

U.S. Department of State
Europe/Regional, Political and Economic Affairs, Room 6519
Washington, D.C. 20520
Phone: 202/647-2395

Besides its role in diplomacy and foreign policy, the Department of State (DOS) assists U.S. business in more than 140 countries. Local officials promote U.S. trade and investment interests. The State Department provides assistance in developing trade contacts and in resolving disputes with foreign governments. The level of service depends on the consular officer at each site, some being more helpful than others.

The DOS operates the U.S. Mission to the European Communities in Brussels, and this can serve as a contact point. Personnel can assist in advising you on who to see when in town. The address is:

U.S. Mission to the European Communities
Boulevard du Régent 40
1000 Brussels
Phone: 32 513 44 50

In addition, the commercial counselor at the U.S. embassy in Brussels can recommend a brief list of reputable lobbyists to help present your views to the Commission.

State Department publications of interest to business include:

The European Community's Program to Complete a Single Market by 1992, July 5, 1988, an overview of 1992.
Key Officers of Foreign Service Posts, publication #7877, providing the names of key contacts for U.S. business representatives. For a copy, contact the Office of Commercial, Legislative, and Public Affairs of the State Department at 202/647–1942.

The U.S. International Trade Commission
The United States International Trade Commission (USITC)
500 E Street, N.W.
Washington, D.C. 20436
Phone: 202/252–1000

The USITC is an independent government agency that determines the degree of injury inflicted on U.S. companies in cases of trade violations concerning intellectual property and dumping. Its judgment is used to determine the penalty to be levied in such trade cases. There are six commissioners, appointed for nine-year terms, three from each political party.

The U.S. Trade Representative
The United States Trade Representative (USTR)
600 17 Street, N.W.
Washington, D.C. 20506
Phone: 202/395–3320

Reporting directly to the President, the trade representative is charged with coordinating and setting U.S. trade policy, and is the President's principal adviser on international trade policy. The USTR represents the United States at all GATT activities, OECD discussions, and other multilateral meetings regarding trade. USTR officials can be particularly helpful in providing current information on trade policy.

USTR heads the interagency government task group for 1992, and produces specific policy recommendations for the President regarding 1992.

USTR officials have sector and geographic expertise. For issues regarding Europe, call 202/395–3320. These officials are called on from time to time to testify before Congressional hearings. Transcripts of evidence presented by USTR officials at these hearings are available from USTR.

USTR publications include:

An initial assessment of certain economic policy issues raised by aspects of the EC's program, Document no. 1288, December 1988.
Annual Report of the President of the United States on the Trade Agreements Program, published annually.

State Assistance

An often effective local source of information and help is your state government. You should be eligible for assistance so long as you operate in the state; therefore, if you have multistate operations, you should be able to participate in the programs of each one of them.

Services vary, but at the very least each should be able to help you make contact with Washington-based programs. The Massachusetts Industrial Finance Agency, for example, streamlines the Export/Import bank loan application process, enabling qualifying Massachusetts businesses to get financing through the program much faster than if they had gone directly to Washington.

States also have a variety of export programs, training seminars, trade shows (both in-state and overseas), and other ties to federal agencies like the SBA and Department of Commerce.

The Council of American States in Europe (CASE) is an umbrella organization that loosely coordinates the twenty-five state offices that operate in Europe. These liaisons serve two functions: (1) to attract European foreign direct investment (FDI) to their state, and (2) to provide assistance for their companies exporting to Europe. These offices vary in effectiveness, so look for tangible results and ask for references. The following states and one commonwealth all have offices in Europe:

Alabama	Kansas	Ohio
Arkansas	Kentucky	Pennsylvania
California	Maryland	Puerto Rico
Connecticut	Michigan	Rhode Island
Florida	Minnesota	South Carolina
Georgia	Missouri	Texas
Illinois	New York	Virginia
Indiana	New Jersey	Wisconsin
Iowa	North Carolina	

Private Assistance

With fourteen offices in Europe, the American Chamber of Commerce offers a variety of services and publications for its members. European AMchams represent companies of American parentage and have 18,000 members. AMcham's message to the Community is professional and effective. It has established itself as a credible source in the eyes of Commission officials and is consulted on many issues.

AMcham's most effective work is produced by the variety of committees it sponsors. The quality and intensity of each working group, comprising executives from AMcham's membership, of course varies according to the people on the committee. As a member, you would have the opportunity to participate in these activities.

Another benefit of AMcham is its publications group. Ask for a list of the many quality information packets that the Brussels office produces.

Of particular interest are the updates on EC directives, published twice a year, and the introductory booklet on the Community.

Each AMcham provides market data and a comprehensive list of agents, distributors, lawyers, and bankers. The two most important AMchams in Europe are:

American Chamber of Commerce in Belgium
The EC Affairs Manager
Avenue des Arts 50, Box 5
B-1040 Brussels, Belgium
Phone: 32/ 2 513 68 92

American Chamber of Commerce in France
Secretariat
Avenue George V 21
75008 Paris
Phone: 33 1 4723 80 26/70 28
Telex: 650286

Contact your local Chamber or regional Commerce Department in the States for the locations of other overseas branches and for further information.

Port Authorities

There are more than 165 local port authorities dotting the American shoreline. Although not geared to the small exporter, they do offer an assortment of services ranging from export advice to help with customs declarations and tariffs. They also offer export publications. Contact the American Association of Port Authorities for a list of members and individual services:

American Association of Port Authorities
Export Trading Division
1010 Duke Street
Alexandria, Va. 22134
Phone: 703/684–5700
$35 fee for a member handbook (1988 price)

Note

1. Ellen Schweppe, "Getting export financing," *Business Credit*, June 1989.

Euro-Discounts: Country Profiles and Government Relocation Incentives

Tax breaks, investment credits, union cooperation, and direct financial handouts are available to companies willing to locate their facilities in certain areas of the Community, especially in economically depressed places like Scotland and the Saarland in West Germany. This directory describes the ABCs of what's available and how American companies can qualify.

Finding a "Good Deal"

In the mid-1980s British officials bragged about Britain's comparatively low business taxes and fast-improving productivity, but American business people yawned. However, a repackaged "Europe 1992" campaign presenting Britain as the best way into the world's largest market woke them up. The revamped campaign generated over 2,000 responses in 1988.[1]

Each EC member state offers relocation incentives in the hopes of attracting some foreign direct investment in Europe. Government perks include tax holidays, subsidies for employee training, buildings at bargain prices, subsidized loans, and discounts on utilities. Factoring these benefits into an investment decision can make or break a venture.

General Tips for Securing Relocation Incentive Packages

First, contact the foreign direct investment (FDI) office in the United States of the country you are interested in. Besides providing information on incentive packages, these offices usually offer market data and country statistics, and they can help you find suppliers, distributors, and employees. They will also get you up to speed on such things as local tax, accounting, and legal procedures. Refer to member state profiles in this directory for addresses at the beginning of each country description.

Because financial assistance in most instances can be granted only before a project begins, it is important to do the following:

1. Discuss the project early with government officials.
2. Prepare a brief two- or three-page description of your project for use in these discussions, so that you can determine early whether the project has a chance of qualifying.
3. Support your application with a complete business plan and a three-year pro forma financial statement.

Don't expect prime real estate to come with incentives. These programs are offered for a reason. They're usually available for locations in depressed economic areas that are characterized by high unemployment, low skill levels, and/or poor infrastructure. Sometimes programs are available for specific industries (usually declining ones).

Incentives are generally offered for plant and equipment, buildings, land, research, and training. As with all contracts, read the fine print; some grants are subject to performance criteria and others may become repayable if the project turns out to be commercially successful.

Keep in mind why these programs are offered. Your proposals will be evaluated in terms of what they can bring in the way of jobs, technology, economic growth, and exports. Pitch your project in those terms.

View government as a partner, not as an adversary. Nurture the relationship the way you would a valued customer. As in any project approval process, well-thought out proposals, concisely presented, that fit with program objectives stand the best chance of gaining support.

If you export from one of the member states, you most likely will be eligible for export assistance, including special financing, trade show support, marketing analysis, and general export advice.

When moving overseas, don't forget formalities like business licenses, VAT registration, Social Security registration, and incorporation rules. Also, examine all local labor laws governing hiring, firing, layoffs, and worker participation before investing.

Finally, don't shape your choice of corporate location solely around incentives. These should complement and enhance your decision for locating in a particular area. Facility location should fit strategically with your other operations.

Incentive Updates and More Sources to Check

Programs are likely to change from year to year, so to keep current you should obtain the most recent version of the following:

European Regional Incentives 1989, European Policies Research Centre, University of Strathclyde, £49.00. Contact Trish Lovell, Bowker-

Saur Ltd., Borough Green, Sevenoaks, Kent TN15 8PH, England (*phone*: 0732/884567; *fax*: 0732/884530). This annual work summarizes the regional incentives offered by EC member states and Sweden. It provides good country comparative data and analyzes recent changes in country offerings.

The Structural Funds of the European Communities, The London Chamber of Commerce. Contact 69 Cannon Street, London, EC4N 5AB (*phone*: 01/248-4444).

Corporate Location Europe, The European Economic Development Magazine. Contact Century House Information Limited, 22 Towcester Road, Old Stratford, Milton Keynes MK19 6AQ, England (*phone*: 0908/560-555; *fax*: 0908/560-470). This provides up-to-date information on factors critical to the European investment decision, such as good comparative analysis of wage rates, productivity, taxation, energy costs. Country supplements have a wealth of information.

Many service firms such as the Big Six accounting/consulting firms also offer data bases, information packets, and assistance in evaluating locations and government incentive packages.

European Community Incentive Programs

The EC offers a variety of specialized incentive programs. Here's a list of the major offerings, with a brief overview of each:

• *European Structural Funds.* Designed to put the different member states on a par with each other with regard to infrastructure, industrial strength, and labor skills. Over 14 billion ECU have been set aside by the Commission for the period 1988 to 1993; funds are earmarked for depressed areas, labeled as "least favored areas." DG-16, the Regional Directorate, supervises the regional structural funds. Regions have different allowable percentages of subsidy. For example, up to 45 percent of an investment in Portugal can be subsidized, but no more than 10 percent in West Germany.[2] Portugal, Greece, Ireland, and parts of Spain and Italy are expected to receive 60 to 70 percent of these funds, for which there are three programs:

1. *European Regional Development Fund (ERDF).* Intended for the development and structural adjustment of less-developed and declining regions. Close to $4 billion was spent in 1988. Member states submit five-year development plans to the Commission. Once approved, the member states allocate the money.

2. *European Social Fund (ESF).* Created to assist in the implementation of employment and vocational training. Grants are avail-

able for young people and less favored workers. Close to $4 billion was spent in 1988. The program is currently under review.

3. *European Agriculture Guarantee and Guidance Fund (EAGGF or FEOGA).* Provides discretionary grants of up to 25 percent of fixed capital costs for projects that tend to raise the prices paid to primary producers for agricultural and fisheries products, e.g., food processors and marketers. Projects must be in receipt of national aid and cost more than $40,000.

• *Integrated Mediterranean Programmes (IMPs).* Established in 1985 to develop the Mediterranean areas of Greece, Italy, and France. The programs are financed out of the structural funds, the European Investment Bank, and a special Community budget.

• *European Coal and Steel Community (ECSC) Loan Program.* Provides companies that create jobs for unemployed coal and steel workers secured loans of up to 50 percent of fixed assets invested. Eight-year term, four-year repayment holiday, low interest schedule. Contact:

The Directorate of Credit and Investments
Commission of the European Communities
Bâtiment Jean Monnet
Kirchberg
Luxembourg
Phone: 352/430 131 90

• *European Investment Bank.* Offers favorable loans for industrial and infrastructure projects in "Assisted Areas" that strengthen the European economy. Loans are available for up to 50 percent of the project. Contact:

European Investment Bank
Boulevard Konrad Adenauer
Plateau de Kirchberg
Luxembourg L 2950
Phone: 352/4379-1
Fax: 325/43 77 04

Member State Incentive Programs

Member states have a host of individual programs to attract foreign direct investment and to boost certain industries within their own borders. This section provides a brief description of what each country offers in addition to some industrial facts about each member state. You'll also find a

European Community Statistics

	Population (Millions)	1988 GDP ($ Billions)	1988 GDP ($ Per Capita)	Average 1989 Unemployment
Belgium	9.8	$ 147.5	$14.889	13.3%
Denmark	5.1	107.7	21.112	9.2
France	55.6	944.8	16.902	10.0
Greece	9.9	53.0	5.248	13.4
Ireland	3.6	31.3	8.943	17.9
Italy	57.3	820.2	14.314	16.6
Luxembourg	0.4	6.3	15.750	1.4
Netherlands	14.7	227.0	15.338	13.8
Portugal	10.3	41.0	4.184	12.4
Spain	38.7	339.4	8.703	16.4
United Kingdom	56.8	802.1	14.072	7.6
Germany	60.9	1,206.8	19.590	7.9
EC-12	324.2	4,727.2	14.581	11.0*
United States	246.2	4,861.8	19.479	5.5*
Japan	123.0	2,841.3	23.100	2.5*

*Unemployment Data for EC-12, the United States, and Japan are as of 1988.
Source: U.S. Mission to the European Community, *Management Horizons.*

U.S. contact (when available) from which you can obtain more detailed information. Although 1992 may result in curtailment of some of these programs, expect each country to maintain its own FDI agency, just as individual states in the United States compete against one another for FDI. The next section discusses member state subsidies for national industries and Brussel's attempts to slow the money flow.

Community Rulings on Member State Incentives

DG-IV, the Competition Directorate, is attempting to curtail member state subsidies to declining industries. This is an attempt to set Community-wide priorities, improve efficiencies, and synchronize member state industrial policies. Expect more programs to come out of Brussels and fewer from the member states themselves.

Brussels receives this authority through Articles 92 to 94 of the Treaty of Rome, which state that member state subsidies are incompatible with the concept of a common market if they distort trade competition within the Community.

Comparative Price Levels in Western Europe, mid-1989
(Purchasing Power Parities)
Country
(national currency)

	Aus Sch	Bel BFr	Den DKr	Fra FFr	Ger DM	Gre Dr	Ire IR£	Ita L	Neth Fl	Nor NKr	Por Esc	Spa Pes	Swe SKr	Swi SFr	UK £
Austria (Sch)	100	114	84	109	101	161	118	120	119	78	192	142	86	83	118
Belgium (Bfr)	88	100	74	96	88	142	104	105	105	68	169	125	75	73	103
Denmark (DKr)	119	136	100	130	120	192	141	143	142	93	230	169	102	99	140
France (FFr)	92	104	77	100	92	148	108	110	109	71	177	130	78	76	108
Germany (DM)	99	113	83	108	100	160	118	119	118	77	191	141	85	82	117
Greece (Dr)	62	71	52	68	62	100	73	74	74	48	119	88	53	51	73
Ireland (IR£)	85	96	71	92	85	136	100	101	101	66	163	120	72	70	100
Italy (L)	83	95	70	91	84	135	99	100	99	65	161	118	71	69	98
Netherlands (Fl)	84	96	70	92	85	136	99	101	100	65	162	119	72	70	99
Norway (NKr)	129	147	108	141	130	208	152	154	153	100	248	183	110	107	152
Portugal (Esc)	52	59	44	57	52	84	61	62	62	40	100	74	44	43	61
Spain (Pes)	70	80	59	77	71	114	83	84	84	55	136	100	60	58	83
Sweden (SKr)	117	133	98	127	118	189	138	140	139	91	225	166	100	97	138
Switzerland (SFr)	121	137	101	131	121	194	143	144	143	94	232	171	103	100	142
United Kingdom (£)	85	97	71	93	85	137	100	102	101	66	164	121	73	70	100

Note: The table is to be read vertically. Each column shows the number of specified national monetary units needed in each country listed to buy the same representative basket of consumer goods and services. In each vertical column this "basket" costs a hundred units in the country whose currency is specified.

Example: £100 spent in the UK would have to be increased to £108 equivalent if spent in France; only FFr57 spent in Portugal would buy as much as FFr100 similarly spent in France.

Source: OECD Main Economic Indicators (1989) based on quarterly national consumer price indices.

The Commission fears that governments will be tempted to use subsidies to counter increased competition as national barriers fall and the single European market becomes a reality.[3] A December 1988 ruling obliging member states to obtain authorization before handing out any subsidy worth more than 12 million ECU to firms in the car industry was an attempt to create a level playing field within the Community.[4]

In 1988 the Commission forced the governments of member states to reclaim about $1.2 billion in illicit state aid disbursed over a four-year period (1983–1987).[5] Most of the aid had gone to state-owned corporations or declining industries. In the summer of 1989, the Commission actually took legal action against West Germany and Spain for refusing to seek approval from Brussels before paying subsidies to their automakers.

While Brussels attempts to curtail the subsidization proclivities of member states, it's also attempting to get its own house in order. Over 80 percent of all Community aid to member states has been devoted to agriculture (26 billion ECU in 1987).

Belgium

The Belgium Embassy
Investment Office
3330 Garfield Street, N.W.
Washington, D.C. 20008
Phone: 202-333-6900

Location advantages:	Near the heart of Europe, close to the Commission.
Location disadvantages:	Large government bureaucracy.

Belgium is located in the region where the Germanic tribes of the north met the Latinized Celtic peoples of the south in the first century A.D., making it the true crossroads of Europe. Although the country did not become independent of the Netherlands until 1831, the Flemish culture in the north and the French culture in the south share certain basic similarities.

The country is divided into three distinct regions, Flanders in the north and west, Brussels in the center, and Wallonia in the south. The regional governments administer separate incentive programs. Note that French is spoken in Brussels and Wallonia, and that Flemish, a variant of Dutch, is spoken in Flanders. (If you don't speak Flemish, use English rather than French.)

Two specific high-tech programs are offered by the Belgian government. The tax free zone package is for new businesses that have a minimum of ten employees and no more than 200. The following sectors qualify: information technology, software, micro- and optoelectronics, office automation, robotics, telecommunications, and biotechnology. Incentives include ten-year tax breaks and registration fee exemptions. Applications are made to the Tax Free Zone Management Secretariat in Brussels.

The innovation scheme, coordinated by the Ministry of Finance in Brussels, is offered to high-technology companies that formed during the period 1984 to 1993 and have fewer than a hundred employees. The program offers an assortment of liberal tax reductions.

The maximum subsidy for smaller firms is 21 percent of investment, for larger companies, 24 percent. Several employment and training incentives are available. Reduction in salary and social security costs are obtainable for small and mid-size firms. Tax incentives for new job creation, training grants, and employee search assistance are provided.

Marketing regions

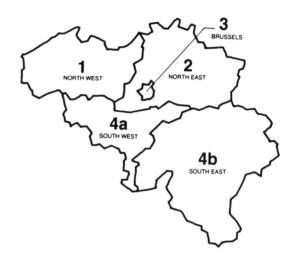

BELGIUM AND LUXEMBOURG

	Households ('000s)	%
1	800	22
2	1,100	30
3	500	14
4a	600	17
4b	600	17
Total	**3,600**	**100**

Standard regions

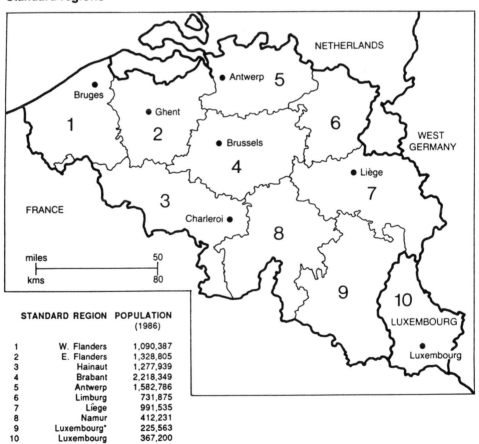

STANDARD REGION		POPULATION (1986)
1	W. Flanders	1,090,387
2	E. Flanders	1,328,805
3	Hainaut	1,277,939
4	Brabant	2,218,349
5	Antwerp	1,582,786
6	Limburg	731,875
7	Lïege	991,535
8	Namur	412,231
9	Luxembourg*	225,563
10	Luxembourg	367,200

* Province of Belgium

Source: Euromonitor.

The Flanders Investment Opportunities Council (FIOC) in Brussels administers all Flemish programs. It provides grants, tax breaks, and assistance in finding partners and suppliers. Flemish emphasis is on high-technology projects and personnel development. Because Flanders has no raw materials, it looks to an educated population as its major resource, and commits 20 percent of its total budget to schooling.

Brussels, host to the European Commission and headquarters of NATO, makes an excellent location for those who want to be near the pulse of 1992 activity. More than 1,000 U.S. subsidiaries operate in Brussels.[6] Although Brussels does not have incentive programs of its own, the Brussels Regional Ministry handles the general Belgian programs.

Wallonia, the southern French-speaking region of Belgium, has traditionally been the home of heavy industry like iron and steel. To diversify from smokestack to silicon chip industries, the region offers several programs to attract new technology ventures. The Regional Company for Investments in Wallonia (SRIW) acts as an agent to raise venture capital and provides advice for new business ventures and other types of financing. Many parts of Wallonia qualify for European Regional Development Fund monies.

Other Facts About Belgium

- The currency is the Belgian franc, worth approximately 2.8 cents.*

- The combination of Germanic and Latin culture in Belgium makes it an excellent European test market.

- Belgian infrastructure is well regarded. Antwerp is the third-largest seaport in the world; the Belgian railway system has the densest network in the world; its motorways are considered outstanding; and Brussels airport claims to have the fastest air cargo handling and distribution center in the EC.

- Belgium derives 80 percent of its GNP from exports, the highest percentage of any industrialized country.[7]

- Companies with one hundred employees or more must set up worker councils as a means of facilitating communication between labor and management. Termination of employees often requires compensation of four months' pay. Contact the Ministry of Economic Affairs for details.

*All currency equivalents in this directory are as of March 1990.

Denmark

Consulate General of Denmark
Commercial Counsellor
825 Third Avenue, 32nd floor
New York, N.Y. 10022
Phone: 212/223-4545
Fax: 212/754-1904

Location advantages:	Close ties to Scandinavian countries, educated work force, strong language skills.
Location disadvantages:	Stringent regulatory controls, especially in the areas of labor and consumer and environmental protection.

Scandinavian roots combined with a European future best describe Denmark. It keeps its feet in the Community but its heart in the Nordic country. Denmark is an excellent location from which to service all of northern Europe while still maintaining access to the rest of Europe.

Historically, Denmark has not promoted FDI because Danish business was concerned over increased competition. However, during the 1980s, both business and government came to realize that FDI benefits all Danes. A revamped program begun in 1989 targeted investment in telecommunications, information technology, and food processing.

Denmark has few regions of high unemployment; consequently, not many relocation incentives are offered. In designated regional development areas, some programs are available. Assistance includes grants for financing the initial cost of establishment, and subsidies for retraining employees.

Investment grants of up to 35 percent are available for manufacturing equipment. Local government authorities in regional development areas may erect industrial buildings for leasing or sale to industrial firms. Special loans are available in these areas to cover up to 75 percent of construction costs. Special financial incentives are available for shipbuilding. Certain Danish grants contain a clause stating that if a project is successful, the grant may become repayable. Contact the Directorate of Regional Development for more information.

The Danish Ministry of Labor organizes training courses for unskilled workers engaged in new occupations. Training courses are typically divided into three phases, with the government paying for the course and for workers' wages during the first two phases, and partially subsidizing the last phase.

Marketing regions

DENMARK

	Households ('000s)	%
1	600	27
2	700	32
3	900	41
Total	2,200	100

Standard regions

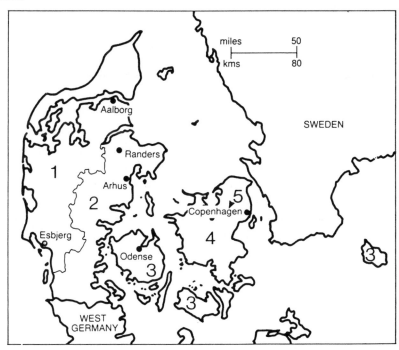

STANDARD REGION	POPULATION (1986)
1	N/W Jutland	1,194,528
2	S/SE Jutland	1,162,435
3	Fyn, Lølland, Bornholm	759,751*
4	Sjaelland	492,202
5	København	1,547,357

*(incl. part of Sjaelland Island)

Source: Euromonitor.

Other Facts About Denmark

- The currency is the Danish krone, worth approximately 15 cents.

- Denmark has stringent environmental and labor laws. Legislation sets the maximum weekly hours a business can be open, places restrictions on the number of hours it can be open on specific days, and forbids opening on Sundays and public holidays. These laws are in the process of being changed, so check with the Embassy for the most current information.

- Patents are granted for a period of twenty years starting from the date of application for registration. Denmark has not ratified the European Patent Convention.

- Only 1,000 people in Denmark earn over $130,000 a year. Those making $30,000 a year or more are considered wealthy.[8]

- Denmark has the highest per capita spending on education of any EC country.

- Two autonomous regions, Greenland and the Faroe Islands, enjoy a special relationship with Denmark. Although Greenland was granted EC status with Denmark's membership, it opted out because of a dispute over EC fishing quotas. Greenland is associated with the EC through the Overseas Lands and Territories (OLT) Agreement which also applies to other countries. The Faroes, a former European Free Trade Association (EFTA) member, enjoys rights in the EC similar to those enjoyed by Sweden and Norway.

- Denmark is still a member of the Nordic Council, which brings it together with Norway, Sweden, Finland, and Iceland to discuss areas of common concern. The region entitles its citizens to take up residence and work in any of the Nordic countries.

- Danish commitment to health and human welfare is strong. Roughly $2,400 per capita a year is invested in social and medical programs.[9]

France

French Industrial Development Agency (FIDA)
610 Fifth Avenue, Suite 301
New York, N.Y. 10020
Phone: 212/757-9340
Fax: 212/245-1568

FIDA is the U.S. representative for the government agency Délégation à l'Aménagement du Territoire et à l'Action Régionale (DATAR).

Marketing regions

FRANCE

	Households (millions)	%
1	3.9	20
2	2.3	12
3	1.8	9
4	1.6	8
5	2.0	10
6	1.8	9
7	1.9	10
8	2.4	13
9	1.8	9
Total	19.5	100

Standard regions

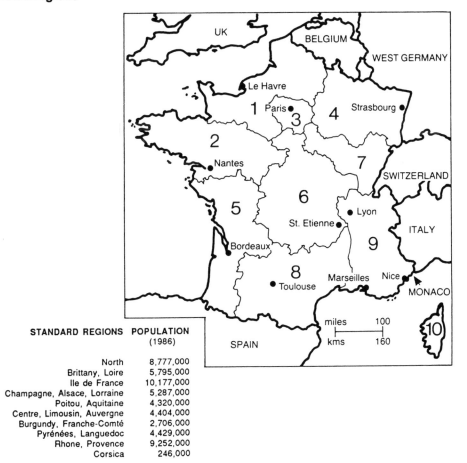

	STANDARD REGIONS	POPULATION (1986)
1	North	8,777,000
2	Brittany, Loire	5,795,000
3	Ile de France	10,177,000
4	Champagne, Alsace, Lorraine	5,287,000
5	Poitou, Aquitaine	4,320,000
6	Centre, Limousin, Auvergne	4,404,000
7	Burgundy, Franche-Comté	2,706,000
8	Pyrénées, Languedoc	4,429,000
9	Rhone, Provence	9,252,000
10	Corsica	246,000

Source: Euromonitor.

FIDA also has offices in Chicago (*phone:* 312/661-1640), Los Angeles (*phone:* 213/879-0352), and Houston (*phone:* 713/526-1565).

Location advantages:	Situation in the middle of Western Europe, modern transportation infrastructure, large internal market (55 million).
Location disadvantages:	An often difficult bureaucracy, stiff labor laws.

The disappointing results of the French socialist programs of the early 1980s prompted a capitalist revival in French society. Business is booming and France's 1992 cheerleading has greatly enhanced the internal market's chances for success.

French efforts to attract FDI are quite organized. DATAR provides companies with business information on France, site selection studies, financial and fiscal incentives, and information on French business partners.

Grants of up to 25 percent of an investment are available for land, buildings, and equipment purchases during the first three years of operation. Eligibility criteria include:

- The investment must be in certain specified areas of France only.
- A minimum of twenty jobs must be created within three years.
- A minimum of $3 million is required.

A joint French-EC program for the northeastern part of France provides grants of up to 37.5 percent of an investment

Local subsidies and job training grants are available; contact local authorities for details. On the national level, tax credits for training and R&D investments are also available

Three special enterprise zones—Dunkirk, La Ciotat, and La Seyne— provide ten-year tax exemptions (certain restrictions apply) if a company sets up operations there.

Other Facts About France

- The currency is the French franc, worth approximately 17 cents.
- Certain acquisitions in France require prior declaration to the French Treasury Department. Check with FIDA for more details.
- France has one of the most digitized telecommunications networks in the world.
- Close to 70 percent of France's energy comes from nuclear power.
- A business permit is required of any non-EC national appointed as manager or officer of a French subsidiary of a foreign-based company. Contact your nearest French Consulate for more information.

• Sales distributorship contracts cannot include the following: non-competition clause, price fixing clause, exclusive territorial clause.

• Employee rights are governed by the French Labor Code. Depending on the number of employees in a company, one of three types of workers' councils must be established in your organization. Labor is entitled to certain rights of information and has the right to approve of certain changes in working conditions. These groups serve as a means of communicating formally with management. Contact FIDA for more details. But if the European Company Statute is passed, and a company elects to incorporate under that law, it would supersede member state labor laws.

• Until 1986, France relied heavily on price controls to fight inflation. The December 1986 ordinance eliminating this policy has let the market freely determine prices. Besides Community price controls on agricultural products, steel, and coal, France still has some form of price controls on a few health, energy, and transportation products and services.

• Nine free trade zones in France grant special duty waivers and fast customs service.

Greece

Embassy of Greece
Office of the Economic Counselor
1636 Connecticut Avenue, N.W.
Washington, D.C. 20009
Phone: 202/745-7100
Fax: 202/265-4291

Location advantages:	Good ports, low wages, warm weather.
Location disadvantages:	Poor infrastructure, unskilled labor.

At the crossroads of three continents, laced with bountiful harbors and secure waterways, Greece has been home to shipping interests that have thrived throughout the centuries. Combined with a sun-drenched climate, an assortment of classic islands, and a heritage second to none in the world, Greece makes an interesting location for many companies.

The Ministry of National Economy runs many of the Greek programs. They are administered locally by the Departments of Regional Development (DRD). Contact the Greek Embassy in New York for details on all programs.

Incentives are available for so-called productive investments, which are defined rather liberally and apply to most manufacturing and services

Marketing regions

GREECE

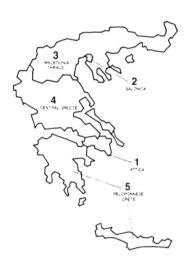

	Households ('000s)	%
1	1,050	37
2	220	8
3	550	19
4	550	19
5	470	17
Total	2,840	100

Standard regions

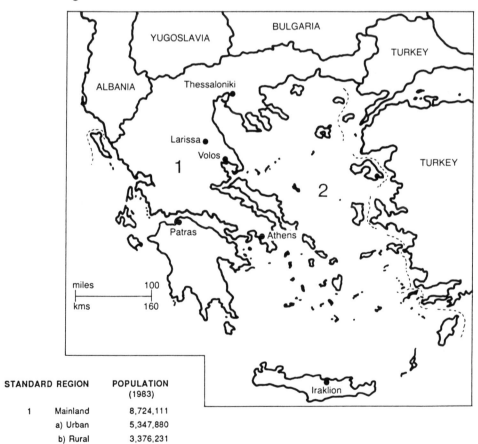

STANDARD REGION		POPULATION (1983)
1	Mainland	8,724,111
	a) Urban	5,347,880
	b) Rural	3,376,231
2	Islands	1,122,154

Source: Euromonitor.

sectors, including tourist projects. Program offerings include grants, reduced tax rates, interest subsidies, tax allowances, and increased depreciation rates. The country is divided into four areas, and incentives are based on a rising scale from Area A to Area D. Certain depressed areas, designated as special zones, offer even more generous perks. Special programs are offered for high-technology sectors, shipping, and biotechnology.

Greek industrial estates (VI. PE.) are industrial parks, fully equipped with infrastructure to support manufacturing, ship building, and the processing and storage of agricultural products. They are located in four areas of the country. Incentives include price breaks on land, fewer permit requirements, and financial assistance.

The Hellenic Business Development and Investment Company S.A. (HBDIC) is a corporation established by the Greek Ministry of National Economy with General Dynamics, General Electric, and Westinghouse. Its goal is to promote Greek business activity and improve exports. The company participates in business development projects and can act as an agent to secure other partners, including financing.

Other Facts About Greece

- The currency is the Greek drachma, worth approximately .61 cents.

- Certain restrictions on imported capital and repatriation of profits exist in Greece. The laws are complex and are in the process of being liberalized, so contact the Greek authorities for the latest information.

- When Greece was admitted to the EC in 1981, a transitional schedule to harmonize tariffs, duties, and VAT with general Community policies was devised. That process for the most part was completed in 1988. A phaseout of subsidizing exports to the EC was completed by 1990 and is scheduled to be completed for exports to non-EC countries by 1992.

- Greek labor laws provide workers with certain protections regarding health, safety, and termination. Many of the laws are being harmonized with Community legislation. Contact the Ministry of Labor for more information.

- Greek participation in the Community-sponsored Integrated Mediterranean Programmes (IMP) has resulted in substantial funding to improve Greek infrastructure. Projects to modernize motorways, airports, public transportation, energy production, and other basic public services are in the works.

- Although agriculture plays a lesser role in the Greek economy today than it did ten years ago, it still constitutes 17 percent of the country's GNP. Manufacturing is considered Greece's secondary sector and tourism its tertiary sector.

• Greek shipping is a major source of foreign currency earnings.

• Although exports to Arab states once represented more than 10 percent of all Greek exports (mostly food and construction materials), sagging oil prices and an oversupply of building materials have caused a decline in the importance of shipments to these countries.

• The Hellenic Industrial Development Bank (ETBA) has undertaken several large-scale projects to improve Greek capability in raw material production, ship building, and energy utilization.

Ireland

Industrial Development Authority of Ireland (IDA)
Two Grand Central Tower
140 East 45th Street
New York, N.Y. 10017
Phone: 212/972-1000
Fax: 212/687-8739

IDA also has offices in Atlanta (*phone:* 404/351-8474), Boston (*phone:* 617/367-8225), Chicago (*phone:* 312/644-7474), Cleveland (*phone:* 216/991-6055), Houston (*phone:* 713/965-0292), Los Angeles (*phone:* 213/829-0081), and Menlo Park, California (*phone:* 415/854-1800).

Location Advantages:	Cost-effective, an educated and young English-speaking work force, low-cost office rents, low corporate tax rate.
Location Disadvantages:	Weak infrastructure relative to other northern European countries.

Although Ireland is one of the poorest northern European countries, it has a surprising amount of high-tech capability and is committed to attracting software and other information technology companies.

The IDA provides assistance with site selection, manpower, and legal formalities, and offers help even after you have settled in. Government incentives include:

• Training grants of up to 100 percent
• Employment grants
• Equipment grants of up to 60 percent in development areas
• Rent subsidies and rent-free periods
• Low-cost financing

Certain grants are subject to performance criteria, and others may become repayable if the project is commercially successful.

Marketing regions

IRELAND

	Households ('000s)	%
1	455	52
2	251	29
3	106	12
4	58	7
Total	870	100

Standard regions

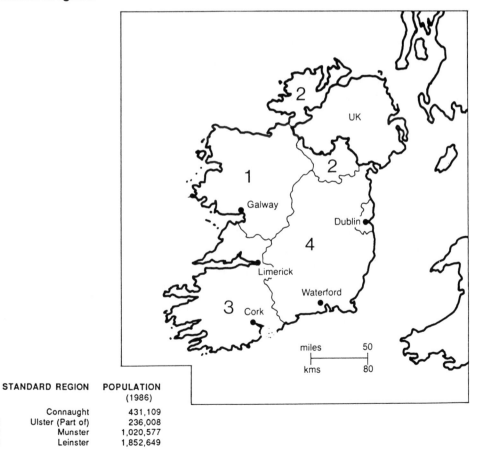

STANDARD REGION		POPULATION (1986)
1	Connaught	431,109
2	Ulster (Part of)	236,008
3	Munster	1,020,577
4	Leinster	1,852,649

Source: Euromonitor.

A very attractive feature of Ireland is its 10 percent corporate tax rate on manufacturing profits, established by the 1980 Finance Act; the law remains in force until the year 2,000. Each year, the definition of manufacturing profits becomes more liberal, so check with IDA, even if you're in a service business. In addition, a 75 percent depreciation allowance is granted for certain assets.

Ireland is very interested in attracting software companies. Lotus, Microsoft, and Micropro all operate in Ireland, as do IBM, DEC, and Motorola. One reason high-tech companies prefer Ireland is its educated work force, which on average costs less than comparable workers in other northern European countries. A 1988 survey of new investments by U.S. information technology companies in Europe revealed that Ireland received seventeen of thirty-two such investments.[10]

To attract service businesses to Ireland, the government has created a number of attractive business parks in close proximity to airports, housing, and schools. Contact the IDA for more information.

Other Facts About Ireland

- The currency is the Irish pound, worth approximately $1.56.

- Because Ireland was late in developing its telecommunications system, it now has one of the most advanced telecommunications systems in Europe, with over 60 percent of its trunk-switching exchanges being digital.

- More than 350 U.S. companies operate in Ireland.

- Ireland's work force is young and eager to work. The nation's 1988 unemployment rate was 18 percent. People between the ages of 14 and 45 constitute 39 percent of the population.[11]

- The International Financial Services Centre in Dublin is one of the world's fastest-growing currency dealing centers.

- In late 1989, about $5 billion was pledged to improve Ireland's infrastructure during the 1989–1993 period. The EC is funding about one-third, the Irish government 40 percent, and the private sector the rest.

- Dublin is the only West European capital without a direct transatlantic air connection.

Italy

Italian Trade Commission (ITC)
499 Park Avenue
New York, N.Y. 10022
Phone: 212/980-1500
Fax: 212/758-1050

Location advantages:	Low wages, large market, strong design skills.
Location disadvantages:	Poor infrastructure, rapid government turnover.

Italy's ability to carry on despite almost yearly governmental changes is indicative of the character of the people. For those patient enough to wait for her trains, Italy harbors many surprises and riches, including a largely untapped market and the EC's highest savings rate (23 percent).

Italian incentives are divided by regions, with the poorest southern region offering the most. A combination of cash grants, subsidies, tax breaks, and loans is offered. The Istituto per l'Assistenza allo Sviluppo del Mezzogiorno (IASM), located in Rome, manages the development packages for southern Italy (Mezzogiorno) and the islands of Sardinia, Elba, and Sicily. The current program runs until 1993 and is offered for a wide range of activities including agriculture and services; check with ITC for specific sector exemptions.

Cash grants of up to 40 percent of costs (up to 7 billion Lit.) for construction, reactivation, expansion, modernization, reorganization, or conversion of plants in the Mezzogiorno region are available. A ten-year corporate income tax exemption is available to new businesses in the region, in addition to several other tax breaks. Mezzogiorno also offers special programs for young entrepreneurs aged 18 to 29 who live in the region.

Exemptions and rebates on social security charges and training subsidies are available in many parts of the country, but are more prevalent in the south.

Other Facts About Italy

- The Italian currency is the lira (plural, lire) and is usually abbreviated as Lit; 1,000 lire are worth approximately 79 cents.

- Even though Italy has gone through numerous changes in government, the Christian Democrats have had a plurality in all general elections since 1945.

- There are some restrictions on repatriation of capital, depending on the type of investment (productive or nonproductive) governed by Law 43. The transfer is subject to proof that all taxes due have been paid.

Marketing regions

ITALY

	Households (millions)	%
1	5.4	30
2	3.4	19
3	4.0	22
4	4.9	27
Sardinia	0.4	2
Total	18.0	100

Standard regions

	STANDARD REGION	POPULATION (1988)
1	Valle d'Aosta, Piedmont, Liguria	6,296,819
2	Lombardy	8,925,794
3	Friuli, Veneto, Trentino	6,503,368
4	Romagna	3,952,716
5	Marche, Umbria, Toscana	5,881,466
6	Lazio	5,144,370
7	Abruzzi and Molise	1,597,073
8	Campagna	5,721,847
9	Calabria, Basilicata, Puglia	6,853,175
10	Sicily, Sardinia	6,793,159

Source: Euromonitor.

- The Istituto Mobiliare Italiano (IMI) is a government-owned medium-term credit agency set up mainly for foreign investors. Contact ITC for more information.

- Although no formal employee representation is required in Italy, many companies set up workers' committees (consiglio di fabbrica) to serve as a communication channel between workers and management.

- Italy requires employers to pay workers a semiannual cost of living allowance, a Christmas bonus (also called a "thirteenth" month's salary), and, in many cases, an additional sum called a "fourteenth" month's salary, payable in the summer.

- Price controls are in force for such basic goods as sugar, bread, oil, and pharmaceuticals. They are overseen by the Comitato Interministeriale Prezzi (CIP).

- Pharmaceutical patents are not recognized in Italy.

- Each Italian province has its own Chamber of Commerce. Chambers keep an official register of business enterprises and collect data on local economic activity. There are many business associations throughout Italy; one that many companies belong to is the Confindustria, which serves industry as a communication vehicle with trade unions and public authorities.

- There are several free trade zones in Italy where foreign goods may be introduced without paying customs duties. Contact ITC for details.

Luxembourg

Luxembourg Board of Economic Development
801 2nd Avenue
New York, N.Y. 10017
Phone: 212/370-9850
[*See Belgium for map of Luxembourg.*]

The board also has an office in San Francisco (*phone:* 415/788-0816).

Location advantages:	Good labor relations, liberal corporate structure laws, low VAT rates. Central to all of Europe and near EC decision-making bodies.
Location disadvantages:	The only EC country without a coastline.

Although Luxembourg is the smallest EC member, it is considered an international financial center and is host to several EC institutions. Because of its size, Luxembourg is able to offer personalized service and support for your operations within the Grand Duchy.

The Economic Development Board offers a variety of programs including:

- Building and land at favorable terms for immediate occupancy
- Credit facilities: The state-owned National Credit and Investment Company (SNCI) finances investment and exports from Luxembourg
- Direct financial grants of up to 25 percent for building, equipment, and worker training
- Tax reductions—a 25 percent tax holiday for first eight years of operations, a 14 percent investment tax credit

Other Facts About Luxembourg

- The currency is the Luxembourg franc, worth approximately 2.8 cents.

- Because of its liberal corporate structure laws, more than 6,000 holding companies are based in Luxembourg.

- No restrictions exist on capital and profit transfers out of Luxembourg.

- Confidential banking services in Luxembourg rival Swiss offerings. Over 100 foreign banks operate in the country.

- To attract FDI, Luxembourg has built fully equipped industrial parks ready for occupancy at subsidized rates.

- There hasn't been a strike in Luxembourg for more than sixty years.

- Luxembourg has the lowest VAT rates in the EC.

- Goodyear Tire Corporation is the second-largest industrial employer in Luxembourg.

The Netherlands

Office of the Netherlands Foreign Investment Agency (NFIA)
One Rockefeller Plaza
New York, N.Y. 10020
Phone: 212/246-1434
Fax: 212/246-9769

NFIA also has offices in Los Angeles (*phone:* 213/477-8288) and San Francisco (*phone:* 415/981-1468).

Location advantages:	Excellent port facilities and liberal customs procedures, strong technical and language skills in the work force, liberal corporate structuring.
Location disadvantages:	High corporate tax rate due to heavy social costs.

Marketing regions

THE NETHERLANDS

	Households (millions)	%
1	1.0	19
2	1.5	28
3	0.6	11
4	1.0	19
5	1.2	23
Total	5.3	100

Standard regions

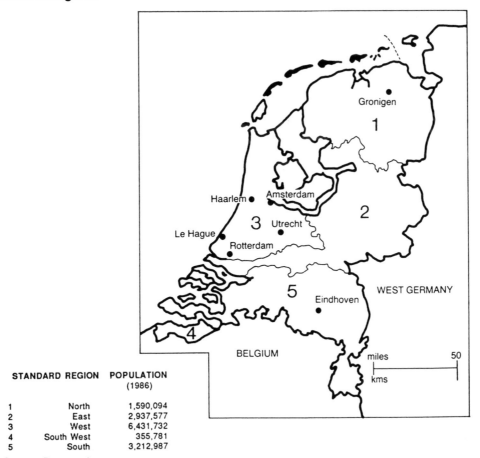

STANDARD REGION		POPULATION (1986)
1	North	1,590,094
2	East	2,937,577
3	West	6,431,732
4	South West	355,781
5	South	3,212,987

Source: Euromonitor.

Throughout their history, the Dutch have been known as Europe's traders principally because their country was blessed with fabulous harbors. Today, nearly half of all cargo unloaded in Holland is destined for other countries, testifying to its claim of being the gateway to Europe.[12]

NFIA, Holland's FDI agency, assists companies in initiating investments or expanding their activities in Europe via the Netherlands. NFIA specializes in high-technology industries like biotechnology, information technology, and medical equipment.

NFIA has helped more than 260 North American companies with their Dutch investments.[13] Services include cost analyses and advice on site selection, marketing, and strategy. NFIA also assists in finding joint venture partners, suppliers, venture capital, bank financing, and with introductions to key Dutch government officials. Dutch government incentives include:

- *Investment Premium Regulation Regional Projects (IPR)*. Cash grants of 25 percent to 90 percent of costs for new building and equipment (excluding land); of up to Dfl (Dutch florins) 18 million for projects in "stimulus-areas."
- *Premium Regulation Development Lelystad (PSOL)*. Cash grants of up to Dfl 30,000 per employee to a maximum of 25 percent of investments for those locating in Lelystad. Some caveats apply; consult NFIA for details.
- *Youth Development Scheme (JOB)*. Provides a subsidy of 33 percent of the minimum wage (including social premium) for a maximum of twelve months. Applies only to youths under age 25 who have been unemployed for at least two years. Up to 10 percent of the work force can participate. The government also offers several training subsidies for youth, the disabled, and dislocated workers.
- *Measure to Support Placement of Employee (MOA)*. Pays a maximum of Dfl 1,000 per month for a six-month period for people hired who have been unemployed for at least a year. Contact the Local Employment Exchange or NFIA

Other Facts About the Netherlands

- The currency is the Dutch guilder, worth approximately 52 cents.
- The Netherlands received $14.2 billion of U.S. FDI in 1987, making it the third-most popular EC country for U.S. investment.[14]
- Rotterdam is the world's busiest harbor.
- The Dutch Silicon Triangle, covering the tri-city area of Eindhoven, Den Bosch, and Nijmegen, is composed of a mixture of Dutch, European, and American firms.

- The Dutch have the second-highest venture capital pool in Europe, exceeding $1 billion.[15] Call NFIA for contacts.

- A Dutch 1992 hot line (called Euro-lijn) has been established to keep local firms abreast of developments.

Portugal

Economic Counsellor
Embassy of Portugal
2125 Kalorama Road, N.W.
Washington, D.C. 20008
Phone: 202/332-3007

The Embassy of Portugal can put you in touch with the Foreign Investment Institute in Lisbon.

Location advantages: Low labor costs, great location incentives.
Location disadvantages: Weak infrastructure, low labor skills.

Since joining the Community in 1986, Portugal's economy has grown 4.9 percent, well ahead of the OECD average of 3.4 percent.[16]

As a response to joining the EC, Portugal in 1988 created three very liberal incentive programs:

1. *SIBR (System of Regional Based Incentives):* Designed to stimulate industrial activity in less-favored regions, SIBR offers cash grants of up to 65 percent per project. The grant is determined by two components: regional location (accounting for 5 to 40 percent of the qualifying expenditure, there being three zones with varying percentages), and job creation potential, under which, depending on the regional zone, a grant could pay from Esc. 200,000 to Esc. 400,000 per job. The number of jobs forecast must be filled within two years of completion of the investment. All tangible fixed assets are eligible, with the exception of land and buildings not directly related to the productive process or to essential administrative activities. To qualify, companies must be financially stable, have technical and managerial skills, and be committed to the investment for a minimum of four years. Contact Instituto de Apoio às Pequenas e Médias Empresas e ao Investimento (IAPMEI) for more details.

2. *SIFIT (System of Incentives for Investment in Tourism):* Designed to encourage investment in tourism projects and to stimulate a balanced regional development. Cash grants of up to Esc. 220 million or 60 percent of the project cost, whichever is less, are available. The amount is determined by location and the number of jobs created. Expenditures on

Marketing regions

PORTUGAL

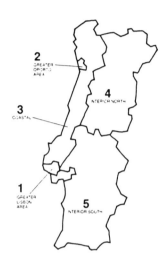

	Households ('000s)	%
1	700	20
2	300	9
3	1,200	35
4	600	18
5	600	18
Total	3,400	100

Standard regions

	STANDARD REGION	POPULATION (1986)
1	Braganca, Vila Real, Braga, Viana do Castelo	1,479,100
2	Guarda, Viseu, Coimbra, Aveiro, Porto	3,387,500
3	Castelo Branco, Leiria, Santarem, Portalegre	1,260,600
4	Setubal, Evora	936,600
5	Beja, Faro	519,100
6	Lisbon	2,124,100
7	Madeira/Azores	523,000

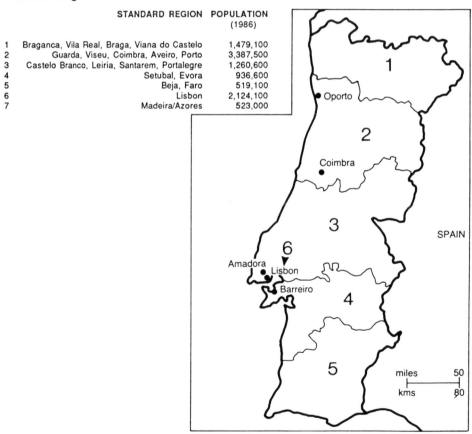

Source: Euromonitor.

buildings, equipment, and infrastructures that contribute to attracting tourists and are used mainly by tourists qualify. Applications should be sent to the Tourism Fund:

Fundo de Turismo
Av. António Augusto de Aguiar, 122—10.0 e 11.0
1000 Lisboa
Telephone: 55 43 56

3. *SIPE (System of Incentives for the Development of Local Potential):* These incentives assist balanced regional development by stimulating local potential in small and medium-size enterprises. Cash grants are available for up to 70 percent of project cost (maximum, Esc. 15 million) for businesses located in most areas. For Lisbon and Oporto the rate is 50 percent. SIPE grants can be used for such things as sectoral studies to identify development potential, technical/economic/financial viability studies, and investment studies. Economic sectors qualifying for SIPE grants include extractive industries, manufacturing, the hotel and restaurant business, car and other vehicle rental activities, travel agents, and transportation. Contact IAPMEI for more information.

Other incentives include:

• *Investment Tax Credits.* Credit against the Industrial Tax liability. The rate is 4 percent and applicable against tax payable on profits for the year in which the equipment enters into use, but it cannot exceed 90 percent of the Industrial Tax liability. Not all assets are eligible; land, cars, and certain other asset catagories are excluded. Tax credits can be carried forward for five years, after which they expire. The incentive cannot be claimed if a similar incentive is being obtained under other legislation.

• *Deductions for Reinvestment of Retained Earnings.* Profits retained in the company or transferred to reserves and reinvested in the company within the subsequent three years can be deducted from the taxable profit during the three years immediately after conclusion of the investment.

• *Job Creation Incentives.* Portugal offers a two-year exemption from social security payments (24.5 percent of employee wages) for employees hired between the ages of 16 and 30. Training subsidies of up to 75 percent are also available. Contact The Employment and Vocational Training Institute (IEFP) for details.

Other Facts About Portugal

• The currency is the escudo, worth approximately .65 cents.
• A special five-year program called Specific Program for the Development of Portuguese Industry (PEDIP) was established by the Commu-

nity to modernize Portuguese industry. Approximately $600 million a year is scheduled to be spent from 1988 to 1992. Coupled with the European Structural Funds, Portugal will receive about $500 million a year from the Community for the 1988–1992 period.

• European Structural Funds have propelled Portugal into the modern age. Having replaced the rickety *Foguete,* the luxurious intercity Alfa train now takes passengers from Lisbon to Oporto. A series of locks enables goods to move more easily from Oporto to the Spanish border, and substantial improvements in motorways, dams, sewers, and farm irrigation have made life easier in areas that until recently were still in the nineteenth century.

• The 1975 Portuguese revolution resulted in the nationalization of virtually all domestic banks and 53 percent of all gross investment. Although a 1976 law permits the state to sell only 49 percent of any state-owned enterprise, a six-year privatization program began in 1989.[18]

• Before Portugal and Spain joined the EC, links between the two countries were minimal. Now highway coordination and other integrated infrastructure projects are moving ahead with speed.

• Nearly $700 million in FDI flooded into Portugal in 1988, an all-time record, and more in one year than the total FDI in Portugal over the previous fifty years.[19]

Spain

Embassy of Spain
Investment Office
405 Lexington Avenue, 44th floor
New York, N.Y. 10174–0331
Phone: 212/661-4959
Fax: 212/972-2494

Location advantages:	Low wages, high growth market, the California of the new Europe.
Location disadvantages:	Low-skilled labor, poor infrastructure.

Spain is alive and vibrant, her people enthusiastic, finally free to express themselves and develop after so many years of confinement and caution. Industrial enthusiasm for post-Franco Spain has resulted in a flood of FDI into the country. Nearly twice as much entered Spain in 1987 as in 1986, close to $5 billion. FDI, however, is subject to a series of formalities. Most investments must be registered at the Investment Register of the Ministry of the Economy. Foreign participation of up to 50 percent in a company's capital is permitted without government approval, but

Marketing regions

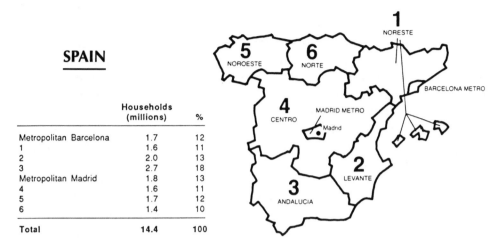

SPAIN

	Households (millions)	%
Metropolitan Barcelona	1.7	12
1	1.6	11
2	2.0	13
3	2.7	18
Metropolitan Madrid	1.8	13
4	1.6	11
5	1.7	12
6	1.4	10
Total	**14.4**	**100**

Standard regions

STANDARD REGION		POPULATION (1982)
1	Galicia	2,781,000
2	Asturias	1,140,000
3	Leon	1,013,000
4	Estremadura	953,000
5	Andalusia	6,153,000
6	New Castille	6,223,000
7	Old Castille	2,118,000
8	Basque, Navarra	2,797,000
9	Aragon	1,161,000
10	Catalonia	6,295,000
11	Valencia	3,761,000
12	Murcia	1,240,000

Source: Euromonitor.

acquisitions over 50 percent must be approved by the Directorate General of Foreign Transactions (DGTE). Further, foreign investors are restricted from the defense, gambling, television, radio, and air transport sectors.

Two major reasons for the increase in FDI are that companies want to exploit Spain's favorable wage conditions and to tap into the EC's fastest-growing market. Wages on average are a third lower than in West Germany, though some experts expect this cost advantage to disappear gradually as the internal market is completed. The combination of low wages and a high-growth market have made scale-intensive ventures like automotive and electronics production quite popular. Spain is the world's seventh-largest auto producer outside North America.[20]

An intriguing consequence of the opening up of Eastern Europe is Spanish concern that the interest other EC countries, especially West Germany, have shown in Spain will be diverted East. Should this prove true, the effect may be countered by Japanese interest; the *International Herald Tribune* claims that Spain's Catalonia region is Japan's most favored investment spot in Europe. Japanese companies have created more than 19,000 jobs in the area over the last few years.[21]

Spain joined the EC only in 1986, and its entry into the Community is being eased by several transitional programs (1986–1992). Custom duties on products imported from EC countries into Spain are being phased out over the period, and tariffs placed on non-EC imports will be harmonized with the Community over the same time frame. Current restrictions also apply to certain services and special products. Check with the Investment Office in New York for details.

Spain is divided politically and administratively into seventeen communities and each has its own incentive programs. Madrid and Barcelona are the most likely communities to examine first.

Spain's general programs are divided by region. There are four regional zones: Zones of Economic Promotion (underdeveloped areas), Zones of Economic Decline, Special Zones (areas experiencing unusual difficulties), and Zones of Urgent Reindustrialization (areas where certain declining industries must be revived).

Certain zones offer investment grants of up to 75 percent of an eligible project. Aid includes direct subsidies, loans, and tax breaks. In addition, the government offers several specialized programs for projects run by small and medium-size firms that generate new jobs.

Spanish sector priorities include mining, processing of ores, natural gas, raw materials for pharmaceutical use, electronics, information technology, autos, and technical inspection of motor vehicles. Several preferential incentives are available for these industries.

The National Employment Institute of the Ministry of Labor and Social Security offers several training programs, including flexible and subsidized employment contracts and tax rebates for job creation.

Other incentives include investment tax credits, job creation tax credits, energy-related incentives, and subsidies for environmental projects.

Other Facts About Spain

▪ The currency is the Spanish peseta, worth approximately .9 cents.

▪ The Fashion Design Promotion Center promotes Spanish fashion designers and companies. It sponsors shows and assists research in new manufacturing techniques.

▪ Spain is one of the more active EC countries in trade with North Africa, the Arab world, and Latin America.

▪ Although Spain has rigid employment contracts that make layoffs difficult, new legislation allowing companies to hire up to 50 percent of its work force on a flexible basis enables firms to make employment adjustments when necessary.

▪ About 25 percent of the products sold in Spain are subject to some degree of price control. Such products as basic food items, pharmaceuticals, transport, telecommunications, and fuel are overseen by the Higher Price Council.

▪ There are free trade zones within Spain where products are exempt from duties and tariffs, VAT, and some regulatory requirements.

▪ Spain's percentage of workers belonging to unions is the second lowest (27.2 percent) in the EC.[22]

▪ Spain's telecommunications company, Telefónica, though lagging behind most of its European counterparts, has committed 7.1 trillion pesetas (through 1992) to improving Spain's system.[23]

The United Kingdom

Invest in Britain Bureau (IBB)
British Consulate General
845 Third Avenue, 11th floor
New York, N.Y. 10022
Phone: 212/593-2258

IBB also has offices in Atlanta, Boston, Chicago, Cleveland, Dallas, Houston, Los Angeles, San Francisco, Seattle, and Washington, D.C. Contact IBB via the British Embassy or Consulate General in these cities.

Location advantages:	Language and cultural similarities, positive historical track record of U.S. investment, strong political ties,

Marketing regions

	Households (millions)	%
1	4.3	22
2	1.2	6
3	1.5	8
4	2.0	10
5	2.9	15
6	2.7	14
7	2.1	11
8	1.0	5
9	1.8	9
Total	**19.5**	**100**

THE UNITED KINGDOM

Standard regions

	STANDARD REGION	POPULATION (1985)
1	North	2,601,300
2	Yorks, Humberside	4,902,600
3	E. Midlands	3,350,800
4	E. Anglia	2,848,000
5	South East	16,854,600
6	South West	4,500,700
7	W. Midlands	5,183,000
8	North West	6,870,700
9	Wales	2,811,800
10	Scotland	5,136,509
11	N. Ireland	1,557,800
12	Isle of Man	55,482
13	Channel Isles	144,494

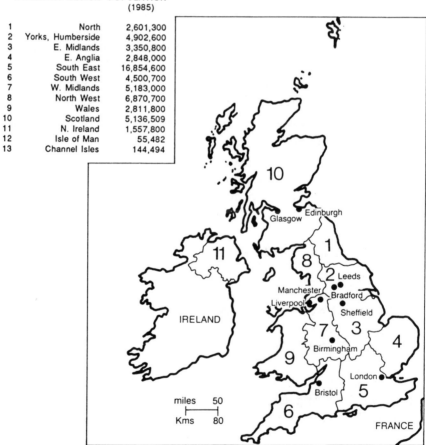

Source: Euromonitor.

	improving productivity rates, an internal market of approximately 58 million.
Location disadvantages:	Unsettled labor relations, cutbacks or elimination of subsidies in some sectors.

Britain is the Number 1 overseas location for American investors. Over 2,000 U.S. companies have invested in the United Kingdom, an investment which at close to $50 billion represents more than one-third of all U.S. investment in the EC.[24]

England is an ideal "first spot" location in Europe because it has the greatest comfort factor for Americans. Language plays a role not only in government negotiations but in labor, management, and community relations. When you send company executives overseas, you don't have to worry that the language will be a barrier for them or their families.

The historical and political relationship between Britain and the United States is another reason for the large U.S. investment in the United Kingdom. The United Kingdom's geographic position is also an advantage; it's easy to reach from the United States, and shipping to the continent is cost-effective—and with the Channel tunnel due to open in 1993, transportation will become even easier.

The Invest in Britain Bureau (IBB), representing England, Scotland, Wales, and Northern Ireland, is the main agency for helping overseas companies locate in Britain. IBB offers assistance and detailed advice on all aspects of investing and locating within the UK. It provides detailed statistics on each geographic region and advice on suppliers of anything from raw materials, parts and pieces, office supplies and equipment to banking and legal services. IBB arranges site location visits and sets up appointments with government personnel.

Finally, IBB assists in obtaining government grants and subsidies. The United Kingdom incentive programs include:

- Grants for capital investment
- Subsidized loans for fixed asset investment and working capital
- Relief from central and local taxation
- Loan and export guarantees
- Subsidized factory building
- Provision of development capital
- Job creation and consultancy advice

The United Kingdom government's Department of Trade and Industry (DTI) also offers a variety of export advice and general consulting services at reduced rates to companies exporting from the United Kingdom.

Industrial aid in the United Kingdom is administered on a quasi-federal basis, with different arrangements applying in England, Scotland,

Wales, and Northern Ireland. A rundown on the principal agencies and government bodies providing incentives follows.

The *Northern Ireland Development Agency* offers the best incentives in the United Kingdom because of the area's high unemployment level and its designation by the European Commission as a "least favored area."[25] These include:

- Up to 100 percent rent grants on factories for up to five years
- Up to 50 percent grants on selective machinery and equipment
- No property tax
- 40–50 percent R&D grants of up to £250,000 per project

Contact the Northern Ireland Development agency through your nearest IBB for more information.

The *Scottish Development Agency* offers many of the services IBB does. Contact:

Suite 810, One Landmark Square
Stamford, Conn. 06901
Phone: 1-800/THE-SCOT or 203/325-8525

The *nationalized coal and steel corporations* each have their own source of funds to help new industries provide jobs for "redundant" (laid off) coal and steel workers.

The *Manpower Services Commission*, responsible for training assistance, offers employee educational advice and provides training grants to upgrade worker skills.

A classification system designates general incentive categories and points to specific geographic locations that offer incentives:

- *Assisted areas* are those regions of the United Kingdom eligible to offer special programs to companies locating within them.
- *Development and intermediate areas* grant even greater incentives.
- *Regional selective assistance* is a discretionary grant for projects that would not proceed without the enhancement of these funds.
- *Enterprise zones*, of which there are twenty-five, grant local tax exemptions and simplified planning procedures in addition to all other United Kingdom programs.
- *Freeport zones*, of which there are six, are areas in which, for customs purposes, goods are treated as being outside the United Kingdom. This includes relief from value-added taxes on imported goods not leaving the "freeport." This program is currently under review.

Other Facts About the United Kingdom

- The currency is the English pound, worth approximately $1.60.
- The city telephone code for London changed as of May 1990 from 01 to either 071 (for inner London) or 081 (for outer London). The country code for the UK remains 44.
- Both Scotland and Northern Ireland have separate legal systems, distinct from that encompassing England and Wales.
- A high-density electronics area near Glasgow has been dubbed Silicon Glen. Such firms as IBM, HP, and Compaq have set up manufacturing facilities there.
- In 1989, inflation averaged 8.5 percent, unemployment 7.6 percent.
- Although labor has been less militant than in the early 1980s and earlier, it can still muster clout, as indicated by the one-day-a-week rail strikes in the summer of 1989.
- The Chunnel under the English Channel, due for completion in 1993, could make United Kingdom railways more prosperous. However, rights of way for new track from the English end of the Chunnel to London are being challenged by local groups.
- Population is approximately 58 million.
- The main urban areas are Greater London (6.8 million), Birmingham (1 million), Glasgow (.73 million), and Leeds (.71 million).

Northern England is industrial and is to the political left. Many there blame Margaret Thatcher for its serious economic decline. Southern England is more prosperous and conservative.

- While industry and retailing have embraced the metric system, many foods are still sold almost exclusively in imperial units.

West Germany

German-American Chamber of Commerce
666 Fifth Avenue
New York, N.Y. 10103
Phone: 212/974-8830
Fax: 212/974-8867

Most of the incentives offered by West Germany are handled by the individual states of the country. The German AMcham can provide you with an overview of West German programs, and the addresses of state offices in the United States are given below.

Marketing regions

WEST GERMANY

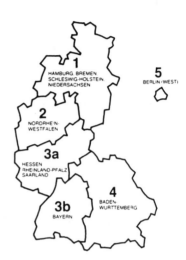

	Households (millions)	%
1	5.3	20
2	7.2	27
3a	3.3	12
3b	4.9	18
4	4.0	15
5	1.0	4
Total	26.3	100

Standard regions

	STANDARD REGION	POPULATION (1987)
1	Schleswig-Holstein	2,612,000
2	Hamburg	1,567,000
3	Bremen	654,000
4	Niedersachsen	7,189,000
5	Nordrhein-Westphalien	16,672,000
6	Hessen	5,552,000
7	Rheinland-Pfalz	3,606,000
8	Baden-Württemberg	9,350,000
9	Bayern	11,043,000
10	West Berlin	1,884,000
11	Saarland	1,041,000

Source: Euromonitor.

Location advantages:	Highly skilled work force, precision manufacturing expertise, largest domestic market in the EC, excellent infrastructure.
Location disadvantages:	High-cost labor and a rigid employee/management relationship called *mitbestimmung*

The German passion for precision, technical excellence, and science makes this country an outstanding location for critical research and development projects and for complex manufacturing.

After World War II, West Germany was divided into eleven *Länder* (similar to states in the United States) to avoid concentration of decision making; consequently, companies wanting to locate in Germany will find that each state (the singular form of *Länder* is *Land*) has its own programs and procedures. In 1969, a coordinating framework was instituted on the Federal level to coordinate each *Land* program, thus making business practices more uniform.

Federal Programs: Germany has abolished several grant programs, relying instead on tax incentives and a stable business environment to attract investment. This new philosophy should result in new tax laws in 1990.

Investment grants are available for specified regions. These areas include the Zonal Border Area (*Zonenrandgebiet,* a 40-kilometer-wide belt of territory along the borders with East Germany and Czechoslovakia) and several other regions throughout Germany called GA areas.

The Zonal Border Area qualifies for several incentives besides the investment grant. These include a freight-transport subsidy; a special depreciation allowance of up to 50 percent of the cost of plant and equipment; and up to 40 percent depreciation for buildings and land (in addition to the standard straight-line deduction).

Small business can qualify for an ERP regional soft loan (*Regionaldarlehen*). This is a project-based loan for companies that can't qualify for the investment grant.

State Programs: State programs vary, depending on the economic strength of the region and the types of industry it supports. Most will be able to give you advice on location, on finding partners and suppliers, and on personnel selection. A change in state government may affect incentive programs. Several states have offices in the United States:

Bavaria
Kallman Associates
5 Marple Court
Ridgewood, N.J. 07450
Phone: 201/652-7070

Berlin
Four Liberty Square, 3rd floor
Boston, Mass. 02109
Phone: 617/542-0158

Hamburg
Hagan and Company
283 Franklin Street, Suite 200
Boston, Mass. 02110
Phone: 617/542-5945
Fax: 617/338-4054

Niedersachsen
P.O. Box 7066
103 Carnegie Center
Princeton, N.J. 08540
Phone: 609/987-1202
Fax: 609/987-0092

Nordrhein-Westfalen
330 Eastover Road
Charlotte, N.C. 28207
Phone: 704/373-0774
Fax: 704/333-6446

Rheinland-Pfalz
30 E. 81 Street
New York, N.Y. 10028
Phone: 212/772-2267
Fax: 212/772-3692

Saarland
5139 South Royal Atlanta
Drive
Atlanta-Tucker, Ga. 30084
Phone: 404/493-4098

Here's a brief overview of what four of the states offer:

1. *Berlin:* The corporate tax rate here is 22½ percent lower than in the rest of Germany. Special subsidized investment financing (4½ percent) is available courtesy of the Marshall Plan. Also available: grants of up to 15 percent for plant and equipment, generous depreciation allowances, and a turnover bonus based on Berlin-added value, under which you can deduct up to 10 percent of sales from pretax profits.

2. *Hamburg:* The Hamburg Business Development Corporation (HWF) offers certain small firms limited office space free for six to twelve months.

3. *North Rhine-Westphalia:* This state offers special programs for many types of projects in steel-producing areas, for small businesses, and for projects that create new jobs. Training grants and subsidies for creating employment for certain disadvantaged workers and aid of up to 18 percent of capital expenditure for manufacturing projects are also available.

4. *Niedersachsen:* Several programs are offered for small business and high-technology projects. Tax-free investment grants are obtainable for establishing or expanding manufacturing in the region.

Other Facts About West Germany

• The currency is the deutsche mark (DM), worth approximately 59 cents.

• Unlike other European countries such as France or Great Britain, West Germany has no clearly definable commercial or industrial capital.

Rather, it has several major centers of business and industrial activity. Generally speaking, the Rhine-Ruhr region hosts the country's heavy industry. Frankfurt is known for banking, Berlin and Munich for electronics, Niedersachsen for automotive production, and Munich and Hamburg for insurance.

- The West German economy is the largest and strongest in Western Europe.

- The German system of codetermination (*mitbestimmung*), under which workers have direct representation on supervisory boards (*Aufsichstrat*, similar to a board of directors), applies only to publicly quoted companies with more than 2,000 employees. Smaller companies must implement a works council, elected by labor to represent its views to management on such issues as wages, working conditions, training, and disciplinary matters.

- Berlin is a great place in which to conduct East-West trade, as compared with Vienna or Scandinavia (the other hot East-West trade spots), because it has the added advantage of being part of the EC. Hamburg is also a good location for trade with the East.

- Hamburg is the third-largest port in Europe and has more foreign consulates than any other metropolitan area except New York.

- North Rhine-Westphalia contains nearly a third of West Germany's population and has the largest economy of all the West German *Länder*.

- Compulsory membership in the Association of German Chambers of Commerce and Industry (DIHT) is required of all companies operating in Germany. There are sixty-nine chambers in the country and forty-three that operate overseas. Over 2 million firms belong to the association. The Chambers provide industry input for government policy, both in Germany and in Brussels. They also offer training programs, special assistance to smaller firms, and export advice via their overseas offices.

Special programs are being created to help spark ventures with Eastern Europe. Contact the German-American Chamber of Commerce in New York for details.

The German-American Chamber of Commerce not only promotes German imports; it also assists U.S. companies locating in Germany. It can help you find locations and partners, and in market research.

Notes

1. "Le défi is back," *The Economist*, May 13, 1989, p. 70.
2. "The Budget Buster of the 1990s?" *The Economist*, July 15, 1989, p. 45.
3. "Battle of Britain," *The Economist*, June 10, 1989, p. 65.

4. "EC acts on auto subsidies," *International Herald Tribune*, August 2, 1989, Business Section, p. 1.
5. Michael Calingaert, *The 1992 Challenge From Europe* (Washington, D.C.: National Planning Association, 1988), p. 50.
6. *Euro Trends Supplement*, 1987-1988.
7. Belgian Ministry of Economic Affairs, "Why your European facility should be in Belgium," 1988, p. 12.
8. Ibid., p. 4.
9. "Copenhagen a taxing situation," *Europe*, July-August 1989, p. 7.
10. Ministry of Foreign Affairs of Denmark, "Facts about Denmark," 1988, p. 67.
11. IDA news release, "Major Apple Investment for Ireland," June 23, 1989.
12. Ellen T. Corliss, "The Emerald Isle Wants American Business Now," *Mass High Tech*, June 5–18, 1989.
13. NFIA brochure, "The Netherlands Foreign Investment Review," 1988.
14. Ibid.
15. Glennon J. Harrison, "European Community: Issues Raised by 1992 Integration," CRS Report for Congress, May 31, 1989, p. 23.
16. Willem Thone, "Holland Hails High-Tech Influx," *Mass High Tech*, February 1–14, 1988.
17. *The Economist*, Financial Index, July 29, 1989, p. 83.
18. "Privatizing begins," *Europe*, July-August 1989, p. 12.
19. "Portugal," *Europe*, September 1989, p. 36.
20. Consorcio de la Zona Franca de Barcelona, "Investing in Barcelona," 1987, p. 68.
21. Investing in Madrid, an IMADE publication, 1987, p. 55.
22. "Catalonia: Looking to Europe," *International Herald Tribune*, May 30, 1989, p. 9.
23. "Investing in Barcelona," p. 33.
24. Excerpt from a *Briefing on Britain*, an information packet provided by the Invest in Britain Bureau.
25. "United Kingdom, 1988," *Corporate Location Europe* supplement, p. 23.

Cooperative R&D Programs

To encourage cooperation among companies operating in different member states, the EC has created several programs, many of which are supplemented by EC funds (up to 50 percent). These programs support Community industrial objectives, so most funding is directed toward high-technology projects. Because EC R&D programs cannot infringe on the principles of free competition, most are limited to precompetitive research.

Foreign companies can participate in these programs, but non-EC companies must normally conduct some form of R&D in the Community to be eligible. Another option is to form a joint venture with a European-based company. This will, in most cases, make the partnership eligible for Community and member state aid. But even if you're not eligible, it's a good idea to know what your European competitors are up to.

This directory describes what's available, how to find partners, and how to qualify for government support. If you don't have a project in mind, don't worry; there are data bases available to identify projects that are looking for partners.

Sharing: Is It Worth It?

Working in a cooperative R&D project poses special challenges, and many researchers question whether the extra effort is worth it. Yet, the 1980s saw an explosion of such projects in Europe, the United States, and Asia. What's driving this unusual cordial behavior among fierce competitors?

For one thing, companies often can't afford to go it alone because the cost of R&D continues to rise dramatically. The semiconductor industry spends, on average, 12 percent of its sales on R&D alone. At the same time, as the complexity of new developments increases, many firms find that they simply don't have the in-house expertise. Further, it often doesn't make economic sense to hire the skills because product life cycles have shortened so much that there isn't enough time to recoup a decent return on an investment undertaken alone. For example, before users came close to exploiting the full potential of Intel's 286 microprocessor, two new generations, the 386 and 486 chips, have appeared on the market. Competition is too fierce to slow down this process; it's innovate or die. To offset the shortened life cycle of new products, companies are joining forces to reduce the increased risk and costs.

Because these cooperative efforts are comparatively new, most participants are still attempting to sort out such issues as personnel management, supervision, control, and culture. Should a company send its best people to such projects? Some argue yes, others say no. It all depends on how important the project is to the success of the firm. Some European companies claim that the Brussels bureaucracy is burdensome and costly, and conclude that the freedom and flexibility of doing a project alone makes better sense.[1]

On the other side, one U.S. high-technology company gave two reasons why participating in EC cooperative R&D programs was a good idea:

1. It enhanced its image as a European company.
2. The research frequently resulted in the formulation of a standard that the company would not have been privy to or would not have been able to influence had it not participated.

The jury is still out on the efficacy of these types of programs. Over the next ten years, theories will emerge and studies will reflect on the experiences companies are going through right now. If you're in a high-technology industry, or if high technology can help your low-tech business, it makes a lot of sense at least to make yourself aware of what's going on. In many cases, the cost of joining, especially for smaller firms, is not that high, and considering what you get for the investment, it may not be a bad option. The rest of this directory describes the programs offered by the Community and by its member states.

Selection Criteria

It's important to understand the motivations of the decision makers who examine your proposal. Although each program has its own rules, project selection is generally based on:

-   The technical competence of the proposer
-   The scientific interest of the proposal, its originality, its relevance

to the scope of the overall program, and its feasibility (including ultimate economic feasibility)
- The likely contribution of the proposed research to the economic strength and competitiveness of the European Community
- The intensity of transnational collaboration (in most cases, proposals not originating from at least two laboratories located in different member states will not be considered for funding)
- The degree of interest expressed in exploiting the research results
- The state of the research, that is, whether it is large enough so that individual member states could not—or could only with great difficulty—do it on their own
- Whether the research leads, where the need is felt, to the establishment of uniform norms and standards (this applies to EC-sponsored R&D as opposed to that sponsored solely by one or more member states)[2]

Concerns You Probably Have

Potential partners for R&D projects include industrial and commercial firms, European-based universities and polytechnic schools, independent research and technology organizations, and European government agencies.

Confidentiality. Although each program has its own guidelines, strict confidentiality and publicity rules are normally part of the contract for any project. With Community-sponsored R&D projects, the Commission is usually empowered to publish the title and objective of the project, the names of the project leaders, the duration of work, and the amount of the Community's financial contribution. Details of the project, communications, and memos, however, are held in strict confidence. Most EC programs have a standard contract. Ask for a copy and have your legal department examine it before signing on.

Intellectual Property Rights. In general, a participating company can license any technology that comes out of the project only on terms that are fair to all other program participants and at no charge to its partners in the project that generated the technology. When the EC itself sponsors a project, it reserves the right to publish research results and to force the companies to grant licenses if they are unwilling themselves to commercialize the technology.[3] Some companies claim that Community rules concerning IPR require them to yield too much to make the effort worthwhile.

European Community Cooperative R&D Programs

Community-sponsored R&D programs are becoming increasingly prevalent because no individual member state can afford to sponsor more than a fraction of the efforts that are required to compete in the global technology race. These projects are geared to improving the competitiveness of European industries, coordinating their activities, and reducing duplication of effort. It is hoped that this will increase efficiency all around and lower the cost to individual companies and member states. By fostering cooperation across borders among industry, research institutes, and universities, the EC hopes to enhance the 1992 process by spreading European technology throughout the Community. Cooperation among member states also helps to establish Communitywide standards. In addition, these programs are designed to counteract the support given national industries by non-EC governments, and to involve smaller companies, which constitute an important source of innovation.

To accomplish these ambitious goals a framework program was created in 1983, and in 1989 it was extended to 1991. The new program calls for over 5 billion ECU of Community funding, which is earmarked for the following purposes:[4]

- To enhance the quality of life (375 million ECU)
- To contribute toward creating a large market and an information and communications society (2,275 million ECU)
- To modernize industrial sectors (845 million ECU)
- To exploit and optimize the use of biological resources (280 million ECU)
- To contribute to the development of energy resources and of science and technology (1,253 million ECU)
- To exploit the seabed and the use of marine resources (80 million ECU)
- To improve European science and technology cooperation (288 million ECU)[5]

To stay current on cooperative R&D, obtain the most recent editions of the following publications, which are available from the EC Information Office in Washington, D.C., or from the EC Publications Office in Luxembourg; addresses for both are in Directory E:

The European Community of Research and Technology, Publication of the European Community, ISBN 92–825–6804–0, 1987. Presents an overview of all EC cooperative R&D efforts.
The Official Journal of the European Community. Similar to the U.S. *Federal*

Register. This lists current legislative proposals and calls for project proposals. Subscribe, or use the EC data base.

Euro-abstracts. A publication of the European Community. This lists the variety of cooperative R&D publications available.

What follows is a list of Community cooperative R&D programs, grouped by the categories established in the framework program. In most instances, the funding listed must be matched by industry. DG addresses and phone numbers are to be found in Directory E.

Quality of Life

Medical and Health Research Programme. Concentrates on major health problems such as cancer, AIDS, age-related health problems, and environment- and life-style-related health problems.[6] The Community coordinates member state activities. For 1987–1991, 65 million ECU have been allocated. Contact DG XII.

Radiation Protection Programme. Designed to improve the conditions of life with respect to safety at work, the protection of man and the environment, and the safe production of energy from atomic fission. The program was first approved in 1985 with 48 million ECU; in 1988, 10 million ECU were added. A new program is planned for 1990–1994. Contact DG XXI.

Predictive Medicine Programme. Aimed at the use and improvement of new biotechnologies for risk forecasting, early diagnosis, prevention, prognosis, and treatment of some human diseases, and for better understanding of the mechanisms of heredity.[7] Approved February 2, 1989, the program was allotted 15 million ECU for 1989–1991. Contact DG XXI.

Environment Programme. Several environmental programs are included in this scheme:

- Protection: 55 million ECU
- Climatology and natural hazards (EPOCH): 17 million ECU
- Science and technology for environmental protection (STEP)
- Pilot projects on technical hazards: 3 million ECU. Contact DG XII.

Information Technologies

European Strategic Programme for Research and Development in Information Technology (ESPRIT). Established in 1984, ESPRIT set out to coordinate and improve European basic research in information technology, including microelectronics, information processing systems, and information technology applications. Its initial budget of 750 million ECU was matched by industry.

One goal of ESPRIT is to improve Europe's supply capabilities. Europe accounts for 30 percent of world demand for information technology products but for only 10 percent of the supply.[8]

Proposals are approved centrally by the ESPRIT management committee, which comprises government-designated representatives from each member state. Criteria include technical merit and the degree of fit with other EC high-technology efforts. Each year, there is a general call for proposals; contact the ESPRIT operations office for dates, or refer to the *Official Journal* (similar to the U.S. *Federal Register*). DG XIII organizes a "Proposers Day," at which potential proposers are briefed at a meeting in Brussels.

Phase II of ESPRIT (1988–1992) has a budget of 1.6 billion ECU (to be matched by industry) and places a new emphasis on ensuring that research results are applied.[9]

Here are some additional facts about ESPRIT:

- DG XIII maintains a "Eurocontact" data base to help participants find partners.
- ESPRIT projects involve an average of 3.5 organizations.[10]
- U.S. companies participated in less than 2 percent of Phase I ESPRIT programs.[11]

A US/EC task force is attempting to improve foreign participation in each other's cooperative programs.

Joint European Submicron Silicon Initiative (JESSI). A 4-billion ECU project (1989–1995) designed to strengthen the European electronics industry. JESSI's scope includes semiconductors, equipment and materials for microelectronics manufacturing, and applications of chips (from computers to VCRs).[12]

JESSI is a European response to the U.S. SEMATECH project (a Department of Defense-sponsored consortium comprising fourteen American semiconductor companies). Because SEMATECH doesn't allow foreign participation, JESSI may prohibit U.S. participation, but some form of compromise may occur over the next few years. There should be opportunity for U.S. firms at some point in JESSI's lifetime.

JESSI is financially supported by ESPRIT, EUREKA, some member states, and corporate funds. For further information, contact:

Planning Group JESSI
Margarete-Steiff-Weg 3
D-2210 Itzehoe
West Germany
Phone: (49) 48 21/ 7 78–0
Fax: (49) 48 21/ 7 13 90

Research and Development in Advanced Communications Technology for Europe (RACE).   Designed to coordinate efforts to establish a coherent European telecommunications network. The aim of RACE is to enable the Community to move towards integrated broadband communications (IBC) based on integrated service digital networks (ISDN).[13] For 1987–1992, 550 million ECU have been allocated. Contact DG XIII.

Development of European Learning Through Technological Advance Exploratory Action (DELTA).   Aims at creating a comprehensive European network using PCs, video data bases, and central host computers to enable students to communicate with teachers in remote locations. 20 million ECU for 1988–1990. Contact DG XIII.

Dedicated Road Infrastructure for Vehicle Safety in Europe (DRIVE). Designed to apply information technology to road transport. 60 million ECU for 1988–1991. Contact DG XIII.

Advanced Informatics in Medicine in Europe (AIM).   This two-year pilot program is designed to apply information technology and telecommunications to health care. 20 million ECU for 1988–1990. Contact DG XIII.

Modernization of Industrial Sectors

Basic Research in Industrial Technology for Europe (BRITE).   Designed to stimulate and coordinate R&D in traditional sectors such as chemicals, textiles, construction, and motor vehicles. Project examples include laser technology, CAD/CAM, membrane technology, advanced materials, and automated manufacturing techniques.[14] Begun in 1985 with 125 million ECU, the program was funded with an additional 60 million ECU in 1986. Contact DG XII.

European Research in Advanced Materials (EURAM).   Established to provide Europe with the capacity to produce advanced materials that are currently imported or manufactured under license. The goal is to develop sophisticated materials for electronics, data processing, telecommunications, the motor industry, shipbuilding, construction, aerospace, biomedical technologies, and other sectors.[15] 70 million ECU for 1986–1989. Contact DG XII.

BRITE/EURAM.   This program builds on the achievements emerging from the first BRITE and EURAM programs. 439.5 million ECU for 1989–1992. Contact DG XII.

Aeronautics Programme.   Two pilot programs (one through 1991, the other through 1993) are designed to enhance Europe's aeronautical technology base. A full program will be developed in 1994. Contact DG XII.

BCR Programme.   R&D in the field of applied metrology and chemical analysis. 59.2 million ECU for 1988–1992. Contact DG XII.

Biological Programs

Biotechnology Action Programme (BAP).   Designed to develop the Community's capacity to master and exploit the applications of modern biology in agriculture and industry. The program began with 50 million ECU in 1985, and an additional 20 million ECU were added in 1988. Contact DG XII.

Biotechnology Research for Innovation; Development and Growth in Europe (BRIDGE).   If approved, the proposed program will further biotechnology research in the Community by building on BAP accomplishments,[16] and there will be 100 million ECU for 1990–1993. Contact DG XII.

European Collaborative Linkage of Agriculture and Industry through Research (ECLAIR).   Designed to promote the useful application of recent developments in the life sciences and biotechnology. 80 million ECU for 1988–1993. Contact DG XII.

Food Linked Agro-Industrial Research (FLAIR).   Designed to focus on the way consumers, industry, and research interact with each other; concentrates on R&D that is closer to the market than to "pure' research.[17] 25 million ECU for 1989–1993. Contact DG XII.

Agricultural Research Programme.   Designed to coordinate Community agriculture R&D. Although the program concluded in 1988, a new program is planned for 1989–1993. Contact DG VI.

Energy

Radioactive Waste Programme. Designed for the management and storage of radioactive waste. For 1985–1989, 62 million ECU were allocated. A new program is planned for 1990–1994. Contact DG XII.

Decommissioning of Nuclear Installations. Encompasses seven different subjects in this area. Extending the program begun in 1984, 31.5 million ECU were allocated for 1989–1993. Contact DG XII.

TELEMAN Programme. An annual research and training program on remote handling techniques in nuclear hazardous and disordered environments. 19 million ECU for 1989–1993. Contact DG XII.

Joint Opportunities for Unconventional or Long-Term Energy Supply (JOULE). Designed to develop nonnuclear energies. 122 million ECU for 1989–1992. Contact DG XII.

Science and Technology

Development Programme. Aimed at promoting increased scientific cooperation between the Community and developing countries. 80 million ECU for 1987–1991. Contact DG XII.

Marine Resources

Marine Science and Technology (MAST). Focuses on coastal and regional seas. The program has four parts: basic and applied marine science, coastal zone science and engineering, marine technology, and supporting initiatives (1989–1992). Contact DG XII.

Fisheries Programme. Includes fishery management, fishing methods, aquaculture, and the upgrading of fishery products. 30 million ECU for 1988–1992. Contact DG XIV.

EUREKA

Launched in 1985, the European Research Coordinating Agency (EUREKA). (EUREKA) is neither a Community program nor a member state program, but rather receives funding from member state budgets. So far EUREKA has involved nineteen countries (both EC and EFTA countries), 1,600 participating organizations, and $5,500 million invested in 300 different high-technology projects.[18] Its activities are closer to market (as opposed to precompetitive) R&D and broader in scope than those of ESPRIT. EUREKA is more of a framework for cooperation than a formalized program with an approved budget. Support ranges up to 50 percent of the project cost (the average being 35 percent).

Nine sectors qualify for EUREKA consideration: biotechnology, communications, energy, the environment, information technology, laser technology, new materials, robotics, and transport.

Each member state has a National Project Coordinator (NPC) who coordinates EUREKA activity in that country and can assist in finding partners and filing applications. The Community has a representative within the EUREKA Secretariat and occasionally participates in projects with a Community appeal. A minimum of two companies and two national governments or institutes must participate to qualify for EUREKA status. A EUREKA matchmaker data base provides companies with a list of projects in search of partners.

In early 1990, a special EUREKA Program was created to help improve the European environment. It promotes collaboration among European companies developing the equipment and services needed to provide greater environmental protection.

For more information on EUREKA, contact:

The Eureka Secretariat
19H, Avenue des Arts, Bte 3
B-1040 Brussels
Belgium
Phone: (32) (2) 217 00 30
Fax: (32) (2) 218 79 06

Member State Cooperative R&D Programs

The following is a brief synopsis of member state research programs that are accessible to any company that conducts R&D in a member state, regardless of the nationality of its ownership. These countries will also assist you in getting involved in Community-run programs. For further information on these programs, contact the offices for foreign direct investment of the appropriate member state. You can find their addresses and telephone number in Directory B.

Belgium

With an emphasis on high-technology research, the government offers interest-free advances for approved prototype and research projects of up

1987 Member State R&D Spending

(ECU Million)	Total R&D	Per Capita R&D (in Thousands)*
Belgium	668	68
Denmark	582	113
France	10,470	188
Greece	104	10
Ireland	121	34
Italy	4,965	89
Luxembourg	—	—
Netherlands	1,790	123
Portugal	111	11
Spain	914	24
United Kingdom	6,824	120
Germany	10,633	174

*1987 exchange rates.
Source: European Commission.

to 50 percent of the total cost. Grants of up to 50 percent are also available. Special programs are in place to encourage activities between university research centers and enterprises operating in Brussels.

Denmark

Several government institutions offer assistance to companies solving technological problems. These agencies also contribute to the spread of information about international technology developments. The government offers grants and loans for product development of up to 75 percent of the project cost.

The Fund for Industrial and Commercial Development grants interest-free loans until the project is complete, and no installments are due until after two years.

At Arhus in Jutland, an innovation center linked to the local university has been set up with the purpose of conducting advanced electronic and biotechnology research.

Denmark participates in all EC programs and provides help in the application process.

France

French technological accomplishments, from the Ariane launch vehicle to the world's fastest passenger train, which whisks travelers at speeds of more than 230 miles per hour from Paris to Lyons, are indicative of the country's commitment to world scientific leadership. Such large-scale government-sponsored projects have projected France to the forefront of other areas like remote satellite sending, aircraft manufacturing, and defense electronics. In telecommunications, Minitel, an interactive video-text network, now operates in over 2 million French households.

The creation of a new Ministry for Research and Technology in 1987 renewed the government's commitment to R&D development. The budget has been increased (reaching $6.6 billion in civilian R&D in 1988), and eleven areas have been identified as priorities: biotechnology, food research, medical research, the social sciences, production technology, electronics, transport, natural resources, new materials, molecular engineering, and the technical needs of the Third World.

A combination of grants and tax credits are available for certain qualifying projects in addition to favorable amortization of R&D investments.

Technopoles, coined from the Greek words *techne* (science and technology) and *polis* (city), have cropped up all over the country. These research science parks are well equipped to support R&D, providing state-of-the-art infrastructure, close proximity to universities and research institutes, and the availability of skilled labor.

France is also the most active participant in the EUREKA program, an idea sparked by President François Mitterrand in 1985.

Greece

Several nonprofit research institutes operate in the country. They range in specialization from manufacturing productivity and plant pathology to atomic energy research.

Ireland

Because Ireland has only 3 million people, it does not sponsor elaborate R&D programs. It does, however, participate in the EC cooperative programs and EUREKA. The Irish government also sponsors several information technology R&D facilities:

- The Software Engineering Laboratory, which offers services to industry.
- The National Software Centre, which provides technical and managerial assistance to software companies.
- The National Microelectronics Research Centre, which is involved

in contract research for the European Space Agency and the EC, and has formed partnerships with several corporations. It serves as a teaching and development center for semiconductor design and fabrication, gallium arsenide technology, and hybrid circuit technology.

Cash grants of up to 50 percent are also available towards agreed costs of R&D expenditures (up to IR£ 250,000 per project). For more information on Irish R&D, contact:

EOLAS
Irish Science and Technology Agency
Glasnevin, Dublin 9
Republic of Ireland
Phone: 353/ 1 370 0101

Italy

Italy is strongly committed to developing technology; the government spent about $1 billion on pure, applied, and development research in 1988.[19] Both national Italian R&D programs and regional programs are available.

Nationally, the Research and Development Fund provides cash grants, and the Technological Innovation Revolving Fund, organized by the Ministry of Industry and Commerce, offers subsidized loans for approved projects. These funds can be applied not only to the costs of the project but consulting studies, technical assistance, and technology transfer as well. Subsidies of up to 80 percent are available. The Research and Development Fund has spent 5 trillion lire since 1982; the Technological Innovation Fund has spent 4.5 trillion lire.[20]

Scientific and technological research centers that employ not fewer than fifteen research staff members can obtain cash grants. Research consortia located in southern Italy (the Mezzogiorno) are eligible for cash grants of up to 80 percent of expenditures or project costs in addition to subsidized loans.

Luxembourg

Because Luxembourg is so small, little is offered. However, eligible R&D projects can qualify for grants of up to 50 percent of project costs.

The Netherlands

The Dutch government has identified several high-technology sectors for special grants:

- *Biotechnology.* The Dutch are attempting to establish the Netherlands as the European biotechnology center. Cooperative R&D programs and university linkages are available to U.S. firms conducting R&D in the country.
- *Medical Technology.* The Dutch have a strong social and economic commitment to health care. The Medical Technology Stimulation Program promotes and coordinates national efforts.
- *Information Technology.* To promote microelectronics, telecommunications, office automation, computer-integrated manufacturing, and software development, the Dutch government spends over $200 million a year on cooperative R&D programs.

The Innovation Stimulation Scheme (INSTIR) program subsidizes small and medium-size information technology businesses for R&D-related wage costs.

Technical Development Loans (TOK) are available to smaller companies (under 20,000 employees) for the development costs of new products, processes, or services that are between the research stage and exploitation. Other R&D grants are available for projects focused on the following subjects: energy savings, wind energy, recycling, the economic and environmental use of coal, water pollution, gas engines, water cleansing installations for internal use, reduction of manure surplus, and environmentally clean production processes and consumer goods.

Portugal

R&D subsidies of up to 50 percent are available for manufacturing and up to 60 percent for scientific research and development.

Spain

Spain has seriously lagged behind most of its Western European counterparts in technology. To rectify this, the government has committed money and created several R&D programs to close the technology gap. Besides aggressive participation in European cooperative ventures, Spain has created several programs, both on the national level and at the local level. Spanish R&D tripled as a percent of gross domestic product (GDP) between 1982 and 1986.[21] The National Plan for Scientific Research and Technological Development includes more than 600 million pesetas for twenty-three programs. The Ministry of Industry and Energy has set the following sector priorities: electronics, automation, energy conservation, fashion and industrial design, mining, and pharmaceuticals.

The Ministry of Education and Science is focused on biotechnology, automation, electronics, artificial intelligence, and advanced chemistry.

The Oficina de Valoración y Transferencíca de Tecnología coordinates relations with industry.

Innovation is encouraged through programs offered by the Centro para el Desarrollo Technológico Industrial (CDTI). In 1986 it committed close to 9 billion pesetas.

The Spanish "community," or local, development agencies can put you in touch with institutes and other government R&D programs. Each region sponsors its own programs. Madrid and Barcelona are the most active. Some universities and private technical institutes make their labs available to industry. Contact the Ministry of Industry and Energy for more information.

The Barcelona-Vallés Science Park brings together high-tech infrastructure (i.e., fiber-optic cabling), technically orientated companies, and institutes to encourage innovation and cooperation. Sharp, Hewlett-Packard, and Olivetti are some of the companies located there.

The United Kingdom

In 1988 the United Kingdom scaled back many programs and moved away from supporting near-market R&D projects.[22] Nevertheless, it still participates in several collaborative projects, which fall under the jurisdiction of the Department of Trade and Industry (DTI). Contact:

Department of Trade and Industry (DTI)
Bridge Place
88–89 Eccleston Square
London SW1V 1PT
Phone: (44) (1) 730 9678

There are nine regional DTI offices, and there's a special 1992 hot line, (1) 200 1992. DTI offers a variety of services similar to those offered by the U.S. Department of Commerce; if you have U.K. operations in the United Kingdom, they'll assist you.

General Criteria for Projects. Government support will be considered only when it is essential to the scope or scale of the project. Applicants must prove that projects would not go ahead without this support.

Besides participating in EC-sponsored programs, the United Kingdom offers the following:

• *The LINK Initiative.* Fosters cooperation between industry and universities in the United Kingdom. Project proposals in these areas are welcomed: nanotechnology; molecular electronics; advanced semiconductor materials; industrial measurement system sensors; and eukaryotic genetic engineering. Link offers support of up to 50 percent of project costs. For more information, contact the LINK secretariat at the DTI: (1) 212 6402.

▪ *Advanced Technology Programmes.* Encourage precompetitive research in new technologies to build up United Kingdom capabilities and accelerate their application. Project proposals are welcomed for: gallium arsenide applications; advanced robotics; national electroncs research initiatives; resources from the sea; superconductivity; and information engineering. At least three partners are required, and two must be capable of exploiting the research. The program offers financial support of up to 50 percent of project costs. For more information, contact DTI regional offices or the Invest in Britain Bureau in New York.

▪ *General Industrial Collaborative Programmes.* Encourage collaborative projects that will benefit many companies, particularly small and medium-size companies. Contact DTI for more information.

▪ *Small Firms Merit Award for Research and Technology (SMART).* Encourages potential commercial projects that lack funding. SMART also helps small firms to develop and market new ideas in selected areas and helps them to mature. The awards are for up to £50,000 and are open to any manufacturing firm operating in the United Kingdom that has fewer than 200 employees, and is not part of a group with 200 employees or more in total; SMART awards are also available to individuals who are United Kingdom citizens or foreign national residents. Contact DTI for more information.

West Germany

West Germany is the world's leading nonmilitary R&D spender per capita.[23] Of all government R&D funds, 80 percent are spent in the fields of electrotechnology, chemistry, the automotive industry, engine building, precision mechanics, and optics.[24]

West Germany has more than 499 scientific and R&D institutions that cooperate with industry, 250 being located in the Hamburg area and 186 in Berlin. The Max Planck Association and the Fraunhofer Gesellschaft are two well-known German research institutes that have facilities throughout the country.

The German Ministry of Science and Technology (BMFT) coordinates federal domestic R&D programs. Grants are available for up to 50 percent of the costs of a project. Since West Germany is divided into seventeen states, each offers its own programs. Incentives include credit guarantees, grants, loans, and technical assistance. Contact state development agencies for details (refer to Directory B). In some areas, local authorities also offer programs.

The annual report of the federal government on research provides a comprehensive view of West Germany's R&D activities.

Notes

1. James W. Dudley, *1992 Strategies for the Single Market* (London: Kogan Page, 1989), p. 213.
2. *The Official Journal of the European Communities*, No. L 302/1, October 24, 1987, p. 23.
3. David Levy, "Technology Collaboration in Europe," Harvard Business School Case no. N9–389–130, 1989, p. 11.
4. *The Official Journal of the European Communities*, No. L 3021, October 24, 1987, p. 3.
5. Ibid.
6. "Inventory of Specific Programmes within the framework programme," *European Affairs*, Spring 1989, p. 102.
7. Ibid., p. 103.
8. Northern Telecom Report, 1987.
9. *The Official Journal of the European Communities*, Volume 31, L 118, May 6, 1988, p. 36.
10. Commission of the European Communities, "ESPRIT the first phase: Progress and results," 1987, p. 3.
11. Levy, "Technology Collaboration in Europe," p. 10.
12. Robert S. Williams, "JESSI," Harvard Business School Case no. 9–389–135, March 1989, p. 1.
13. *The European Community of Research and Technology*, A European Community Publication, 1987, p. 24.
14. Ibid., p. 28.
15. Ibid., p. 30.
16. *The Official Journal of the European Communities*, January 1989, p. 12.
17. "Inventory of Specific Programmes within the framework programme," *European Affairs*, Spring 1989, p. 106.
18. "Invitation: EC Chip Project," *International Herald Tribune*, June 22, 1989, p. 15.
19. "Underwriting Research," *International Herald Tribune*, June 17–18, 1989, p. 13.
20. Ibid.
21. Consorcio de la Zona Franca de Barcelona, *Investing in Barcelona*, 1987, p. 62.
22. "The Research and Technology Initiative," The Department for Trade and Industry, 1988, p. 7.
23. "West Germany, the logical choice for investment in Europe," published by the Federal States of West Germany, 1988, p. 11.
24. Ibid., p. 13.

Directory D | The Directives and Legislation

The directives,* legislation, and proposals listed in the following pages address the Euro-hazards issues described in Chapter 3 and the industrial sectors described in Chapter 5. The *List of European Community 1992 Directives and Proposals* gives the status and *Official Journal* number of all directives. It can be obtained at:

Single Internal Market Information Service
Office of European Community Affairs
U.S. Department of Commerce
Room 3036
14th and Constitution Avenue, N.W.
Washington, D.C. 20230
Phone: 202/ 377–5276

Directives, Legislation, and Proposals to Watch

Intellectual Property (IP)

- Border enforcement against importation of counterfeits
- Trademarks: First directive
- Community Trademark Office Proposal (CTO): The CTO proposal creates an office that establishes a single trademark as valid throughout the Community. The office would have the authority to grant, monitor, and enforce trademarks
- Regulation on Community trademarks
- Regulation on the rules needed for implementing the Community trademark regulation
- Community Trademark Office regulation on fees
- Regulation on rules of procedures for the Boards of Appeal of the Community Trademark Office

*Directives are listed roughly in order of importance.

- First directive to approximate the laws of member states relating to trademarks: to ensure that national trademarks will compete on equal terms with the proposed Community trademark
- Proposal for a regulation of the fees payable to the Community Trademark Office
- Proposal for a Community Patent Convention
- Proposal for a Council directive on the legal protection of biotechnological inventions
- Council Directive 87/54 of 16 December 1986 on the legal protection of topographies of semiconductor products: to protect against copying the designs of integrated circuits
- Proposal for a Council directive on the legal protection of computer programs

Merger Control

- Merger control regulation
- Tenth directive on cross-border mergers
- Proposal for a directive on takeover bids

Standards

There are more than 200 directives aimed at harmonizing European standards. Some sector-specific directives, like the one on gas emissions standards for motor vehicles, are given in the next section of this directory. The directives listed here deal only with standards formulation, testing, and certification in general.

- Member state notification to Commission of pending standards
- Extension of information procedures on standards and technical rules

Social Dimension

- European Company Statute: Would allow a company to incorporate on an EC-wide basis. In exchange, the company would have to accept one of several systems of worker participation, information, and consultation.
- Community Charter of Fundamental Social Rights: Lists twelve basic rights covering such issues as fair wages, sexual equality, worker participation, training, and the right to join a union.
- Health and Safety Framework Directive: Would establish minimum EC-wide health and safety rules.
- Tenth Company Law Directive: Companies subject to worker participation under the European Company Statute could form a cross-border merger to avoid this requirement.

- Establishment of a general system of mutual recognition of higher-education diplomas.

Government Procurement

- Two directives adopted October 11, 1988 permit the exclusion of offers on goods and materials containing less than 50 percent EC content. When such bids are considered, however, a 3 percent preference will be given to equivalent offers on goods containing more than 50 percent content. This is similar to the U.S. "Buy America" program, which provides for preference being given to products that have at least 50 percent U.S. content.
- Opening up public procurement in sectors previously closed to open tenders: water, energy, and transportation.
- Application of Community rules to procedures for the award of public works contracts: Modifies an earlier directive to open up the awarding of government contracts.
- Coordination of procedures on the award of public supply contracts: Modifies directives to open up supply contract bidding by requiring listing of supply contracts in the EC's *Official Journal.*
- Directives 71/305 (public works) and 77/62 (supply contracts) provide judicial remedies for dealing with member states that continue to favor national companies.
- Public procurement in the field of services (engineering, consultancy, and software).

Harmonization of Veterinary and Phytosanitary Measures

Because there are so many directives in this area, we have listed only some of the more visible ones. In addition, new ones are being added all the time. You can identify the rest by contacting your trade association or the Commerce Department.

- Proposal amending Directive 81/852 concerning veterinary medicinal products
- Amendment to Directive 72/462 on health and veterinary inspection problems upon importation of bovine animals and swine and fresh meat from third countries
- Proposal to amend the annex to Directive 76/895 concerning residues of pesticides in and on fruit and vegetables (ethoxyquin and diphenylamine)
- Proposed directives on the contained use of genetically modified micro-organisms
- Proposed directives relating to the environment of genetically modified organisms

Import Quotas

There are no quantitative restriction (QR) directives yet.

Reciprocity

- Second Banking Directive
- Investment services
- Liberalization of capital movements

Rules of Origin and Local Content

- Television without frontiers directive.
- VCRs: Must contain 45 percent local content.
- Photocopiers: Origin is determined to be where the most sophisticated component is made. This stance is based on the European Court's ruling that Japan's Ricoh photocopiers assembled in California cannot be considered American.

The directives and legislation listed on the following pages address the industry-specific issues described in Chapter 5.

Company Law

- Regulation of a European Economic Interest Grouping (EEIG)—the Fifth Company Law Directive
- Eleventh Company Law Directive
- Fourth Company Law Directive
- Seventh Company Law Directive

Automotive

- Roadworthiness tests for motor vehicles and their trailers; type of approval of motor vehicles and their trailers
- Rearview mirrors on motor vehicles
- Weights, dimensions, and characteristics of certain road vehicles
- Braking devices of motor vehicles and trailers
- Engine power of motor vehicles
- Motorcycle replacement exhaust systems
- Approximation of laws relating to weights and dimensions of certain motor vehicles
- Approximation of laws relating to tires of motor vehicles and their trailers
- Limitation on values for gaseous emissions of cars (vehicles below 1400 cc)
- Gaseous emissions, commercial cars (diesel engines)

- Amendment to Directive 70/220 on air pollution by gases from car diesel engines
- Tire pressure gauges for motor vehicles
- Field of vision of motor vehicle drivers

Chemicals

- Restrictions on the marketing of dangerous substances
- Supervision and control within the EC of transfrontier shipment of hazardous wastes
- Protection of workers through the banning of certain chemical agents and activities
- Restrictions on the marketing and use of asbestos
- Restrictions on the marketing and use of PCBs
- Minimum standards for disposing of PCBs
- Liquid fertilizers
- Good laboratory practices, nonclinical testing of chemicals

Consumer Products

- Misleading Advertising Directive
- Product Liability Directive
- Doorstep Selling Directive
- Toy Safety Directive
- Price Indication Directive
- Recommendation on payment systems
- Food additives
- Food labeling
- Compulsory nutrition labeling of foodstuffs intended for sales to consumers
- Consumer protection in the indication of the price of foodstuffs
- Consumer protection respecting the indication of prices for non-food products
- Price transparency in the prices of medicines and social security refunds
- Household appliances—airborne noise
- Lawnmower noise
- Approximation of laws in member states relating to appliances burning gaseous fuels

Banking

- Second Banking Directive
- First Banking Directive

- Liberalization of short-term capital movements
- Solvency ratios for credit institutions
- Own Funds Directive
- Directive on the annual accounts of banks
- Commission recommendation on monitoring and controlling large exposures
- Deposit insurance
- Code of conduct for electronic payment
- Mortgage Credit Directive

Investment Services

- Liberalization of short-term capital movements
- Framework for investment services with the securities field
- Liberalization of such operations as transactions in securities not dealt in on a Stock Exchange, admission of securities on the capital market, and long-term commercial credits
- Coordination of requirements for the drawing up, scrutiny, and distribution of the prospectus to be published when securities are offered for subscription or sale to the public
- Harmonization of the concept of own funds
- Harmonization of taxes on transactions in securities
- Listing Particulars Directive
- Interim Reports Directive
- Insider Trading Directive
- Market Risk Directive
- Information to be published when major holdings in the capital of a listed company are acquired or disposed of

UCITS

- UCITS Directive
- Liberalization of units in collective investment undertakings for transferable securities

Insurance

- Second Non-Life Insurance Services Directive
- First Non-Life Insurance Services Directive
- Freedom of establishment for agents and brokers
- Second Directive on Direct Life insurance
- Insurance contracts
- Annual accounts—insurance undertakings
- Winding up of insurance undertakings

- Coordination of laws relating to legal expenses insurance
- Credit insurance
- Motor vehicle liability insurance

Information Technology

- Plan of action for information services market
- Procurement: phased open bidding, whereby full international notification of contracts will be required by the end of 1992
- Towards a competitive Communitywide telecommunications market in 1992
- Standardization in the field of information technology and telecommunications
- Mutual recognition of standards and certification of telecommunications equipment
- Recommendation on the coordinated introduction of ISDN
- Establishing an internal market for telecommunications services with Open Network Provision (ONP)
- Competition in the markets for telecommunications terminal equipment
- Mutual Recognition of type approval for telecommunications terminal equipment
- Pan-European mobile telephones
- Legal protection of topographies of semiconductor products
- Radio interferences (electromagnetic compatibility)
- Legal protection of computer programs
- HDTV standards: Obliges member states to broadcast by satellite using the MAC standard
- Telecommunications tariff harmonization
- Policy on VANS and ONA

Pharmaceuticals and Medical Devices

Pharmaceuticals
- EC-wide drug registration
- Regulation of new products
- Patient information
- Harmonization of conditions for distribution
- Testing of medical specialties
- Coordination of provisions respecting certain activities in the field of pharmacy
- Good laboratory practices in nonclinical testing of chemicals
- Price transparency in the prices of medicines and social security refunds

- Amended proposal for a Council directive relating to measures regulating the pricing of medicinal products for human use and their inclusion within the scope of national health insurance systems

Medical Devices
- Active implantable electromedical equipment
- Electromedical devices
- Invitro diagnostic
- Sterile products

Service Industries and the Professions

- Mutual recognition of admissions standards and qualifications

Shipping and Transportation

Transportation in General
- Action program for transport infrastructure to complete an integrated transport market by 1992
- Proposal for instituting a process of convergence of rates of VAT and excise duties
- Opening up of public procurement in the transport sectors
- Opening up of public procurement in the energy, water, and transport services

Air
- Price competition, liberalization of flight allocation, and increase in passenger-sharing arrangements
- Regulations on air transport and coordination of capacity, revenues, tariffs, and slot allocations at airports
- Code of conduct for computerized reservations systems (regulation)

Road Haulage
- Single Administrative Document (SAD)
- Liberalization of road haulage
- Road transport goods, freedom to provide services by nonresident carriers within a member state
- Weights, dimensions, and characteristics of certain road vehicles
- Test methods for industrial trucks

Road Passenger Transport
- Council directive on package travel, including package holidays
- Road transport passengers, freedom to provide services by nonresident carriers within a member state

- Road transport, common rules for the international carriage of passengers by road

Shipping
- Freedom to provide services regulation
- Coordinated action regulation
- Unfair pricing practices regulation
- Competition regulation
- Inland waterways, goods and passengers, freedom to provide services by nonresident carriers within a member state
- Maritime transport, goods and passengers, freedom to provide services in the sea transport sector within a member state by nonresident carriers

Publications

Further information on virtually any aspect of 1992 can be obtained from the EC's Publications Office in Luxembourg and from its information offices in the United States. Many publications are free and others are priced modestly. The EC also issues *Publications of the European Communities*, which is updated annually.

Office for Official Publications of the European Communities
2 rue Mercier
2895 Luxembourg
Phone: 352 499 28-1
Telex: 1324 PUBOF LU

European Community Information Service
2100 M Street, N.W.
Washington, D.C. 20037
Phone: 202/862-9500
Telex: 64 215 EURCOM NW

European Community Information Service
3 Dag Hammarskjold Plaza
305 East 47 Street
New York, N.Y. 10017
Phone: 212/371-3804
Telex: 012 396 EURCOM NY

European Community Information Service
44 Montgomery Street, Suite 2715
San Francisco, Calif. 94104
Phone: 415/391-3476
Fax: 415/391-3641

The Commission

The Commission can be contacted in Brussels at the following address:

Rue de la Loi 200
1049 Brussels, Belgium
Phone: 32 235 11 11
Telex: 21877 COMEU B

The Directorates-General can all be contacted in Brussels at the same address and numbers, except as noted below. Some also have offices in Luxembourg, and these addresses* are included here.

Directorates-General

DG I   External relations
DG II   Economic and financial affairs
DG III   Internal market and industrial affairs
              Task force: small and medium-size enterprises
DG IV   Agriculture
DG V   Employment, social affairs, and education

> Bâtiment Jean Monnet
> Rue Alcide De Gasperi
> 2920 Luxembourg
> *Phone:* 352 430 11
> *Telex:* 3423 COMEUR LU

DG VI   Agriculture
              Brussels address and phone number are the same as that for the
              Commission, but the telex is 22037 AGREC B
DG VII   Transport
DG VIII   Development
DG IX   Personnel and administration

> Bâtiment Jean Monnet
> Rue Alcide De Gasperi
> 2920 Luxembourg
> *Phone:* 352 430 11
> *Telex:* 3423 COMEUR LU

DG X   Information, communication, and culture
DG XI   Environment, consumer protection, and nuclear safety
DG XII   Science, research, and development joint research center
DG XIII   Telecommunications, information industries, and innovation

*Source: EC Directory of the Commission, Brussels, 1989.

Bâtiment Jean Monnet
Rue Alcide De Gasperi
2920 Luxembourg
Phone: 352 430 11
Telex: 2752 EURDOC LU

DG XIV	Fisheries
DG XV	Financial institutions and company law
DG XVI	Regional policy
DG XVII	Energy
DG XVIII	Credit and investments
	Has no office in Brussels; can be contacted at:

Bâtiment Jean Monnet
Rue Alcide De Gasperi
2920 Luxembourg
Phone: 352 430 11
Telex: 2331 EUCRED LU

DG XIX	Budgets
DG XX	Financial control
DG XXI	Customs union and indirect taxation
DG XXII	Coordination of structural instruments
DG XXIII	Enterprise

The Council
The Council of Ministers can be reached at:

Rue de la Loi 170
1048 Brussels, Belgium
Phone: 32 234 61 11
Telex: 21711

European Parliament
The Parliament can be reached at the following locations:

Seat of the Secretariat
Centre Européen
Plateau du Kirchberg
2929 Luxembourg
Phone: 352 430 01
Telex: 3493 and 2894

European Parliament
Rue Belliard 97–113
1040 Brussels, Belgium
Phone: 32 234 21 11
Telex: 26988 and 26989

Palais de l'Europe
Place Lenôtre
67006 Strasbourg, France
Phone: 33 88 37 40 01
Telex: 890129 and 980130

Parliament has eighteen standing committees, which cover specific areas of Community policy. These are:

Political Affairs Committee
Committee on Agriculture, Fisheries, and Food
Committee on Budgets
Committee on Economic and Monetary Affairs and Industrial Policy
Committee on Energy, Research, and Technology
Committee on External Economic Relations
Committee on Legal Affairs and Citizens' Rights
Committee on Social Affairs and Employment
Committee on Regional Policy and Regional Planning
Committee on Transport
Committee on the Environment, Public Health, and Consumer Protection
Committee on Youth, Culture, Education, Information, and Sport
Committee on Development and Cooperation
Committee on Budgetary Control
Committee on Institutional Affairs
Committee on Rules of Procedure and Verification of Credentials
Committee on Women's Rights
Committee on Petitions

The Court of Justice
The European Court of Justice is located at:

Palais de la Cour de Justice
P.O. Box 1409
2920 Luxembourg
Phone: 352 430 31
Telex: 2510

Index